Old West—New West

Old West— New West

Centennial Essays

Edited by
Barbara Howard Meldrum

University of Idaho Press
Moscow, Idaho
1993

University of Idaho Press, Moscow, Idaho 83844-1107
Copyright © 1993 by Barbara Howard Meldrum
Printed in the United States of America. All rights reserved.
97 96 95 94 93   5 4 3 2 1
Design by Karla Fromm
Cover painting by Sue Congleton

Material in Chapter 8 is taken from "Introduction," from *The Journals of Lewis and Clark* by Frank Bergon, Editor; copyright © 1989 by Frank Bergon; used by permission of Viking Penguin, a division of Penguin Books USA Inc.; material in Chapter 3 is from *West of Everything: The Inner Life of Westerns* (New York: Oxford University Press, 1992); material in Chapters 4, 5, and 20 is used courtesy of *Western American Literature*, Logan, Utah; material in Chapter 6 appeared in an earlier version in *Great Plains Quarterly* (January 1992); material in Chapter 7 is used courtesy of the Church of Jesus Christ of Latter-day Saints Archives, Salt Lake City, Utah; material in Chapter 13 is used courtesy of the *South Dakota Review* 28, no. 1 (Spring 1990): 46-61; material in Chapter 17 is used courtesy of Ursula Le Guin and is from *Always Coming Home* (New York: Bantam, 1987); the illustration in Chapter 17 is used courtesy of Margaret Chodos-Irvine; in Chapter 18 letters in the Papers of Lucullus Virgil McWhorter are used courtesy of the Washington State University Libraries, Pullman, Washington; Mourning Dove's manuscript materials and letters are used courtesy of Mary Lemery and Charles Quintasket.

Library of Congress Cataloging-in-Publication Data

Old West—New West : centennial essays / edited by Barbara Howard Meldrum.
    p. cm.
    Includes bibliographical references and index.
    ISBN 0-89301-163-0
    1. American literature—West (U.S.)—History and criticism.
2. Western stories—History and criticism. 3. West (U.S.)—Intellectual life.
4. West (U.S.) in literature. I. Meldrum, Barbara Howard.
PS271.04 1993
810.9′3278—dc20
                                           92-29828
                                                 CIP

To the Memory of
Wallace Stegner (1909–1993)

who broadened and deepened our understanding of both the Old and New West through stories that "rigged up" for us "a line between past and present."

Contents

Part 3
Writing in the New West

Part 4
Other Voices: Ethnic Diversity, Old West and New

Part 5
New Directions for the New West

Acknowledgments

The essays in this collection owe their existence to the Western Literature Association annual conference held in Coeur d'Alene, Idaho, October 11–14, 1989. Many individuals and groups contributed time, talents, and financial resources to make that conference a success. Major funding came from the University of Idaho as well as Washington State University; substantial support was provided by North Idaho College, Eastern Washington University, Lewis-Clark State College, and the Canadian Consulate. Additional support came from Boise State University and Gonzaga University. Nearly twenty members of the Western Literature Association served as referees for the many manuscripts submitted for acceptance in the conference program.

Special thanks are extended to the John Calhoun Smith Memorial Fund, administered by the University of Idaho, for financial support which brought keynote speakers to the conference and supported the editing and publication of this essay collection.

Barbara Howard Meldrum
University of Idaho
January 1993

Introduction

Barbara Howard Meldrum

A century has passed since Frederick Jackson Turner, a young history professor at the University of Wisconsin, presented his landmark essay, "The Significance of the Frontier in American History," to a special conference of the National Historical Association, which met in conjunction with the World's Columbian Exposition in Chicago, July 1893. Turner opened his essay by referring to a recently published report on the 1890 census that declared the American frontier no longer existed. We now know that the author of that report was neither accurate nor authoritative in his pronouncement.[1] We also know that the report was by no means the crucial trigger leading to Turner's formulation of his frontier thesis, for his concepts evolved over a period of several years.[2] Nor did historians greet Turner's theory with a shock of recognition or a call to arms—it wasn't controversial because it was virtually ignored. No wonder, perhaps, for Turner read his paper as the fifth one of an evening program following a hot Chicago day at the fair. The public was also singularly unimpressed with the historians' proceedings: the *New York Times* detailed the arrival at the exposition of a Norwegian replica of a Viking ship, but committed only three lines to the historical congress meeting the same day.[3]

Nonetheless, Turner's paper inaugurated a new era in American historiography with his formulation of the frontier thesis: ("The existence of an area of free land, its continuous recession, and the advance of American settlement westward, explain American development.") He asked important questions and outlined areas needing further investigation. Although historians today eschew the Turnerian label, his influence is still felt.[5] Literary critics are also indebted to Turner's influence; countless articles implicitly or explicitly work with Turner's concepts, and one recent book uses his thesis as a model for a theory of American literature.[6] Obviously, Turner captured something real in America's experience of the westward movement; theories without substance don't endure. For all the necessary qualifying, rebutting, and substituting, Turner's theories are still with us. So too, the myths engendered by the westering experience—or by fantasies of what that westering should be, or was conceived to be—are still very much alive.

One of the legacies of Turnerian theory as well as of popular literature of the West has been an assumption about the legitimate subject matter and theme of western literature: it is to be about the Old West, a West that, as Wallace Stegner put it, "has been mythicized almost out of recognizability."[7] William Kittredge has noted that western writers have generally either succumbed to the myths or engaged in myth bashing—possibly an essential stage in freeing our literature from the shackles of a frontier past.[8] However, as Kittredge and others point out, there are today many western writers who look at the old myths in fresh new ways, or avoid the myths entirely, or simply write of the New West outside the tunnel vision of frontierism. Literary critics are also exploring new ways of interpreting western literature —ways that shed new light on literature from or about the Old West, and that reveal the dynamics of contemporary writing from the New West.

The essays in this volume focus on reassessments of Old West literature and history, and approaches to New West literature. They were first presented as papers at the twenty-fourth annual conference of the Western Literature Association held in Coeur d'Alene, Idaho, October 1989. The host institution, the University of Idaho, was celebrating its centennial, and 1989–90 marked the state centennials of Idaho, Washington, Montana, North Dakota, South Dakota, and Wyoming. These commemorative events, together with the century mark of the census that came to be regarded as the official closing of the frontier, sparked the theme of the conference: The Old West—The New West. Several keynote speakers were invited to address plenary sessions, and writers of the New West presented readings of their works as scholars met to reassess the Old West and formulate new directions in critical views of both the Old and New West. More than 165 papers were presented, in addition to the keynote addresses, the readings by New West writers, and several panel discussions. Not all presentations focused on the conference theme, but many did. Selections from these papers are included here, together with the addresses by invited speakers. Several of these essays appeared in print while this volume was in preparation; that reviewers working independently found them publishable is an implicit endorsement of quality. One essay from the 1988 conference is also included: Nancy Cook's "Investment in Place: Thomas McGuane in Montana." This essay won the J. Golden Taylor award for the best conference paper submitted by a graduate student; because of that distinction and the fact that the topic so well fit the theme of this volume, it is included here, together with the 1989 award-winning entry by Nathaniel Lewis. Perhaps it is characteristic of the current status of western literary studies that these two prize-winning essays were written on Montana subjects by graduate students enrolled in eastern schools.

The fact that Turner presented his ground-breaking thesis at a conference held in a somewhat incongruous setting may have its counterpart in the Coeur d'Alene conference. The Columbian Exposition must have been a strong competitor for the attention of those academics who dutifully attended sessions of papers. Coeur d'Alene had its own attractions, in the natural beauty of the lakeside setting as well as the commercial developments of the resort and surrounding community. Turner had to forego the fair while he finished writing his paper in his Chicago room;[9] most of the Coeur d'Alene conference papers were accepted after completion, so only last-minute revisions would have kept scholars in their hotel rooms. Nonetheless, the deadlines of presentation often stimulate creative synthesis. This pheomenon may well be one of the best justifications for academic conferences.

Addresses by two distinguished historians, Gerald D. Nash and Patricia Nelson Limerick, open this volume. Nash, whose scholarship has focused on the twentieth-century West, provides a useful overview of Turner's contributions to western historiography, outlines the major shortcomings of Turnerian interpretations, and highlights the changes in the West itself and in interpretations of the West that have occurred during the century since Turner first formulated his frontier thesis. Nash draws from recent scholarship on the West (including his own) to define the major new perspectives put forth by contemporary scholars. Limerick, whose style is as engaging in the lecture hall as it is in print, calls for a revamping of the western myth to include the tragic dimension. Arguing that Turner's thesis implicitly espoused a comic, happy-ending view of American history, she shows how the novelist Raymond Chandler incorporated into his fiction a view of the West that Turnerian historians ignored or failed to see. Chandler's West—and Limerick's—is not a "mythic region steeped in evasive innocence," but a "realistic region that has known sin." Neither Nash nor Limerick calls for utter repudiation of Turnerian history; both urge new formulations that, for Nash, enlarge the frame of reference and, for Limerick, bring about a radical shift of emphasis.

The second group of essays in this collection, "Paradigms of the Old West," opens with Jane Tompkins's address, which focuses on popular Westerns and the Old West myths they express. Building on her earlier essay in *South Atlantic Quarterly* (1987), Tompkins argues that the Western emerged as a revolt against women, religion, and culture of the Victorian era, when "the ability to manipulate language conferred power"; the Western "equates power with 'not-language,' " and not-language with "being male." Linked with that macho silence is violence: "Silence is a sign of mastery, and goes along with a gun in the hand." This essay closes with more questions than it answers, suggesting that the silence used to control may really be an escape or evasion of the inner self.

As I was editing this volume, I happened to reread Tompkins's essay during the days leading up to the Gulf War. The timing could not have been more appropriate. Trampas and the Virginian, moving toward an inevitable shoot-out, were recast as Saddam Hussein and George Bush, who "would rather die than settle the argument by talking to one another"—but of course, others would do the dying for them. Popular Westerns are not history, but fantasy—a fantasy that endures because it so often fits so well our own era, yet seems distanced by the historical trappings of bygone days. Popular Westerns are intensely political, as Max Westbrook's essay demonstrates. Zeroing in on one of the most popular Hollywood Western combos, John Ford and John Wayne, Westbrook brilliantly dissects the uses of western mythology that true westerners often find objectionable: an appropriation of western history that identifies myth with reality and makes "a very un-American message seem American." The Western as a genre evolved to feed the tastes of an eastern audience, yet it has gained a legitimacy comparable to the Buffalo Bill identity at first assumed by William Cody, then eventually believed by him when playing the role could no longer be separated from living it.

Forrest Robinson's essay defines new historicism as it can be used to illuminate much of the literature of the American West. Indeed, Westbrook's essay seems to be a new historicist study without the terminology. Westbrook is most certainly exposing patterns of evasion, instances of bad faith, and subversive subtexts in Ford's Western films. Westbrook, however, encourages us to read the subtexts and eliminate the cultural lies that reinforce undemocratic Americanism; Robinson gives credence to the likely necessity of bad faith for the survival of society. Or, perhaps the difference lies with the choice of subjects: Westbrook focuses on popular Westerns, whereas Robinson chooses texts by Mark Twain, Jack Schaefer, and E. L. Doctorow, with passing reference to a host of others—Cooper, Cather, Stegner, Morris, and more—closing with a respectful yet incisive reassessment of Henry Nash Smith's role in western literary criticism.

Tompkins, Westbrook, and Robinson work with the mythologies of the frontier and the ideologies of American democracy that emerged during the era of the Old West. The remaining essays in this group focus on individual writers. Betsy Downey scrutinizes domestic violence in Mari Sandoz's biography of her father and substantiates that text's representation of social realities that prevailed during the pioneering, settlement period of the Old West—whether specific dates fall chronologically before or after the symbolic closing date of the frontier. We are pointedly reminded that violence, so often linked with the male world of popular Westerns, was all too often present within family households. While not claiming that domestic violence was a direct result of frontier conditions, and while we all know that the passing of the frontier has unfortunately not meant the passing of brutality within the family, Downey's analysis does reveal intrinsic relationships between pioneering social conditions and the prevalence of domestic violence. Paula Harline's essay focuses on families quite different from Sandoz's pioneers, but ones that constituted a significant segment of western history. Through Harline's sensitive analysis of diaries and autobiographical writings of Mormon women engaged in polygamous relationships, we enter the inner world of a particular group of western women and find there haunting reminders of commonalities in human experience though the immediate context may be alien to our own backgrounds.

By this point, readers may well begin to believe that contemporary criticism of western literature focuses on the dark side, possibly overcompensating for the rosy optimism of an Old West that seemed driven by Manifest Destiny. Such a reaction may well be justified; if so, perhaps the emphasis seeks the kind of equality that affirmative action strives to achieve in another sphere. There are, of course, also solid critical studies that find something to praise in the Old West. Concluding this group are three essays that pursue a more positive tack. Frank Bergon takes a fresh look at the journals of Lewis and Clark and demonstrates that these records of an epic journey reveal a composite rather than individualistic (western?) heroism and an affirmation of communal values experienced through the necessities of interdependence. As such, they are exemplary for Americans today. Susan Maher's discussion of Frances Hodgson Burnett's fiction reveals two significant, positive uses of western mythology. By first writing about a Nevada girl's conquest of English society in *A Fair Barbarian* and following that work with her enormously popular *Little Lord Fauntleroy,* Hodgson Burnett nationalized the western myth by transforming the East-West dichotomy within the United States to a European-American one. She also made the American embodiment of values a distinctively western one by appropriating for her heroine the moral energy and crudeness of the West as an "antidote to a civilized world's malaise." If Daisy Miller was the East's ambiguous and ambivalent counterpoint to European civilization, Hodgson Burnett's Octavia Bassett was an American, and recognizably western American, representative who promoted a positive cultural synthesis through the power of her character and even her western manners. Writing during the frontier era and as a nonwesterner, Hodgson Burnett showed that the mythology of the Old West could be used as a cultural bridge.

Willa Cather was drawn to certain aspects of the Old West for subject matter and confirmation of values. For her, the breaking point between Old and New was not the 1890 census but the disillusionment following World War I—her world "broke in two" in 1922.[10] Gary Brienzo studies her 1931 novel, *Shadows on the Rock,* in the context of the historical sources she used and concludes that she selectively drew from these sources to create an Old West in which the values she felt were now lost, existed as perhaps they never did in fact. Such uses of the past may bring Cather closer to the techniques of popular Westerns than she or her critics would care to place her. She did win an eastern audience while many of her contemporary westerners did not; in some respects her fiction may have been written for easterners as were the popular Westerns. This is not to deprecate her work; her place in the western as well as national canon of literature seems secure. She did not, however, receive unqualified praise from some of her contemporary western writers. Vardis Fisher once called Cather's early works " 'romantic' tosh,"[11] and Sophus Winther—whose naturalistic portrayal of a rugged Nebraska frontier was praised by Mari Sandoz—recognized his own Nebraska in Sandoz's *Slogum House* and with that recognition said good-bye to "the world [Willa Cather] saw in Nebraska by means of visioning [her] heart's desire and never really seeing Nebraska at all."[12]

Marilynne Robinson bridges the Old and the New West in her address that opens the section, "Writing in the New West." She was asked to comment on writing in the West today—what relevance one's western background has, whether it is a help or a hindrance, whether the West of today is so removed from the Old West that there is little difference between East and West. She brilliantly addresses these issues, and more, in her essay. The title, "My Western Roots," is my invention, because Robinson did not provide one. I hope readers will not miss the irony, for her roots are not simply western American but Western civilization, and beyond. Giving western individualism a new significance and suggesting optimism from a philosophical premise that concedes a dialectic only between bad and worse, she both heartens and challenges us.

The critical essays in this section focus on individual writers of the New West. First is Sheila O'Brien's comparative study of Marilynne Robinson's novel, *Housekeeping* (1981), and the film version of it. The novel is New West art, whereas the film, in departing slightly from the text and mood of the novel, projects an Old West image. O'Brien's comparisons not only illuminate Robinson's work but help to define just what New West literature is. Helen Lojek chooses two contemporary plays to show how Old West myths can be "read" in real life in the New West. Each drama portrays central characters who are easterners going West to pursue a life modeled on Old West myths. One reads the myth as realism and meets with disaster; the other reads the myth didactically and selectively, gaining direction and a sense of purpose for his own life.

Nathaniel Lewis further illuminates the characteristics of New West writing in his study of contemporary Montana fiction. Using Kenneth Burke's model of symbolization, he shows how writers such as William Kittredge, Patricia Henley, Jim Harrison, Rick Bass, and many others are not only "demolishing the comfortable and false old myths" but also "creating unfamiliar new ones." These fictions use violence of action as well as of words in painfully confronting the realities of a New West that likely shares more commonality with "today's America" than with the historic or mythic past of the Old West. Taking a different approach, Nancy Cook examines Thomas McGuane's fiction in the context of his efforts to place himself and identify himself within his adopted home state of Montana. She concludes that McGuane has not divested himself from Old West myths—that he has, in fact, imposed those myths on the contemporary West and is thus inevitably disappointed by the New West.

Elizabeth Simpson views Montanan Ivan Doig's work through the eyes of the folklorist and thereby calls to our attention another way in which writers can give us a "personal and possessed past" that forms a bridge to the life of the present, in spite of the obvious changes and apparent discontinuities that surround us today. Through stories and traditions and occupational communities that exist independently of place, the history of individuals is passed on; this heritage forms the cultural matrix from which writers such as Doig create their art. Simpson's essay elucidates one aspect of Doig's work; the Western Literature Association recognized and honored Doig at the Coeur d'Alene conference by awarding him the Distinguished Achievement Award and inviting him to read from his latest work in progress. Doig and other Montana writers figure prominently in any discussion of New West literature, as the three varied essays included in this collection demonstrate, for many excellent writers are writing in, about, or from Montana today. That critical approaches are as varied as those represented here reflects not only the multiple possibilities of contemporary criticism but the complexities of the works the critics address.

Closing the section on New West writers is Mary Catherine Harper's essay on Ursula Le Guin's *Always Coming Home.* Though a native Californian and an Oregon resident for many years, Le Guin is not usually regarded as a western writer. Yet she most surely is one in ways that defy facile categorization. Harper's essay appropriately eschews Old West—New West dichotomies, for Le Guin's fiction, especially *Always Coming Home,* repudiates dualities as instances of either-or thinking. As Harper's analysis shows us, Le Guin creates a future civilization in northern California that reflects values of earlier Native American cultures as well as oriental yin-yang philosophy. The unifying concept of Le Guin's complicated presentation in prose and poetry is "He goes backward, looks forward." Perhaps this concept, if acted upon, would be the creative connection between Old and New West that eludes so many of us.

This collection has intentionally focused on Anglo-American writers because the concept of the frontier and the Old West—New West theme emerge from the Anglo-American westering experience. A useful corrective, however, comes from study of those writers whose ethnic heritage provides a radically different conception of the significance of the frontier in American life. Alanna Brown opens a pair of essays focused on ethnic issues with a study of the ways one Native American writer, Mourning Dove, drew from her own and her people's experiences of exploitation, using the language and the modes of Anglo-American culture to express her story but asserting her identity as Indian in a gesture that for her meant the difference between survival and the nonentity of the half-blood. Jerry Dickey's discussion of playwright David Henry Hwang reminds us that our conceptions of the Old West are largely conditioned by our identification with the Anglo-American moving frontier and that our New West perspectives still relate to that historical past. Native Americans, however—as well as the Asians who labored for the white man in the mines, on the railroads, and in the homes of wealthy Old Westerners —obviously experienced the frontier era very differently. These essays on ethnic diversity in the West can but suggest the range of possibilities for critical study of subjects that are beginning to receive more attention. Mourning Dove speaks for the Native Americans during the transition from frontier era to the twentieth century; Hwang and other New West ethnic writers tap the resources of their own racial and cultural backgrounds as they create fictions that legitimize and celebrate their own identities and that invite us to see ourselves through others' eyes.

Concluding this volume of essays is an important challenge to the western literary critic—a call for ecological criticism. Glen Love, in his Past President's Address to the 1989 conference, reminds us of the anthropocentric nature of western civilization's history of conquest and urges us to move from ego-consciousness to eco-consciousness. Poised as we are on the edge of ecological catastrophe, we as critics can respond responsibly by privileging "literature which recognizes and dramatizes the integration of human with natural cycles of life." Love calls attention to a distinctively western version of pastoral in which "the green world . . . asserts its greater significance to the main character" and urges increased attention to the genre of nature writing.

Included here, then, are essays that represent fairly accurately the overall content of the 1989 Western Literature Association conference on The Old West—The New West. Obviously, a single volume cannot provide comprehensive treatment of such a broad topic; the intent here has been to include a number of theoretical essays together with more specialized studies. Though the intent is to represent the range of possibilities, one omission readers may notice is any extended discussion of western poetry. That omission is unfortunate, for not only are there many fine poets today in the West, but the conference program did include a number of papers on poetry. Admittedly, however, the emphasis fell disproportionately on fiction writers. Perhaps this is indicative of an oversight on the part of western literary critics. As far as this volume is concerned, selections were made to provide a coherent essay collection that tells its own story. I could have included conference papers on the poetry of Robinson Jeffers and David Wagoner as examples of ecocriticism, but I chose instead to conclude the volume not with examples but with a challenge. In another paper presented at the conference, Cheryll Burgess urged us to "direct our pioneering spirit toward creating a livable planet." That is a new frontier for western literary critics; it is a new frontier for Americans—for all people—a challenge to use our energies in creative, life-giving ways. Frederick Jackson Turner inaugurated the era of American exceptionalism with his frontier thesis a century ago; today, as Glen Love and other contributors to this volume have pointed out, the West is not an isolated region and our concerns are global ones.[13] Marilynne Robinson provides the appropriate motto for this volume in these lines from her conference address: "The real frontier need never close. Everything, for all purposes, still remains to be done."

Notes

1. Gerald D. Nash, "The Census of 1890 and the Closing of the Frontier," *Pacific Northwest Quarterly* 71 (July 1980): 98–100.

2. Ray Allen Billington, *The Genesis of the Frontier Thesis: A Study in Historical Creativity* (San Marino, Calif.: Huntington Library, 1971), especially chap-

ters 3, 6, and 7. Also see Martin Ridge's Introduction to *Frederick Jackson Turner: Wisconsin's Historian of the Frontier,* ed. Martin Ridge (Madison: State Historical Society of Wisconsin, 1986), 1–12.

3. Billington, *Genesis,* 166–67, 170–71.

4. Frederick Jackson Turner, "The Significance of the Frontier in American History," in Ridge, *F. J. Turner,* 26.

5. See, for instance, the Introduction to Michael P. Malone and Richard W. Etulain, *The American West: A Twentieth-Century History* (Lincoln: University of Nebraska Press, 1989). A recent survey of members of the Western History Association, the Western Writers of America, and a group of editors and publishers reveals sharp divisions of opinion as to whether the West is defined by the frontier process (a Turnerian view) or is a geographically identifiable place. See Walter Nugent, "Where Is the American West? Report on a Survey," *Montana: the Magazine of Western History* 42, no. 3 (Summer 1992): 2–23.

6. "Historically the existence of a frontier of settlement, and of unsettled and even unknown lands beyond, has generated in the American literary imagination a set of images, attitudes, and assumptions that have shaped our literature into a peculiarly American mold." David Mogen, Mark Busby, and Paul Bryant, eds., *The Frontier Experience and the American Dream* (College Station: Texas A&M University Press, 1989), 3. See also Harold P. Simonson, *The Closed Frontier: Studies in American Literary Tragedy* (New York: Holt, Rinehart, and Winston, 1970).

7. Wallace Stegner, "History, Myth and the Western Writer" (1967), in *The Sound of Mountain Water* (New York: Doubleday, 1969), 199.

8. William Kittredge, *Owning It All* (Saint Paul, Minn.: Graywolf Press, 1987), 170–74.

9. Billington, *Genesis,* 165–66.

10. Willa Cather, *Not Under Forty* (New York: Alfred A. Knopf, 1936), v.

11. Vardis Fisher, "Hometown Revisited: The Antelope Hills, Idaho," *Tomorrow* 9 (Dec. 1949): 19.

12. Sophus K. Winther, review of Mari Sandoz's *Slogum House* (1937), typescript in editor's possession. (Winther reviewed books for several publications during this period, but a published source for this review has not been identified.) For Sandoz's comments on Winther, see her review, "Danes on the Prairies," *Saturday Review of Literature,* Mar. 28, 1936, 21.

13. Some recent historians have called attention to global influences on the American West, and have described the West as a world subregion. See especially Richard White, *"It's Your Misfortune and None of My Own": A New History of the American West* (Norman: University of Oklahoma Press, 1991); Patricia Nelson Limerick et al., eds., *Trails: Toward a New Western History* (Lawrence: University Press of Kansas, 1991), especially the essays by Limerick, Donald Worster, Richard White, Michael P. Malone, and William G. Robbins; Donald Worster, *Rivers of Empire* (New York: Pantheon Books, 1985).

Bibliography

Billington, Ray Allen. *The Genesis of the Frontier Thesis: A Study in Historical Creativity.* San Marino, Calif.: Huntington Library, 1971.

Cather, Willa. *Not Under Forty.* New York: Alfred A. Knopf, 1936.

Fisher, Vardis. "Hometown Revisited: The Antelope Hills, Idaho." *Tomorrow* 9 (Dec. 1949): 18–23.

Kittredge, William. *Owning It All.* Saint Paul, Minn.: Graywolf Press, 1987.

Limerick, Patricia Nelson, Clyde A. Milner II, and Charles E. Rankin, eds. *Trails: Toward a New Western History.* Lawrence: University Press of Kansas, 1991.

Malone, Michael P., and Richard W. Etulain. *The American West: A Twentieth-Century History.* Lincoln: University of Nebraska Press, 1989.

Mogen, David, Mark Busby, and Paul Bryant, eds. *The Frontier Experience and the American Dream: Essays on American Literature.* College Station: Texas A&M University Press, 1989.

Nash, Gerald D. "The Census of 1890 and the Closing of the Frontier." *Pacific Northwest Quarterly* 71 (July 1980): 98–100.

Nugent, Walter. "Where Is the American West? Report on a Survey." *Montana: the Magazine of Western History* 42, no. 3 (Summer 1992): 2–23.

Ridge, Martin, ed. *Frederick Jackson Turner: Wisconsin's Historian of the Frontier.* Madison: State Historical Society of Wisconsin, 1986.

Sandoz, Mari. "Danes on the Prairies." *Saturday Review of Literature,* Mar. 28, 1936, 21.

Simonson, Harold P. *The Closed Frontier: Studies in American Literary Tragedy.* New York: Holt, Rinehart, and Winston, 1970.

Stegner, Wallace. "History, Myth and the Western Writer." *American West* 4 (May 1967): 61–62, 76–79. Reprint in *The Sound of Mountain Water,* 186–201. New York: Doubleday, 1969.

Tompkins, Jane. "West of Everything." *South Atlantic Quarterly* 86 (Fall 1987): 357–77.

Turner, Frederick Jackson. "The Significance of the Frontier in American History" (1893). In *Frederick Jackson Turner: Wisconsin's Historian of the Frontier,* edited by Martin Ridge, 26–47. Madison: State Historical Society of Wisconsin, 1986.

White, Richard. *"It's Your Misfortune and None of My Own": A New History of the American West.* Norman: University of Oklahoma Press, 1991.

Winther, Sophus K. Review of Mari Sandoz's *Slogum House* (1937). Typescript.

Worster, Donald. *Rivers of Empire: Water, Aridity, and the Growth of the American West.* New York: Pantheon Books, 1985.

Part I

Turner and After:
Perspectives on Western History
and Literature

1. New Approaches to the American West

Gerald D. Nash

The celebrations of the centennials of the northern states provide us with a unique opportunity to assess an Old West that is visibly passing, and to try to comprehend a New West that is following in its wake. Just as in 1890 the generation of Frederick Jackson Turner was keenly aware that they were witnessing the passing of one era and the opening of another, so today we are conscious of the fact that a century of statehood represents a true landmark in the history of the West, and the beginning of a new stage of development whose outlines are not yet visible. Like Turner in 1890, we too stand at the brink of a new century. Celebrations such as centennials serve a most useful function. They call attention to the passage of time. The closing years of centuries in particular provide a spur to reflection and contemplation; they offer opportunities for self-assessment and they challenge us to divine the future of our respective interests in the study of the West.

Turner contemplated the statehood of western states; we contemplate the statehood centennials. Turner's creative thinking during that crucial decade of the 1890s culminated in a perception that has dominated historical writing about the West, has shaped both fictional and nonfictional literary endeavors, and has sunk deep into the popular consciousness of the American people for nearly a century. Indeed, one would be hard put to think of another field of literature or history in which the ideas of one individual had as profound or pervasive an impact as did those of Frederick Jackson Turner. Now, a century later, the time is particularly appropriate to review the paths that students of literature and history in the West have followed. Are our inherited concepts still valid? Is it time to abandon them or to adapt them to the state of knowledge about the West a hundred years later? Just what is the relationship between the Old West and the New?

The dimensions of Turnerian perspectives are well known. Turner postulated two significant hypotheses. His most famous formulation was the theory concerning the influence of the frontier on American life. That pronouncement coincided with statehood for Idaho, Washington, Montana, Wyoming, North Dakota, and South Dakota.[1] The coincidence of the Turner theory and statehood for these territories within a few years of each other was not accidental. A direct relationship existed between the rapid settlement of these areas and the perceptions of Turner and his generation that they were witnessing the passing of an era that they recalled nostalgically. As their memories dimmed in later years they remembered the past as even more of a golden age than when they had first glimpsed it in their youth. When they became old they enshrined it romantically in their imaginations.

Turner did not have much success with his second major idea, interpreting the West as a section or region (he used these terms interchangeably). As the settlement of the frontier proceeded, he argued, it was replaced by the formation of the West as a region. As in his development of the frontier hypothesis, Turner was not entirely original. He borrowed many aspects of his sectional hypothesis from Josiah Royce, who had developed its outlines three decades earlier. Turner labored on his theory of sections for more than thirty years after 1890. He did not formulate it in final form until the last decade of his life, beginning in 1922. During these years he believed firmly that his theory of sections was at least as significant as his theory of the frontier. But, alas, when he first publicized it in 1922, and more fully in 1926, he received a less than enthusiastic reception. Most scholars, whether students of literature, history, or the social sciences, were singularly unimpressed. As his biographer, Ray Allen Billington, told the story:

> He did his best, but the result was a sad anticlimax. "The significance in American history of the advance of the frontier and of its disappearance is now generally recognized," he began boldly.... "I wish to consider with you another fundamental factor..., namely, the Section." Then came the usual history of

the sectional conflicts of the nineteenth century. . . . Yet he had little to add to a story that was already well known to historians and was by no means convincing. The address . . . stirred none of the excitement of his frontier thesis.[2]

His address to the Wisconsin State Historical Society on sections thus was a deep disappointment. But he continued to argue the theme on the lecture circuit in succeeding months, without much success. His audiences remained small and skeptical. Still, he was convinced that ultimately his sectional theory would win wide acceptance. "I am possessed with the idea," he wrote to his good friend, Arthur M. Schlesinger, Sr., "that twenty years or so from now my Sections paper will travel along with my frontier as interpretations." Twenty years passed, yet the theory did not have many more adherents in 1946 than it had in 1926.[3]

Thus it is the theory of the frontier that is most widely associated with Turner, although his own perceptions of western history were much broader. He ranged across the whole spectrum of American history, into the social sciences, psychology, the natural sciences, and somewhat less into the cultural dimension of American life. Yet, in spite of his avowed broad outlook, it was his frontier theory that became his most significant legacy for later generations.

In the course of the twentieth century, however, shortcomings of the frontier hypothesis became apparent. That was hardly surprising. Turner was very much a creature of his own age and reflected its particular prejudices and outlooks. What was relevant to the generation of the 1890s was hardly timely for those in later years. If there is truth to the adage that each generation reinterprets the past according to its own perspectives, then the aging of the thesis was to be expected and certainly cast no discredit on Turner. Nevertheless, in the absence of other broad theories the Turnerian framework continued to dominate successive generations of scholars, and even now enjoys considerable support.[4] The centennial raises the question, however, whether it is time, not necessarily to reject the Turner theory, but to consider other approaches to an understanding of the West that might be equally or perhaps even more fruitful. A Model T may not be as useful on the high-speed turnpikes of today as it was on the country roads of an earlier age.

What have been some of the problems that the Turner theory has presented to students of the West? In the first place, it did not apply

problems with Turner

very well to the West of the twentieth century. While many aspects of the Turner hypothesis provided suggestive explanations for western development before 1890, the thesis did not appear too useful in explaining the growth of the West after that time. The reaction of many writers and historians before 1970 was merely to ignore the West of the twentieth century and to focus almost all of their attention on the frontier. But is it possible in 1993 simply to ignore or dismiss an entire century in the development of the West as a region?

Second, the dimensions of the Turner thesis seemed increasingly narrow. It left out huge chunks of the western experience. It contributed relatively little to an understanding of cultural and intellectual life of the West; it largely ignored cultures other than the Anglo-American in the area, whether Indian, Hispano-American, or black. And it allotted very little attention to at least one-half of the population, namely, women, who had their own role in the West. At best, it provided only a partial glimpse of the western experience.

Third, while the Turner thesis explained a great deal about the Old Northwest (Turner's own native region, which he knew so well), it was much less revealing about many other subregions of the West. These included what were once known as the Great American Desert, the Great Plains, the arid Southwest, and the old Spanish Borderlands. Nor did it apply very well to the development of California, or the states of the Pacific Northwest, or the northern tier of states that celebrated their centennials in 1989 and 1990.

Despite such obvious shortcomings, however, between 1893 and 1993 the Turner thesis continued to have a large cadre of adherents. Perhaps this was because Turner was more than just a historian. He was also a poet. It would be naive to assume that the Old West before 1890 was nothing more than a historical event, a phase in regional and national growth. It was much more than that, of course. As we are all aware, it was—and is—an essential part of American myth. It is a land of the imagination, a golden age of America's past that may not have existed in fact but continues to endure in the minds and hearts of millions of Americans. Thus, while many can concede the disappearance of much of the West as a physical frontier, they cannot as readily admit to the disappearance of this West from their imaginations. This West is a mythical land that enshrines American hopes and dreams. Such an emotional attachment to the Old West—as distinguished from an intellectual comprehension of the region—may do much to explain the persistence of the Turner thesis long after it out-lived much of its initial usefulness.

But, it may be asked, what reasons suggest the desirability of considering other approaches to the study of the West? First, one must mention the passage of time, which has created new perspectives. Turner wrote about the era he knew best, namely, the late nineteenth century. He extended the perspectives of his own times to earlier eras. But the passage of one hundred years has obviously created different outlooks. One of these is to raise doubts about the significance of the year, 1890, as a watershed. Clearly, the western frontier did not disappear in 1890. What Turner did was uncritically to accept statements by the superintendent of the U.S. census in 1890. Note that Turner never mentioned that individual by name, whether consciously or unconsciously, and took his pronouncements at face value. The person involved was one Patrick Porter, an English immigrant who was a journalist and a popular writer on a great variety of subjects. He was not an expert on either demography or the interpretation of statistical analysis. In fact, he accepted the position of superintendent of the census as a temporary position between journalistic stints.[5] Although thousands of historians have followed Turner in citing Porter's report, very few have bothered to identify him by name or to assess his competence. But as eminent geographers who were Turner's contemporaries pointed out, specifically Isaiah Bowman, the western frontiers did not disappear in 1890. Frontier-type settlement, Bowman noted, continued steadily in the United States (and western Canada) between 1890 and 1930.[6] Indeed, between 1905 and 1915 more than 500,000 Americans participated in a land rush to the western Canadian provinces, a rush that was one of the largest of its kind. When compared to the censuses of 1900 or 1910, that of 1890 was not especially distinctive. From the perspective of 1990, therefore, 1890 may not have been as significant a watershed as contemporaries believed. But without quibbling about 1890, it is apparent that the passage of time has produced changed perspectives on the West.

Does the West since 1890 have greater significance in national life than it did in the preceding century? That's a difficult question to answer. Certainly the aggregate wealth of the region is much greater. Certainly its population is far larger. Indeed, the census of 1980 revealed that the center of population in the United States for the first time in its history was located west of the Mississippi River. That symbolized the westward shift of people that occurred during the one hundred years following 1890. Similarly, the shift of economic power was reflected in the increase of large corporations with headquarters west of the 98th meridian. Moreover, by 1990 the West had far greater political power in national affairs, reflected in an increasing number of congressional seats as a result of reapportionment. Since 1928 six Presidents have been identified with the West—Hoover, Eisenhower, Johnson, Nixon, Reagan, and Bush. In short, it is difficult to ignore the extraordinary growth of the West since 1890, and historians and students of the literary West need to confront the reality as well as the myths surrounding its existence.[7]

Generational changes also contribute to changing perspectives on the West. Every generation has a particular outlook on its own and on other cultures that is significantly shaped by contemporary events of particular eras. These events usually have their greatest impact during the first twenty-five years of an individual's lifetime. This is not to suggest that people never change their minds over a span of years. Yet their worldview, their Weltanschauung, their perspective on life and on culture is often stamped by the particular events or ideas of their youth, frequently the most impressionable years of their lives. The philosopher José Ortega y Gasset recognized this tendency when he defined culture as

> only the interpretation which man gives to his life, the series of more or less satisfying solutions he finds in order to meet the problems and necessities of life, as well as those which belong to the material order and the so-called spiritual ones. . . . Culture is the conception of the world or the universe which serves as the plan . . . riskily elaborated by man, for orienting himself among things, for coping with his life, and finding a direction amid the chaos of his situation.[8]

The theologian Martin Marty developed this theme further. He warned that the concept of "generations" could be taken too literally in a biological sense. Still, in seeking to grasp something as elusive as culture, the generational handle can be quite valuable. Differing interpretations of historical data—such as those pertaining to the West—often appear along generational lines. Marty noted that

> Ortega was almost certainly too mechanical in his idea that cultural generations occurred fifteen years apart; he was more sub-

tle when he recognized that several generations are coevals alive at the same time. Those who have undergone a similar set of experiences at decisive stages in their life-careers tend to develop common outlooks. This is as true of those within the culture who endow with meaning both their fortune and their suffering —as it is of those who recognize and label the cultural change they perceive.[9]

In other words, the passage of generations results in differing views or perspectives over time, which in turn result in altered understanding of the significance of the West in the nation's life. The task of students of literature and history is to identify, record, and analyze these changes.

It could be argued that a consideration of new approaches to the West is necessitated also by the rich and diversified scholarship that the region has inspired in the past century. Scholars have written about the West as a frontier, of course, but also as a region, as an urban civilization, and as an element of myth. These varying perspectives have done much to broaden our awareness of the complexities of both cultural as well as environmental influences that have shaped the West. Thus, (the passage of time, change over generations, and fruitful scholarship dictate an expansion of perspectives on the West without necessarily rejecting older hypotheses such as those of Turner.)

If such a premise has some validity, then the question arises concerning alternative approaches available to students of American literature and history who have a special interest in the West. One alternative is to extend our chronological frame of reference. Another is to utilize a multicultural perspective. Viewing the West as an urban civilization also yields new insights. A fourth approach is ideological. These are not mutually exclusive, and are readily susceptible to interdisciplinary research.

The possibility of extending our chronological frame of reference for the West to the period after 1890 has already been mentioned. That would certainly do much to alter our image of the West in both literature and history. Even if the Old West and the New West reflect many continuities, still the changes and differences between them are at least as striking as the continuities. Let us briefly contrast this twentieth-century West with its predecessor of the nineteenth century. The twentieth-century West has become an urban civilization with a multicultural and multiracial population. That differentiates it from an earlier age characterized by a far more homogeneous society dominated by people of English or northern European background. The twentieth-century West boasts a diversified economy based on manufacturing and advanced technology, tourism, and a military-industrial complex. The nineteenth-century West relied on a pre-industrial, natural-resource-based economy, mainly agriculture, mining, and cattle. The twentieth-century West is one beset by serious environmental limitations, by the fragility of ecological balance, and by a keen awareness of the need for prudent resource management. By contrast, the nineteenth-century West seemed to promise virtually unlimited resources to Americans, available for almost unfettered exploitation. The twentieth-century West reflects a rather prosaic style of politics, characterized by blandness and loose party and regional identity. The nineteenth-century West had a highly distinctive political style stressing individualism, colorful personalities, and strong party loyalties. The twentieth-century West has established itself as a bold innovator in many phases of American cultural life. The nineteenth-century West could not claim a cultural life of its own, but reflected its eastern origins. To summarize, the twentieth-century West embodies an urban, multicultural society, a diversified economy, a limited environment, a nondescriptive political outlook, and has become a dynamic cultural pacesetter.[10] Is it time to give greater prominence to the West that has emerged during the past one hundred years, or should we continue to fix our gaze primarily on the nineteenth-century West?

If perspectives change, new cultural symbols will be needed as well. Instead of the Anglo-Saxon cowboy of the nineteenth century as the West's role model, typical twentieth-century western heroes may be white, black, brown, yellow, or red, and the "he" may as likely be a "she." Instead of mountain men, cattle growers, miners, or farmers, representative figures of the twentieth-century West may be corporate executives, scientists, engineers, government bureaucrats, or military officials. Instead of explorers and fur trappers, the denizens of the western environment may be professional land-management specialists, environmentalists, or naturalists. Instead of colorful political personalities—the local sheriff, the county courthouse politician, or the congressional orator—the twentieth century has bland media personages who follow national trends and are disinclined to much innovation. And the dance halls and saloons of nineteenth century western culture are hardly proper symbols for the region a hundred years later. Major art museums, concert halls, great scientific laboratories, and distinguished educational institutions have come to be representative of the West. And in popular culture, for good or ill, Hollywood, Las Vegas, and Disneyland set standards for all of the United States, and indeed, for much of the world.

Another approach to the study of the West is the multicultural perspective, to view the region as a mingling of peoples with differing ethnic, racial, and cultural backgrounds. Historians adhering to this perspective give much less emphasis to environmental influences than did Turner. Instead, they focus on the primacy of cultural identity. Initially, the approach was developed after 1960 by practitioners who focused on blacks, Chicanos, Native Americans, and women in the hope that the history of each particular group would provide a key to a better understanding of western history. Although the various specialists dealt with specific segments of the population, they did share a common assumption. They believed that the United States in the twentieth century was not a melting pot but a society characterized by ethnic, racial, and cultural diversity. Their studies made previously invisible people in the West visible. Women, blacks, Orientals, Chicanos, and Indians now came to take a more prominent place in the history of western growth. Thus, the mingling of peoples and the interaction of cultures contributed to a new, broader approach to the study of the West.

A consideration of alternatives to the Turner thesis cannot ignore the emerging urban perspective on the West. In the past twenty years urban historians have demonstrated persuasively that the history of the West since the middle of the nineteenth century has in large part been a history of towns and cities. Even the most remote outlying ranches and sparsely populated areas of the West were affected by neighboring urban communities. Although Turner initially ignored this urban dimension, he became quite conscious of it near the end of his career. In fact, he predicted in 1926 that an urban interpretation would grip the attention of historians in the next several decades. Towns and cities set the pace for life-styles throughout the region. As early as 1949 Carey McWilliams noted that in the West—in contrast to the more densely populated East—even small urban enclaves had an influence far greater than their size would imply, often extending for hundreds of miles beyond their boundaries. A city such as Reno, Nevada, which had about twenty-five thousand people in

1940, nevertheless served as the major metro-political center for the entire state of Nevada in that decade, with influence radiating hundreds of miles in various directions.[11]

As in other academic disciplines, some scholars have adopted an ideological approach in writing about the development of the West. Reflecting a national trend, they often embrace New Left political perspectives, or variations of them. This is especially true of some of those scholars who were trained in the 1960s. Although varying in their perspectives, they have a strong anticapitalist bias and a distinctly negative view of most aspects of American society, with few exceptions. They criticize American capitalism as a particularly exploitative and destructive system—not only of the cultures of the people whom it subjugated, largely the minorities, but also of the environment. The influence of Herbert Marcuse's *One Dimensional Man* is evident in some of these writers, such as Leslie Fiedler, Richard Slotkin, and Richard Drinnon, even when they do not cite him specifically.

The contributions of ideological historians are varied. A major asset has been their focus on the big picture, on worldwide and national trends of which the West is only a part. The approach can provide a broad context, one that is at times missing in the work of more narrowly specialized scholars. Ideological historians have demonstrated that the West is not unique, that some aspects of its development shared characteristics common to other regions or nations. This emphasis contrasts with the Turner thesis, which viewed the West as a distinct and unique historical phenomenon. On the other hand, the one-sided negative analysis of writers such as Marc Reisner, Peter Wiley, and Robert Gottlieb is as distorting as Turner's thesis was in exclusively stressing the positive aspects of the frontier experience.

Interdisciplinary approaches, often through American Studies, have been particularly useful in the perception of the West as myth. The West has attracted the attention of scholars in a wide range of fields. Social scientists, in geography, psychology, cultural anthropology, sociology, political science, and economics—to name only a few—have developed important concepts and methods with which to explore the West. In the humanities, scholars of literature, folklore, art, and music history have made similar contributions, which students of American Studies have utilized. Individuals such as Henry Nash Smith, Leo Marx, and William Goetzmann come to mind.[12] Clearly, the interaction of diverse disciplines provides another alternative to the frontier thesis as students of western literature contemplate the Old West and the New.

The alternatives to the Turner thesis discussed in this essay are certainly not the only models available to literary scholars of the West. But they are suggestive of some of the fruitful research of the past generation. As we contemplate the one-hundredth anniversary of the closing of the frontier, the time is ripe for changing our image of the West. A whole century has passed since the West was a frontier. Can we ignore that stark reality, or do we have an obligation to convey it to the American people, to the mass media, and to westerners themselves? Some of the approaches that scholars have developed in the past century are broad and integrative, yet it would be futile to expect a successor to the Turner thesis at this time. The academic profession in 1993 is very different from that of one hundred years ago. Then it was composed of no more than several hundred individuals, mostly men, who had remarkably similar ethnic, social, and cultural backgrounds. By and large, they were white Anglo-Saxon Protestants. A century later the profession numbers not several hundred, but more than twenty thousand. The members are remarkably diverse in their racial, ethnic, gender, social, and cultural backgrounds. In view of such diversity it would be unrealistic to expect the kind of consensus on a conceptual framework that greeted Turner. But the concepts that have been developed do relate the singular features of the western environment to the cultural impact of the people who settled it. They can identify unique and distinctive characteristics of the West as a region, not only before 1890 but for the century thereafter. They can explain the processes of change over time, and can serve as useful vehicles for research.

Much has changed in the West since the 1890s; in many respects it has lost some of its distinctiveness and become more like the rest of the nation. Nevertheless, it still retains important, unique characteristics not the least of which is its natural environment. Attractive climates, natural resources, and open spaces distinguish the West from other regions in the United States. And not to be ignored is its historical tradition, whether rooted in myth or in reality, which has given to the West a particular mystique. As we contemplate the centennials of the northern states, as we contemplate one hundred years of western development since the supposed closing of the frontier, let us sharpen our perspectives on the region by supplementing Turner's frontier hypothesis with the more up-to-date models of the West that have emerged from intensive and fruitful researches of the wide range of writers and scholars during the past three generations.

Notes

1. For Turner's 1893 essay see Frederick Jackson Turner, *The Frontier in American History* (New York: H. Holt, 1920), or Ray Allen Billington, *Frederick Jackson Turner: Historian, Scholar, Teacher* (New York: Oxford University Press, 1973); see also John D. Hicks, *The Constitutions of the Northwest States,* University of Nebraska Studies Series, vol. 23 (Lincoln: University of Nebraska Press, 1924).

2. Billington, *Turner,* 395–98; Earl S. Pomeroy, "Josiah Royce," *Pacific Historical Review* 40 (Nov. 1970): 9–16.

3. Turner's letter to Arthur M. Schlesinger, Sr., May 5, 1925, is in Wilbur Jacobs, ed., *The Historical World of Frederick Jackson Turner* (New Haven: Yale University Press, 1968), 164–65.

4. See, for example, E. David Cronon, "Revisiting the Vanishing Frontier: The Legacy of Frederick Jackson Turner," *Western Historical Quarterly* 18 (Apr. 1987): 157–76. For a more extended discussion of the controversy over Turner see Gerald D. Nash, *Creating the West: Historical Interpretations, 1890–1990* (Albuquerque: University of New Mexico Press, 1991), 11–13, 23–28, 33–36, 41–47, 52–68. This essay is a by-product of this comprehensive study of the course of western history in the century after 1890.

5. Gerald D. Nash, "The Census of 1890 and the Closing of the Frontier," *Pacific Northwest Quarterly* 71 (July 1980): 98–100.

6. Isaiah Bowman, *The Pioneer Fringe* (New York: American Geographical Society, 1931), iii, 139. See also Nash, *Creating the West,* 31–33, for a fuller discussion of this point.

7. Gerald D. Nash and Richard Etulain, eds., *The Twentieth-Century West: Historical Interpretations* (Albuquerque: University of New Mexico Press, 1989), 409–10.

8. José Ortega y Gasset, *Gesammelte Werke* (Stuttgart: Deutsche Verlags-Anstalt, 1954–56), 2:207, 464; 3:403–4, 411, 464.

9. Martin Marty, "Religion in America since Mid-Century," *Daedalus* 111 (Fall 1988): 150–51; See also Karl J. Weintraub, *Visions of Culture* (Chicago: University of Chicago Press, 1966), 266–67.

10. Nash and Etulain, *Twentieth-Century West,* 407–8.

11. Gerald D. Nash, *The American West in the Twentieth Century* (Albuquerque: University of New Mexico Press, 1977), 1–7; Carey McWilliams, Introduction to Ray B. West, ed., *Rocky Mountain Cities* (New York: W. W. Norton, 1949), 8. On Turner, see Jacobs, ed., *Turner,* 153; Billington, *Turner,* 492–93.

12. Henry Nash Smith, *Virgin Land* (Cambridge: Harvard University Press,

1950); Leo Marx, *The Machine in the Garden* (New York: Oxford University Press, 1964); William H. and William N. Goetzmann, *The West of the Imagination* (New York: Norton, 1986).

Bibliography

Billington, Ray Allen. *Frederick Jackson Turner: Historian, Scholar, Teacher.* New York: Oxford University Press, 1973.

Bowman, Isaiah. *The Pioneer Fringe.* New York: American Geographical Society, 1931.

Cronon, E. David. "Revisiting the Vanishing Frontier: The Legacy of Frederick Jackson Turner." *Western Historical Quarterly* 18 (Apr. 1987): 157–76.

Goetzmann, William H. and William N. *The West of the Imagination.* New York: Norton, 1986.

Hicks, John D. *The Constitutions of the Northwest States.* University of Nebraska Studies Series, vol. 23. Lincoln: University of Nebraska Press, 1924.

Jacobs, Wilbur, ed. *The Historical World of Frederick Jackson Turner.* New Haven: Yale University Press, 1968.

Marty, Martin. "Religion in America since Mid-Century." *Daedalus* 111 (Fall 1988): 149–63.

Marx, Leo. *The Machine in the Garden.* New York: Oxford University Press, 1964.

McWilliams, Carey. Introduction to Ray B. West, ed. *Rocky Mountain Cities.* New York: W. W. Norton, 1949.

Nash, Gerald D. *The American West in the Twentieth Century.* Albuquerque: University of New Mexico Press, 1977.

———. "The Census of 1890 and the Closing of the Frontier." *Pacific Northwest Quarterly* 71 (July 1980): 98–100.

———. *Creating the West: Historical Interpretations, 1890–1990.* Albuquerque: University of New Mexico Press, 1991.

Nash, Gerald D., and Richard Etulain, eds. *The Twentieth-Century West: Historical Interpretations.* Albuquerque: University of New Mexico Press, 1989.

Ortega y Gasset, José. *Gesammelte Werke.* 4 vols. Stuttgart: Deutsche Verlags-Anstalt, 1954–56.

Pomeroy, Earl S. "Josiah Royce." *Pacific Historical Review* 40 (Nov. 1970): 1–20.

Smith, Henry Nash. *Virgin Land.* Cambridge: Harvard University Press, 1950.

Turner, Frederick Jackson. *The Frontier in American History.* New York: H. Holt, 1920.

Weintraub, Karl J. *Visions of Culture.* Chicago: University of Chicago Press, 1966.

2. What Raymond Chandler Knew and Western Historians Forgot

Patricia Nelson Limerick

Frederick Jackson Turner, everyone knows, was the father of western American history. Fields and movements, as a rule, have fathers. They seldom have mothers, and they never have uncles or aunts. I suppose it is all a great tribute to the power of patriarchy, that this pattern of fatherly phrasing is so universal and so taken for granted. But it is in western history, where paternity has been so thoroughly narrowed to Turner and the speech he gave in 1893, that the pattern of thought most calls for change.

We have, at long last, come to the end of the Turnerian patriarchy. Let us, then, take this opportunity for a useful change in tone and spirit, and call the leaders of the various movements that have broken up that empire of white male dominance aunts and uncles, rather than mothers and fathers. Especially in some cultures, aunts and uncles can play very central roles in bringing up offspring, but they often play those roles in a less controlling, less dominating way.

Recasting our search for non-Turnerian approaches to the American West as a search for uncles and aunts is one way to ease the pain of the paradigm shift now under way in western American history. Instead of making a wrenching break from the family tree, we can shift the emphasis: we can move our loyalty from *one* father to a set of aunts and uncles, from Frederick Jackson Turner alone, to a kinship network of Josiah Royce, Angie Debo, Georgia O'Keeffe, Bernard DeVoto, Joseph Kinsey Howard, Wallace Stegner, maybe even Turner himself, and, yes, Raymond Chandler.

Why Raymond Chandler? Initially, to be frank, because I wanted some way to relate to an audience at the Western Literature Association. If I were to assign myself the task of reading or rereading some body of western literature, then Raymond Chandler was my first choice. I had not read Chandler in ten years, but I had a distinct memory that his was a West that would have shaken Turnerian western historians to their toes—*if* they had taken it seriously.

But why on earth would they have taken Chandler seriously? And why would I now? I refer to the "Grand Canyon" running between historical studies and literary studies, between fact and fiction, between the hard and the soft, between concerns of reality and concerns of aesthetics. I refer to that Grand Canyon, in order to celebrate it. I have, heaven knows, suffered a bit myself from the depth of this divide. A number of my interesting colleagues in western history have, at times, found me "too literary" in my interests and style, and therefore of doubtful authenticity as a historian.

But think for a moment about the Grand Canyon. Is either side, either rim, anywhere near as interesting as the interior of the canyon? A moment's thought makes it clear that the center of excitement is in the canyon itself, not in the safe plateau on either rim. And yet this disciplinary nonsense has caused us, historical scholars and literary scholars, to devote our attention to one side or the other, resolutely looking away from the center of interest, the canyon itself.

In case this figure of speech is itself, as they say, too literary, let me say explicitly that what I am talking about is the search for meaning in the western past, the search for patterns, the search for themes and organizing ideas. That meaning lies, like the Colorado River, at the floor of the canyon where the literary scholar's search for meaning and the historian's search for meaning would intersect, if we would let them. For both western historians and western literary scholars in the late twentieth century, the search for the meanings of the American West resembles the position of Raymond Chandler's Philip Marlowe in the midst of one novel: "I won't say the pieces [are] beginning to fall into place, but at least they [are] getting to look like parts of the same puzzle."[1]

And so I propose Raymond Chandler as the first uncle of western American history. It may seem odd to select an intellectual kinsman for historians from the other side of the canyon, but it has a considerable logic. Reading Raymond Chandler in the right spirit gives western historians a way of easing their field into the modern age, whether or not that approach seems altogether proper according to conventional disciplinary boundaries.

Let us begin with the obvious: Raymond Chandler is a hell of a writer, and most western American historians are not. Of course, flatness of prose is not a distinctive affliction of western history. Crummy writing is a sad state of affairs throughout the scholarly profession, and, in spite of their more frequent exposure to fine writing, literary scholars have not themselves risen above the academic norm. It may be that western historians, fleeing the association of their field with cheap, popular entertainment, have tried even harder to wrap their writings in shades of academic gray, but reading a Chandler novel provides one way to realize that this academic experiment has been tried long enough. Western historians have proven that they can take exciting stories, and deaden them into full academic respectability. That mission accomplished, it might be worthwhile to watch a capital "S" stylist at work, and see what we can learn.

What we learn could be of enormous consequence for western history, and for the chance that western historians might be heard by the general public. The crisis of western history, as Richard White of the University of Washington has said, is a crisis of storytelling.[2] The old frontier-based western history, White says, was essentially a comedy. Pioneers took on the continent, struggled, and won, and with the happy ending in hand, the hardships and struggles became inconsequential.

The so-called new western historians, White says (and here, I fear, I am myself a prime example), have given up comedy and turned to irony. Now the pioneers take on the continent, with dreams and hopes of profit and progress, and instead run head-on into uncooperative natives and nature. Both natives and nature clearly cannot experience this collision as comedy, and, for that matter, neither can the pioneers. Efforts to introduce new, economically productive crops also introduce weeds and pests. Efforts to save the heathen ruin the heathen. Plowing becomes erosion. Dams to conserve water prove better at evaporating water. And so it goes, one ironic outcome after the other, and the new western historian sits there like an insufferable sportscaster, safe in the press box, narrating a game that is made up almost entirely of incomplete passes and fumbles.

The old western historians, Richard White says, have played with an advantage. They have an appealing, comic story of victory and progress, and we offer an ironic story of intentions stymied. In any variety of contests for an audience's loyalty, comedy beats irony in every match.

But tragedy can carry power equal to, or greater than, comedy. And here, indeed, we hit the central peculiarity of the American myth of the West. Most myths—take, for instance, Greek myths—have a central component of tragedy. Other cultures have myths that face up to tragedy, to defeat, to failure, to sin. (Manifested in movies, popular novels, and Turnerian western history, the American myth of the West brushes off these central elements of human experience.) Other people's myths face up to human depravity and to human despair, but ours remains a "Happy Face—Have a Nice Day" myth, which cannot provide much consolation or guidance in troubling times.

But not in Raymond Chandler's books. Or in his life.

Chandler's parents married in Laramie, though he was born in Chicago and spent much of his childhood in England. "I was conceived in Laramie, Wyoming," he wrote, "and if they had asked me, I should have preferred to be born there. I always like high altitudes."[3] If they had asked me, I would have preferred the symbolic wholeness of Chandler's being born in Wyoming, but I will settle, if I must, for "conceived in Laramie." His father deserted his mother early on, and Chandler, his biographer says, "rarely spoke of his father except occasionally to call him 'an utter swine.' "[4] In later years, a tour of duty working for Southern California oil companies failed to redeem Chandler's faith in human nature, and he remained, from Laramie to Los Angeles, a man who could write of himself, "I have lived my life on the edge of nothing."[5]

That strange and troubling line gives me considerable confidence in Chandler's status as an interpreter of western history. Or perhaps I should say the reverse: that a western historian baffled by that sentence is a western historian whose reflections I would take with some cynicism. "I have lived my life on the edge of nothing," written two years before Chandler's death, was a recognition not forced on him by a deathbed, but a recognition he lived with for years. It is a sentence that is the certification of a man who will not crumble if western experience disillusions him, certification of a man who can stand his ground and look directly at sin and despair, certification of a man who can, even if he writes fiction, face facts.

Now we get to my central topic: what Raymond Chandler knew, and western historians forgot. Let me take up, first, the more concrete elements of western reality that Chandler in the most matter-of-fact way acknowledged and included, even as the mainstream western American historians either ignored them, or seemed genuinely to have forgotten that such elements existed.

Let us start with a big element of western reality: the existence of women. Absent from Turnerian, frontier history, women entered the field first under the auspices of what we might call "conjunction history." In conjunction history, you keep all the conventional operating assumptions and you simply, from time to time, insert the phrase "and women." This approach may be hard on the typesetter, but it is not hard on the mind. Indeed, that is its principal charm: conjunction history requires no thought at all.

One would not put Raymond Chandler forward as an enlightened, ahead-of-his-time nonsexist, but there is nonetheless an undeniable achievement in his track record: his plots would go nowhere without women. Take the women out of the books, and the plots would be aimless and lifeless. The women are, moreover, a surprisingly diverse crowd: a few mindless blondes, certainly, but there are also plenty of complicated women with complicated histories, women whose characteristics extend considerably beyond the categories "whore" or "goddess." Perhaps most valuable, there are women who are murderers.

This is my premise: if one wants to move beyond conjunction history, the most crucial step is to defeat the "Bride Comes to Yellow Sky" notion of the woman as the civilizer, the woman whose genteel, white presence represents the final defeat of wilderness. In that campaign, what could be a better countersymbol than one of Chandler's women, holding a gun in hand and putting that gun to use? There is something to be grateful for in a moment, for instance, when a character remarks that the use of an ice pick suggests that a woman did the murder.[6] "Women's work" acquires, thereby, a whole new dimension. Utterly reversing the madonna of the prairies, the saintly helpmate, the bride coming to Yellow Sky, or the schoolteacher pleading with the Virginian not to fight, Chandler's murderous women recapture the whole range of human character for women. Capable of starting the shooting as well as stopping it, women regain their legitimate claim on greed, envy, anger, desperation, and sin. They can be agents in the decline of civilization, as well as in its advance. They can be forces of wilderness, as well as forces fighting back wilderness. Chandler's willingness to give moral complexity to both women and men permits us to imagine a reversal of the stereotyped scene: we can now see the Virginian pleading with the schoolteacher to put her guns away; we can now see the menfolk looking worried and gathering at the church to discuss how they can persuade their womenfolk to accept the restraints of civilization. Our minds and imaginations thus exercised and elasticized, it becomes possible to allow the women of western history their full human reality.

The second item, in Chandler's remembering and western historians' forgetting, is the existence of minorities. *Farewell My Lovely* begins in a Los Angeles neighborhood evolving from white to black. You could read the works of traditional western historians for a long, long time and not find a comparable scene. Similarly, Hispanics appear regularly in Chandler's books, considerably more regularly than they appeared in conventional western histories. The Mexican border is a clear feature of his setting; Raymond Chandler did not fall into the western historian's trap of acting as if the American conquest of the Southwest put the cultural, social, and economic conflicts of the region to rest.

Blacks and Hispanics are certainly present in Raymond Chandler's West, but as with gender, one would not want to put Chandler forward as a model of enlightened attitudes toward race. A number of stereotypes are in full force in his writing, and yet a number of those stereotypes are also vigorously questioned. The murder in the bar, at the start of *Farewell My Lovely,* gives Chandler the occasion to reflect with some bitterness on the newspaper world's indifference to the death of a black man, and on the police department's unwillingness to make such a death into an occasion of vigorous investigation. More subtly, in *The Long Goodbye,* Chandler introduces a black chauffeur, Amos. Chandler's detective, Philip Marlowe, at first mocks the chauffeur with a reference to T. S. Eliot, but the chauffeur turns the tables a few scenes later by knowledgeably quoting Eliot to Marlowe.[7] Similarly, when a Hispanic cabdriver tells Marlowe that he is not Mexican, that many people of Hispanic origin cannot speak Spanish, Marlowe responds by saying, "*Es gran lástima. Una lengua muchísima hermosa,*" a proposition with which the cabdriver then agrees—in Spanish.[8] They may not be *great* moments in interracial and intercultural understanding. Still, if you put them up against the treatment of Hispanics and blacks in conventional western history, they look pretty good. Put them up against the present-day movements to declare English the official language of a number of states, and Chandler's sentiments—"*Es una lengua muchísima hermosa*"—look very good indeed.

On a third matter, on the existence of class divisions in the West, Chandler gets his highest score yet. His greatest gift as a writer may well have been the description of neighborhoods and business places. From the enclave in celebration of private property in the suburb of Idle Valley to the ratty rooming houses of Bay City, from the elite and polished offices of successful companies to the petty tragedy of ill-kept buildings for fallen professionals, Chandler used physical spaces to embody his recognition that divisions of wealth and status made the world of western America go round, just as much as they powered the rotation of the worlds of the eastern United States and in Europe.

Recognizing the importance of class divisions permitted Chandler a fourth achievement: the acknowledgment of corruption, and especially corruption that occurred along the fault line between money and power. Repeatedly, describing criminals or describing successful businessmen, Chandler indicated that the dividing line between the two groups was a fuzzy one. Given the power of the profit motive in western development, the line between legitimate business and illegitimate crime was not an easy one to draw. "That's the difference between crime and business," a friend of Marlowe says in *The Long Goodbye*. "For business you gotta have capital. Sometimes I think it's the only difference." But Marlowe reminds him that this is not much of a difference at all: "Big time crime takes capital too."[9]

What bearing on western history would all that have? To use the most available and current illustration, consider the Exxon *Valdez*'s effect on Prince William Sound. Consider Rockwell International's management of Rocky Flats nuclear weapons assembly plant in Colorado. Consider the injuries inflicted on workers in Cripple Creek, or Ludlow, or Bisbee, or, for that matter, Coeur d'Alene. Consider the Central Pacific Railroad's utter indifference to the death of Chinese workers in the construction of the track, or consider the Southern Pacific's manipulation of California politics. Raymond Chandler made no direct reference to these matters, but he knew and said directly that the monomaniacal pursuit of profit could be the equivalent of crime, a deep, systemic crime that, as often as not, carried the support of written law and of law enforcement.

Drawing a portrait of a compromised system of justice and governance, Chandler made his fifth contribution: he made it clear what "maturity" meant in models of western development. The "life cycle" metaphor was omnipresent in white Americans' thinking during western expansion; white Americans quite universally referred to towns and settlements as being "born" and then aging into "maturity." But this is where white American thinking dropped the metaphor. Having appropriated "birth" and "maturity" from the human life cycle, western boosters called a halt. Western settlement would halt at maturity, and the full cycle into decay and death would simply be denied.

No such luck, a Chandler novel says clearly. If you get birth and maturity, each novel says, you also get decay and death. You get corruption and gangsters and politicians who put on cowboy hats and ride horses and get elected, even though their heads are emptier than Death Valley.[10] "This is a big town now," Marlowe tells another character. "Some very tough people have checked in here lately. The penalty of growth."[11]

History is not to be evaded, each novel says; characters can flee and deny and cover up evidence and kill off witnesses as much as they like, but the past will not be denied. Each novel, of course, follows that very formula: someone attempts to evade history, and a variety of forces converge to cut off that evasion. Principal among those forces is, of course, the detective himself, Philip Marlowe, the fellow who surely must use the words "tough" and "trouble" more often than any other real or created figure of western American life. And that brings me to my sixth point: that Raymond Chandler gives an important lesson to western historians by telling us that the investigation gets nowhere until the investigator is himself or herself at risk.

Philip Marlowe gets hit on the head a lot. The superficial response would be to say that these are just violent books, functioning under a plot requirement that makes it necessary for someone's head to get hit every twenty or thirty pages. But the deeper meaning is considerably more important. Marlowe usually passes a point where a smart person would withdraw. "Nothing made it my business but curiosity," Marlowe put it on one occasion, and his curiosity was one of the few western resources that came without limits.[12] "I'm a romantic," he tells a policeman. "I hear voices crying in the night and I go see what's the matter. You don't make a dime that way. You got sense, you shut your windows and turn up more sound on the TV set."[13] He persists in his inquiries, because he is curious and because he has, tough guy or not, a fool's faith in justice. He persists, and his persistence usually earns him an attack and an injury. "Common sense says go home and forget it, no money coming in," Marlowe says. "Common sense always speaks too late."[14]

And here we reach the center of Raymond Chandler's value as an uncle to western history: he reminds us that you do not learn anything of importance until you put yourself at risk. Most academic historians have retreated to the protective fiction that historians are the equivalent of scientists in white lab coats, as detached, disengaged, invulnerable observers. Western historians, like most other historians, have tried to evade the fact that you are not going to figure out much of significance until you put yourself at risk. Each time a blow descends on Philip Marlowe's head the western historian receives a reminder that this is a rough field, that western history is full of intense and bitter conflicts, and there is no way to investigate that history without putting one's own head at risk of sharp blows from unexpected directions. "Are you honest?" one character asks Philip Marlowe, to which he replies, "Painfully," an answer that is not only true, but is the answer western historians should aspire to give.[15] "Nobody's in my complete confidence," he tells one character.[16] In every novel, Marlowe places himself deep in the exercise that western historians postponed until the last few years, the exercise of investigating the disparity between what people *said* they were doing and what they actually did. Pit Marlowe against "that class of people [who] can convince themselves that everything they do is right," a class of people well represented in every phase of western history, and the rationalizations and justifications begin to peel off, like paint peeling from constant exposure to the Pacific's salt air.[17]

When I was a kid, at family reunions, I wanted my Uncle Carlos to talk. He was a genial man, and perfectly pleasant to nieces, but he would not tell the stories I wanted him to tell. What stories? Uncle Carlos had been a guard at San Quentin, and much of that time he spent with the death row crowd.

When Uncle Carlos retired, he did what he had wanted to do for a long time, and took college courses, including one in philosophy. If we imagine Uncle Carlos now writing novels, it is that sort of uncle that I think we have in Raymond Chandler—an uncle who has looked at human depravity, at evil, at sin, and who has also studied philosophy. Not the sort of uncle that you'd go to the circus with, or rather *exactly* the sort of uncle that you'd go to the circus with if you wanted to get beyond the cotton-candy facades of the circus, and to figure out its essence.

Does any of this have any particular bearing on the American West? Aren't mystery novels set everywhere? Is there anything regional in Chandler's thinking? The answer is obvious: of course there is. Place, setting, extraordinary natural landscape invaded by odd humans, Pasadena, Hollywood, orange groves next to cyanide plants, arid lands, oil fields, entire communities where everything and everybody (except Philip Marlowe) is for sale, aircraft factories attracting disoriented midwesterners, high winds, smog, the Mexican border, and the whole thing set on the edge of the continent, poised on the brink of the Pacific Ocean: no one can confuse those qualities of Chandler's writing with the racetracks of Dick Francis, or the drawing rooms of Agatha Christie. In his devotion to place, Chandler was, as usual, ahead of the western historians in noting the tragic element of western environmental history. On one crowded resort beach, he notes "a faint smell of ocean. Not very much, but as if they had kept this much just to remind people that this had once been a clean open beach where the waves came in and creamed and the wind blew and you could smell something besides hot fat and cold sweat."[18] The Southern California setting was the right one, the necessary one, for the man who would write, "I have lived my life on the edge of nothing."

At the end of his novels, it is too late for a comic ending, too late for the conventional conclusion that would bring, at long last, progress and civilization to the West. "I guess somebody lost a dream," a medical intern playing a Fortinbras-like role says at the end of *The Little Sister*.[19] As a summing up line, this one works for many episodes of western history. Transforming the mythic region steeped in evasive innocence to a realistic region that has known sin, Raymond Chandler shows us the way to escape the trivializing routes of comedy and irony, routes that stay on the edges of the canyon. He points instead to a route by which we can at last take our search for meaning directly *into* the canyon, giving western history its fully earned dimension of tragedy.

"A nice neighborhood to have bad habits in," Chandler characterized one section of Los Angeles.[20] If anyone has written a better eight-word description of the West that we live in, the West that history built, I have not found it. A westerner who takes Chandler seriously is a westerner persuaded that it is, at long last, time to improve those habits. "You're a moral defeatist," Philip Marlowe tells Terry Lennox at the end of *The Long Goodbye,* and until recently, it was a charge that Marlowe could as properly have brought against most of the writers of western American history.[21]

Notes

1. Raymond Chandler, *The Little Sister* (1949; reprint, New York: Vintage Books, 1988), 136–37.

2. Richard White, "Trashing the Trails," in Patricia Nelson Limerick, Clyde A. Milner II, and Charles E. Rankin, eds., *Trails: Toward a New Western History* (Lawrence: University Press of Kansas, 1991), 27–29.

3. Quoted in Frank MacShane, *The Life of Raymond Chandler* (New York: E. P. Dutton, 1976), 3.

4. MacShane, *Raymond Chandler,* 4.

5. Quoted in MacShane, *Raymond Chandler,* 1.

6. Chandler, *The Little Sister,* 57.

7. Raymond Chandler, *The Long Goodbye* (1953; reprint, New York: Vintage, 1988), 237, 356.

8. Raymond Chandler, *Playback* (1958; reprint, New York: Vintage Books, 1988), 13.

9. Chandler, *The Long Goodbye,* 188.

10. See Chandler, *The Long Goodbye,* 267–68.

11. Raymond Chandler, *The Big Sleep* (1939; reprint, New York: Vintage Books, 1988), 45.

12. Raymond Chandler, *Farewell My Lovely* (1940; reprint, New York: Vintage Books, 1976), 15.

13. Chandler, *The Long Goodbye,* 280.

14. Chandler, *Playback,* 80.

15. Chandler, *The Big Sleep,* 35.

16. Chandler, *Farewell My Lovely,* 105.

17. Chandler, *The Little Sister,* 223.

18. Chandler, *Farewell My Lovely,* 202.

19. Chandler, *The Little Sister,* 250.

20. Chandler, *The Big Sleep,* 21.

21. Chandler, *The Long Goodbye,* 377.

Bibliography

Chandler, Raymond. *The Big Sleep.* 1939. Reprint. New York: Vintage Books, 1988.

————. *Farewell My Lovely.* 1940. Reprint. New York: Vintage Books, 1976.

————. *The Little Sister.* 1949. Reprint. New York: Vintage Books, 1988.

————. *The Long Goodbye.* 1953. Reprint. New York: Vintage Books, 1988.

————. *Playback.* 1958. Reprint. New York: Vintage Books, 1988.

MacShane, Frank. *The Life of Raymond Chandler.* New York: E. P. Dutton, 1976.

White, Richard. "Trashing the Trails." In *Trails: Toward a New Western History,* edited by Patricia Nelson Limerick, Clyde A. Milner II, and Charles E. Rankin, 26–39. Lawrence: University Press of Kansas, 1991.

Part 2

Paradigms of the Old West

3. Women and the Language of Men

Jane Tompkins

Fear of losing his identity drives a man west, where the harsh conditions of life force his manhood into being. Into this do-or-die, all-or-nothing world we step when we read this passage from Louis L'Amour's 1958 novel *Radigan,* where a woman about to be attacked by a gunman experiences a moment of truth:

> She had never felt like this before, but right now she was backed up against death with all the nonsense and the fancy words trimmed away. The hide of the truth was peeled back to expose the bare, quivering raw flesh of itself, and there was no nonsense about it. She had been taught the way a lady should live, and how a lady should act, and it was all good and right and true...but out here on the mesa top with a man hunting her to put her back on the grass it was no longer the same.... There are times in life when the fancy words and pretty actions don't count for much, when it's blood and death and a cold wind blowing and a gun in the hand and you know suddenly you're just an animal with guts and blood that wants to live, love and mate, and die in your own good time.[1]

L'Amour lays it on the line. Faced with death, we learn the truth about life. And the truth is that human nature is animal. When your back is to the wall you find out that what you want most is not to save your eternal soul—if it exists—but to live, in the body. For truth is flesh, raw and quivering, with the hide peeled back. All else is nonsense. The passage proposes a set of oppositions fundamental to the way the Western thinks about the world. There are two choices—

either you can remain in a world of illusions, by which is understood religion, culture, and class distinctions, a world of fancy words and pretty actions, of "manners for the parlor and the ball room, and . . . womanly tricks for courting," or you can face life as it really is—blood, death, a cold wind blowing, and a gun in the hand. These are the classic oppositions from which all Westerns derive their meaning: parlor vs. mesa, East vs. West, woman vs. man, illusion vs. truth, words vs. things. It is the last of these oppositions I want to focus on now because they stand for all the rest.

But first, a warning. What is most characteristic of these oppositions is that as soon as you put pressure on them they break down. Each time one element of a pair is driven into a corner, it changes shape and frequently turns into its opposite. It's as if the genre's determination to have a world of absolute dichotomies insures that interpenetration and transmutation will occur. For instance, when Burt Lancaster, playing Wyatt Earp in *Gunfight at the O.K. Corral,* declares toward the beginning of the movie, "I've never needed anybody in my life and I sure don't need Doc Holliday," the vehemence of his claim to autonomy virtually guarantees that it will be undermined. And sure enough, by the time the showdown arrives you can hardly tell him and Kirk Douglas (playing Doc) apart: they dress alike, walk alike, talk alike, and finally they fight side by side as brothers. Two who started out as opposites—gambler vs. sheriff, drunken failure vs. respected citizen, rake vs. prude—have become indistinguishable.

Westerns strive to depict a world of clear alternatives—independence vs. connection, anarchy vs. law, town vs. desert—but they are just as compulsively driven to destroying these opposites and making them contain each other.

So it is with language. Westerns distrust language. Time and again they set up situations whose message is that words are weak and misleading, only actions count; words are immaterial, only objects are real. But the next thing you know, someone is using language brilliantly, delivering an epigram so pithy and dense, it might as well be a solid thing. In fact, Westerns go in for their own special brand of the bon mot, seasoned with skepticism and fried to a turn. The product—chewy and tough—is recognizable anywhere:

Cow's nothin' but a heap o' trouble tied up in a leather bag.
(*The Cowboys*, 1972).

A human rides a horse until he's dead and then goes on foot. An Indian rides him another 20 miles and then eats him.
(*The Searchers*, 1956).

A Texan is nothin' but a human man way out on a limb.
(*The Searchers*)

Kansas is all right for men and dogs but it's pretty hard on women and horses.
(*Santa Fe Trail*, 1940)

God gets off at Leavenworth, and Cyrus Holliday drives you from there to the devil.
(*Santa Fe Trail*)

There ain't no Sundays west of Omaha.
(*The Cowboys*)

This is hard country, double hard.
(*Will Penny*, 1968)

When you boil it all down, what does a man really need? Just a smoke and a cup of coffee.
(*Johnny Guitar*, 1954)

In the end you end up dyin' all alone on a dirty street. And for what? For nothin'.
(*High Noon*, 1952)

You can't serve papers on a rat, baby sister. You gotta kill'em or let'em be.
(*True Grit*, 1969)

He wasn't a good man, he wasn't a bad man, but Lord, he was a *man*.
(*The Ballad of Cable Hogue*, 1970)

Some things a man has to do, so he does'em.
(*Winchester '73*, 1950)

Only a man who carries a gun ever needs one.
(*Angel and the Bad Man*, 1947)

Mr. Grimes: God, dear God.
Yaqui Joe: He won't help you.
(*100 Rifles*, 1969)

You haven't gotten tough, you've just gotten miserable.
(*Cowboy,* 1958)

The sayings all have one thing in common, they bring you down.
Like the wisdom L'Amour offers his female protagonist out on the
mesa top, these gritty pieces of advice challenge romantic notions.
Don't call on God, He's not there. Think you're tough? You're just
miserable. What do you die for? Nothin'. The sayings puncture big
ideas and self-congratulation; delivered with perfect timing, they land
like stones from a slingshot and make a satisfying thunk.

For the Western is at heart anti-language. Doing, not talking, is
what it values. And this preference is connected to its politics, as a line
from Louis L'Amour suggests: "A man can . . . write fine words, or he
can do something to hold himself in the hearts of the people" (*Treasure Mountain,* 1972). "Fine words" are contrasted not accidentally
with "the hearts of the people." For the men who are the Western's
heroes don't have the large vocabularies that an expensive education
can buy. They don't have time to read that many books. Westerns distrust language in part because language tends to be wielded most
skillfully by people who possess a certain kind of power: class privilege, political clout, financial strength. Consequently, the entire enterprise is based on a paradox. In order to exist, the Western has to use
words or visual images, but these images are precisely what it fears.
As a medium, the Western has to pretend that it doesn't exist at all. Its
words and pictures, just a window on the truth, are not really there.

So the Western's preferred parlance consists ideally of abrupt com-
mands. "Turn the wagon. Tie 'em up short. Get up on the seat" (*Red
River,* 1948). "Take my horse. Good swimmer. Get it done, boy"
(*Rio Grande,* 1950). Also common are epigrammatic sayings of a
strikingly aggressive sort: "There's only one thing you gotta know.
Get it out fast and put it away slow" (*Man without a Star,* 1955).
"When you pull a gun, kill a man" (*My Darling Clementine,* 1946).
For the really strong man, language is a snare; it blunts his purpose
and diminishes his strength. When Joey asks Shane if he knows how
to use a rifle, Shane answers, and we can barely hear him, "little bit."
The understatement and the clipping off of the indefinite article are
typical of the minimalist language Western heroes speak, a kind of
desperate shorthand, comic, really, in its attempt to communicate
without using words.

Westerns are full of contrasts between people who spout words and people who act. At the beginning of Sam Peckinpah's *The Wild Bunch* (1969), a temperance leader harangues his pious audience; in the next scene a violent bank robbery makes a shambles of the crowd's procession through town. The pattern of talk canceled by action always delivers the same message: language is false or at best ineffectual; only actions are real. (When heroes talk, it *is* action: their laconic put-downs cut people off at the knees.) Westerns treat salesmen and politicians, people whose business is language, with contempt. Braggarts are dead men as soon as they appear. When "Stonewall" Tory, in *Shane,* brags that he can face the Riker gang any day, you know he's going to get shot; it's Shane, the man who clips out words between clenched teeth, who will take out the hired gunman.

The Western's attack on language is wholesale and unrelenting, as if language were somehow tainted in its very being. When John Wayne in John Ford's 1956 *The Searchers* rudely tells an older woman who is taking more than a single sentence to say something— "I'd be obliged, ma'am if you would get to the point"—he expresses the genre's impatience with words as a way of dealing with the world. For while the woman is speaking, Indians are carrying off a prisoner. Such a small incident, once you unpack it, encapsulates the Western's attitude toward a whole range of issues:

(1) Chasing Indians—that is, engaging in aggressive physical action —is doing something, while talking about the situation is not.

(2) The reflection and negotiation that language requires are gratuitous, and even pernicious.

(3) The hero doesn't need to think or talk, he just *knows,* for, being the hero, he is in a state of grace with respect to the truth.

In a world of bodies true action must have a physical form. And so the capacity for true knowledge must be based in <u>physical experience</u>. John Wayne playing Ethan Edwards in *The Searchers* has that experience and knows what is right because, having arrived home after fighting in the Civil War, he better than anyone else realizes that life is "blood and death and a cold wind blowing and a gun in the hand." In such a world, language constitutes an inferior kind of reality, and the further one stays away from it the better.

Language is gratuitous at best; at worst it is deceptive. It takes the place of things, screens them from view, creates a shadow world where anything can be made to look like anything else. The reason no one in the Glenn Ford movie *Cowboy* can remember the proper words for burying a man is that there aren't any. It is precisely *words* that cannot express the truth about things. The distaste with which John Wayne says "the Lord giveth, the Lord taketh away" as he buries a man in *Red River* not only challenges the authority of the Christian God but also expresses disgust at all the trappings of belief: liturgies, litanies, forms, representations, all of which are betrayals of reality itself. The articulation of a creed in the Western is a sign not of conviction but of insincerity.

The features I am describing here, using the abstract language the Western shuns, are dramatically present in a movie called *Dakota Incident,* whose plot turns in part on the bootlessness of words and, secondarily, on the perniciousness of money (another system of representation the Western scorns). Near the beginning a windbag senator, about to depart on the stage from a miserable town called Christian Flats, pontificates to a crowd that has gathered to watch a fight: "There's no problem that can't be solved at a conference table." He adds, "Believe me, gentlemen, I know whereof I speak." The next minute, two gunfights break out on main street; in one of them the hero shoots and kills his own brother.

The theme of loquacity confounded by violence, declared here at the outset, replays itself at the end when the main characters have been trapped by some Indians in a dry creek bed. The senator has been defending the Indians throughout, saying that they're misunderstood, have a relationship with the land, and take from the small end of the horn of plenty. Finally, when he and the others are about to die of thirst, he goes out to parley with the Indians. He makes a long and rather moving speech about peace and understanding and they shoot him; he dies clawing at the arrow in his chest.

In case we hadn't already gotten the point about the ineffectuality of language, we get it now. But no sooner is the point made than the movie does an about-face. The other characters start saying that the senator died for what he believed, that he was wrong about the Indians "but true to himself." They say that perhaps his words "fell on barren ground: the Indians and us." And the story ends on a note of peaceful cooperation between whites and Indians (after the attacking Indians have been wiped out), with talk about words of friendship falling on fertile ground.

Language is specifically linked in this movie to a belief in peace and cooperation as a way of solving conflicts. And though it's clear from the start that only wimps and fools believe negotiation is the way to deal with enemies (the movie was made in 1956 during the Cold War), that position is abandoned as soon as "our side" wins. *Dakota Incident* is not the only Western to express this ambivalent attitude toward language—and the peace and harmony associated with it. Such ambivalence is typical, but it is always resolved in the end. Language gets its day in court and then it is condemned.

When John Wayne's young protégé in *The Searchers,* for example, returns to his sweetheart after seven years, he's surprised to learn that she hasn't been aware of his affection. "But I always loved you," he protests. "I thought you knew that without me havin' to say it." For a moment here, John Ford seems to be making fun of the idea that you can communicate without language, gently ridiculing the young man's assumption that somehow his feelings would be known although he had never articulated them. But his silence is vindicated ultimately when the girl he loves, who was about to marry another man, decides to stick with him. The cowboy hero's taciturnity, like his awkward manners around women and his inability to dance, is only superficially a flaw; actually, it's proof of his manhood and true-heartedness. In Westerns, silence, sexual potency, and integrity go together.

Again, in *My Darling Clementine,* Ford seems to make an exception to the interdict against language. When Victor Mature, playing Doc Holliday, delivers the "To be or not to be" speech from *Hamlet,* taking over from the drunken actor who has forgotten his lines, we are treated to a moment of verbal enchantment. The beauty and power of the poetry are recognized even by the hero, Wyatt Earp (played by Henry Fonda), who appreciates Shakespeare and delivers a long soliloquy himself over the grave of his brother. But when the old actor who has been performing locally leaves town, he tricks the desk clerk into accepting his signature on a bill in place of money. The actor, like the language with which he is identified, is a lovable old fraud, wonderfully colorful and entertaining, but not, finally, to be trusted.

The position represented by language, always associated with women, religion, and culture, is allowed to appear in Westerns and is accorded a certain plausibility and value. It functions as a critique of force and, even more important, as a symbol of the peace, harmony, and civilization that force is invoked in order to preserve. But in the end that position is deliberately proven wrong—massively, totally, and unequivocally—with pounding hooves, thundering guns, blood and death. Because the genre is in revolt against a Victorian culture where the ability to manipulate language confers power, the Western equates power with "not-language." And not-language it equates with being male.

In his book *Phallic Critiques,* Peter Schwenger has identified a style of writing he calls "the language of men," a language that belongs to what he terms the School of Virility, starting with Jack London and continuing through Hemingway to Norman Mailer and beyond. Infused with colloquialism, slang, choppy rhythms, "bitten-off fragments," and diction that marks the writer as "tough," this language is pitted against itself *as* language, and devoted to maintaining "masculine reserve."

Drawing on Octavio Paz's definition of the *macho* as a "hermetic being, closed up in himself" ("women are inferior beings because, in submitting, they open themselves up"), Schwenger shows the connections these authors make between speaking, feeling, and feminization. "It is by talking," he writes, "that one opens up to another person and becomes vulnerable. It is by putting words to an emotion that it becomes feminized. As long as the emotion itself is restrained, held back, it hardly matters what the emotion itself is; it will retain a male integrity." Thus, "not talking is a demonstration of masculine control over emotion."[2]

Control is the key word here. Not speaking demonstrates control not only over feelings, but over one's physical boundaries as well. The male, by remaining "hermetic," "closed up," maintains the integrity of the boundary that divides him from the world. (It is fitting that in the Western the ultimate loss of that control takes place when one man puts holes in another man's body.) To speak is literally to open the body to penetration by opening an orifice; it is also to mingle the body's substance with the substance of what is outside it. Finally, it suggests a certain incompleteness, a need to be in relation. Speech relates the person who is speaking to other people (as opposed to things); it requires acknowledging their existence, and by extension, their parity. If "to become a man," as Schwenger says, "must be finally to attain the solidity and self-containment of an object," "an object that is self-contained does not have to open itself up in words."[3] But it is not so much the vulnerability or loss of dominance speech implies that makes it dangerous as it is the reminder of the speaker's own inferiority.

The interdict masculinity imposes on speech arises from the desire for complete objectivization. And this means being conscious of nothing, not knowing that one has a self. To be a man is not only to be monolithic, silent, mysterious, impenetrable as a desert butte, it is to *be* the desert butte. By becoming a solid object, a man is relieved not only of the burden of relatedness and responsiveness to others, he is relieved of consciousness itself, which is to say, primarily, consciousness *of* self.

At this point, we come upon the intersection between the Western's rejection of language and its emphasis on landscape. Not fissured by self-consciousness, nature is what the hero aspires to emulate: perfect being-in-itself. This is why John Wayne was impatient with the woman who took longer than a sentence to speak her mind. As the human incarnation of nature, he neither speaks nor listens. He is monumentality in motion, propelling himself forward by instinct, no more talkable to than a river or an avalanche, and just as good company.

Woman: That's a pretty dog.
Man: No response.
Woman: Well, it's got a pretty coat.
Man: Silence.[4]

The foregoing account of the Western's hostility to language refers to a mode of behavior—masculine behavior for the most part—that has left an indelible mark on the experience of practically every person who has lived in this country in the twentieth century. I mean the linguistic behavior of men toward women, particularly in domestic situations.

He finds it very difficult to talk about his personal feelings, and intimidates me into not talking either. He also finds it very difficult to accept my affection. . . . I become angry that his need to be unemotional is more important than my need to have an outward show of love. Why do I always have to be the one that is understanding?[5]

When I was married, it was devastatingly lonely—I wanted to die—it was just so awful being in love with someone who . . . never talked to me or consulted me.[6]

My husband grew up in a very non-emotional family and it took a long time for me to make him understand that it's a good thing to let people (especially the ones you love) know how you feel.[7]

The relationship did not fill my deepest needs for closeness, that's why I'm no longer in it. I did share every part of myself with him but it was never mutual.[8]

The loneliness comes from knowing you can't contact another person's feelings or actions, no matter how hard you try.[9]

If I could change one thing—it would be to get him to be more expressive of his emotions, his wants, needs. I most criticize him for not telling me what he wants or how he feels. He denies he feels things when his non-verbals indicate he does feel them.[10]

The quotations come from Shere Hite's *Women and Love: A Cultural Revolution in Progress.* I quote them here because I want to make clear that the Western's hatred of language is not a philosophical matter only; it has codified and sanctioned the way several generations of men have behaved verbally toward women in American society. Young boys sitting in the Saturday afternoon darkness could not ride horses or shoot guns, but they could talk. Or rather, they could learn how to keep silent. The Western man's silence functions as a script for behavior; it expresses and authorizes a power relation that reaches into the farthest corners of domestic and social life. The impassivity of male silence suggests the inadequacy of female verbalization, establishes male superiority, and silences the one who would engage in conversation. Hite comments:

> We usually don't want to see . . . non-communication or distancing types of behavior as expressing attitudes of inequality or superiority, as signs of a man not wanting to fraternize (sororize?) with someone of lower status. This is too painful. And yet, many men seem to be asserting superiority by their silences and testy conversational style with women. Thus, not talking to a woman on an equal level can be a way for a man to dominate a relationship.[11]

For a man to speak of his inner feelings not only admits parity with the person he is talking to, it jeopardizes his status as potent being, for talk dissipates presence, takes away the mystery of an ineffable self that silence preserves. Silence establishes dominance at the same time that it protects the silent one from inspection and possible criticism by offering nothing for the interlocutor to grab hold of. The effect, as in the dialogue about the dog quoted above, is sometimes to force the speaker into an ineffectual flow of language that tries to justify itself, achieve significance, make an impression by additions that only diminish the speaker's force with every word.

When Matthew Garth returns to his hotel room at the end of *Red River,* he acts the part of silent conqueror to perfection. The heroine, who has been waiting for him, warns him that his enemy is on the way to town. The film has her babble nervously about how she came to be there, how she found out about the danger, how there's no way he can escape, no way to stop his enemy, nothing anyone can do, nothing she can do. As he looks down at her, not hearing a thing she says, her words spill out uncontrollably, until finally she says, "Stop me, Matt, stop me." He puts his hand over her mouth, then kisses her. The fade-out that immediately follows suggests that the heroine, whose name is Tess Millay, is getting laid.

The scene invites diametrically opposed interpretations. From one point of view, what happens is exactly right: the desire these characters feel for each other yearns for physical expression. Nonverbal communication, in this case sex, is entirely appropriate. But the scene gets to this point at the woman's expense.

Tess is the same character who, earlier in the film, had been shot by an arrow and had it removed without batting an eyelash, had seduced the young man with her arm in a sling, and refused a proposition from his enemy. In this scene, she is totally undercut. As her useless verbiage pours out, she falls apart before our eyes, a helpless creature who has completely lost control of herself and has to beg a man to "stop" her.

> When I feel insecure, I need to talk about things a lot. It sometimes worries me that I say the same things over and over.[12]

> I can be an emotional drain on my husband if I really open up.[13]

Shere Hite notes that women feel ashamed of their need to talk, blaming themselves and making excuses for the silence of men. "My husband grew up in a very non-emotional family." The heroine of *Red River* cares so much about the hero that her words pour out in a flood of solicitude. But instead of seeing this as a sign of love, the film makes her anxiety look ridiculous and even forces *her* to interpret it this way.

Tess Millay's abject surrender to the hero's superiority at the end of *Red River* is a supreme example of a woman's introjection of the male attitude toward her. She sees herself as *he* sees her, silly, blathering on about manly business that is none of her concern, and beneath it all really asking for sex. The camera and the audience identify with the hero, while the heroine dissolves into a caricature of herself. Sex joins here with blood and death and a cold wind blowing as the only true reality, extinguishing the authority of women and their words.

Someone might argue that all the Western is doing here is making a case for nonverbal communication. If that were true, so much the better. But, at least when it comes to the relations between men and women, the Western doesn't aim to communicate at all. The message, in the case of Tess Millay, as in the case of women in Westerns generally, is that there's nothing *to* them. They may seem strong and resilient, fiery and resourceful at first, but when push comes to shove, as it always does, they crumble. Even Marian, Joe Starrett's wife in *Shane*, one of the few women in Western films who, we are made to feel, is also substantial as a person, dissolves into an ineffectual harangue at the end, unsuccessfully pleading with her man not to go into town to get shot. When the crunch comes, women shatter into words.

A classic moment of female defeat appears in Owen Wister's *The Virginian*, which set the pattern for the Western in the twentieth century. In the passage below, Molly, the heroine, is vanquished by the particular form of male silence that her cowboy lover practices. The Virginian has just passed his mortal enemy on the road with drawn pistol and without a word. But when Molly tries to get him to talk about it, and "ventures a step inside the border of his reticence," he turns her away.

> She looked at him, and knew that she must step outside his reticence again. By love and her surrender to him their positions had been exchanged. . . . She was no longer his half-indulgent, half-scornful superior. Her better birth and schooling that had once been weapons to keep him at a distance, to bring her off victorious in their encounters, had given way before the onset of the natural man himself. She knew her cow-boy lover, with all that he lacked, to be more than ever she could be, with all that

she had. He was her worshipper still, but her master, too. Therefore now, against the baffling smile he gave her, she felt
powerless.[14]

Wister makes explicit the connection between the Virginian's
mastery over Molly and his reticence: his conversational droit du
seigneur. Like Louis L'Amour, Owen Wister sees the relationship
between men and women as a version of the East-West, parlor-mesa,
word-deed opposition. Molly is identified by her ties to the East, her
class background, her education, but most of all by her involvement
in language. Words are her work and her pleasure and the source of
her power. She teaches them in school and keeps company with them
in books, but they cannot protect her from "the onset of the natural
man himself." The man's sheer physical presence is stronger than language and so words are finally the sign of Molly's—and of all women's—inferiority.

This is what lies behind the strange explanation the Virginian offers Molly of his relationship to the villain, Trampas. He says that he
and Trampas lie in wait for each other, hating each other in silence,
always ready to draw. Then he tells a story about a women's temperance meeting he once overheard while staying at a hotel. "Oh, heav-
ens. Well, I couldn't change my room and the hotel man, he apologized to me next mawnin'. Said it didn't surprise him the husbands
drank some." Then reverting to himself and Trampas, the Virginian
remarks: "We were not a bit like a temperance meetin'."[15]

The temperance ladies talk and talk; that is *all* they do. It never
comes to shooting. Meanwhile, they drive their husbands crazy with
their cackle. Drive them to drink, which dulls the feelings men can't
talk about. The Virginian and Trampas (the enemy he passes on the
road) hardly exchange a word; therefore they will kill each other
someday. Their silence signals their seriousness, their dignity and re
ality, and the inevitability of their conflict. Silence is a sign of mastery,
and goes along with a gun in the hand. They would rather die than
settle the argument by talking to each other.

Why does the Western harbor such animus against women's
words? Why should it be so extreme and unforgiving? Is it because,
being the weaker sex physically, women must use words as their chief
weapon and so, if men are to conquer, the gun of women's language
must be emptied? Or is it because, having forsworn the solace of

language, men cannot stand to see women avail themselves of it because it reminds them of their own unverbalized feelings? According to Hite, "It could be argued that, if men are silent, they are not trying to dominate women; rather, they are trapped in their own silence (and their own pain), unable to talk or communicate about feelings, since this is such forbidden behavior for them."[16]

If Hite has guessed correctly, men's silence in Westerns is the counterpart of women's silence: that is, it is the silence of an interior self who has stopped trying to speak and has no corresponding self to whom to talk. Its voice is rarely heard, since it represents the very form of interior consciousness the genre wishes to stamp out. But it does burst out occasionally. In *The Virginian* it speaks in the form of a song, roared by the rebellious cowhands who are getting drunk in a caboose on their way back to the ranch where the Virginian is taking them. They sing,

> I'm wild and woolly, and full of fleas;
> I'm hard to curry above the knees;
> I'm a she-wolf from Bitter Creek, and
>   It's my night to ho-o-wl—[17]

The wolf bitch inside men, what would it sound like if they ever let it out? What would it say? The silence of this inner voice, its muteness, keeps the woman's voice, its counterpart, from being heard. It is replaced by the narrative of the gunfight, the range war, the holdup, the chase. By the desert. The Western itself is the language of men, what they do vicariously, instead of speaking.

——

I used to keep a photograph of the young John Wayne posted on my bulletin board. He has on a cowboy hat and he is even then developing a little of the cowboy squint, that inimitable squint so beloved of millions. But he has not yet gotten the cowboy face, the leathery wall of noncommunication written over by wrinkles, speaking pain and hardship and the refusal to give in to them, speaking the determination to tough it out against all odds, speaking the willingness to be cruel in return for cruelty, and letting you know, letting you know beyond all shadow of a doubt, who's boss.

The other expression, the expression of the young John Wayne, is tender, and more than a little wistful; it is delicate and incredibly sensitive. Pure and sweet; shy, really, and demure.

Where is she, this young girl who used to inhabit John Wayne's body along with "the Duke"? I think of the antiwar song from the sixties, "Where have all the young girls gone?" and the answer comes back, "Gone to young men every one" and the young men in the song are gone to battle and the soldiers to the graveyard. How far is it from the death of the young girl in John Wayne's face to the outbreak of war? How far is it from the suppression of language to the showdown on main street? In *The Virginian* Wister suggests that the silence that reigns between the hero and the villain guarantees that one will kill the other someday. And still he ridicules women's language.

The Western hero's silence symbolizes a massive suppression of the inner life. And my sense is that this determined shutting down on emotions, this cutting of the self from contact with the interior well of feeling, exacts its price in the end. Its equivalent, the force of the bullets that spew forth from the guns in little orgasms of uncontained murderousness. Its trophy, the bodies in the dust. Its victory, the silence of graves. Its epitaph, that redundant sign that keeps appearing in *Gunfight at the O.K. Corral:* BOOT HILL GRAVEYARD TOMBSTONE.

Why does the Western hate women's language? I argued earlier that the Western turned against organized religion, and the whole women's culture of the nineteenth century, and all the sermons and novels that went with them; the rejection took place in the name of purity, of a truth belied by all these trappings, something that could not be stated. But perhaps the words the Western hates stand as well for inner confusion, a welter of thoughts and feelings, a condition of mental turmoil that is just as hateful as are the more obvious external constraints of economics, politics, and class distinctions. Women, like language, remind men of their own interiority; women's talk evokes a whole network of familial and social relationships and their corollaries in the emotional circuitry. What men are fleeing in Westerns is not only the cluttered Victorian interior, but also the domestic dramas that go on in that setting, which the quotations from Shere Hite recall. The gesture of sweeping the board clear may be intended to clear away the reminders of emotional entanglements that cannot be dealt with or faced. Men would rather die than talk because talking might bring up their own unprocessed pain, or risk a dam burst that would undo the front of imperturbable superiority. It may be that the Western hero flees into the desert seeking there what Gretel Ehrlich has called "the solace of open spaces," a place whose physical magnificence and emptiness are the promise of an inward strength and quietude. "Where never is heard a discouraging word, and the skies are not cloudy all day."

Notes

1. Louis L'Amour, *Radigan* (New York: Bantam Books, 1958), 144–45.
2. Peter Schwenger, *Phallic Critiques* (London: Routledge and Kegan Paul, 1984), 43–45.
3. Ibid., 54.
4. Shere Hite, *The Hite Report: Women and Love, A Cultural Revolution in Progress* (New York: Knopf, 1987), 17.
5. Ibid., 18.
6. Ibid., 23.
7. Ibid., 18.
8. Ibid., 19.
9. Ibid., 23.
10. Ibid., 21.
11. Ibid., 25.
12. Ibid., 19.
13. Ibid.
14. Owen Wister, *The Virginian: A Horseman of the Plains* (1902; reprint, New York: Heritage Press, 1951), 256.
15. Ibid., 259.
16. Hite, *Hite Report*, 25.
17. Wister, *The Virginian*, 142.

Bibliography

Angel and the Bad Man (1947, Republic). Directed by James Edward Grant.
The Ballad of Cable Hogue (1970, Warner Brothers). Directed by Sam Peckinpah.
Cowboy (1958, Columbia Pictures). Directed by Delmer Daves.
The Cowboys (1972, Warner Brothers). Directed by Mark Rydell.
Dakota Incident (1956, Republic). Directed by Lewis R. Foster.
Gunfight at the O.K. Corral (1956, Paramount). Directed by John Sturges.
High Noon (1952, United Artists). Directed by Fred Zinnemann.

Hite, Shere. *The Hite Report: Women and Love, A Cultural Revolution in Progress.* New York: Knopf, 1987.

Johnny Guitar (1954, Republic). Directed by Nicholas Ray.

L'Amour, Louis. *Radigan.* New York: Bantam Books, 1958.

———. *Treasure Mountain.* New York: Bantam Books, 1972.

Man Without a Star (1955, Universal). Directed by King Vidor.

My Darling Clementine (1946, Fox). Directed by John Ford.

100 Rifles (1969, Fox). Directed by Tom Gries.

Santa Fe Trail (1940, Warner Brothers). Directed by Michael Curtiz.

Red River (1947, United Artists-Monterey). Directed by Howard Hawks.

Rio Grande (1950, Republic). Directed by John Ford.

Schwenger, Peter. *Phallic Critiques.* London: Routledge and Kegan Paul, 1984.

The Searchers (1956, Warner Brothers). Directed by John Ford.

Shane (1952, Paramount). Directed by George Stevens.

True Grit (1969, Paramount). Directed by Henry Hathaway.

Will Penny (1968, Paramount). Directed by Tom Gries.

Winchester '73 (1950, Universal). Directed by Anthony Mann.

Wister, Owen. *The Virginian: A Horseman of the Plains.* New York: Macmillan, 1902. Reprint, edited by Sidney Clark. New York: Heritage Press, 1951.

4. The Night John Wayne Danced with Shirley Temple

Max Westbrook

John Ford's *Fort Apache*[1] (1948) is the story of Colonel Owen Thursday (Henry Fonda), a pompous egomaniac transferred from a post in Europe to a desert command in Arizona. Colonel Thursday is admirable in his verbal slashing of a corrupt Indian agent, but his sense of honor and integrity is selective. Basically, he is an arrogant snob whose primary purpose is to win fame and glory for himself in order to obtain an assignment to a more prestigious post back east. In a maniacal attempt to capture Cochise (Miguel Inclan), Thursday orders a suicidal charge into an obvious trap and gets his regiment massacred. Being, on occasion, an honorable maniac, he rejects a chance to escape and rejoins the remnants of his troop just in time to share with them a death that has no purpose.

In the final scene, the most controversial in Western films,[2] a few years have passed. Captain York (John Wayne) is now a colonel and the commanding officer. Newspaper reporters are praising Thursday, calling him "almost a legend," the "hero of every schoolboy in America." York does a restrained take—since he knows the praise is blatantly false—and then dodges another round of praise with a neat verbal side step. Asked to confirm a reporter's statement that Colonel Thursday was a "great man" and a "great soldier," York carefully replies, "No man died more gallantly."

Another reporter says "the ironic part of it" is that we "always remember the Thursdays, but the others are forgotten." Immediately, York changes. Instead of incredulous takes and verbal side steps, he

60

speaks with conviction and confidence. The dead are not forgotten, York says, because they are alive in the regiment; and the regiment, thanks to Colonel Thursday, consists of "better men" now and is "a command to be proud of."

As if to confirm his high praise, York imitates Thursday's characteristic language ("Questions, gentlemen?") and dress (the desert cap), then rides off in pursuit of Geronimo and, according to one of the reporters, "more glory" for his regiment.

Since Thursday was an egocentric who got his regiment massacred in a foolish attempt to further his own career, the ending of *Fort Apache* is obviously a contradiction of the film the audience has just seen. Several critics have tried to defend the ending by quoting a famous line from *The Man Who Shot Liberty Valance* (1962): "When the legend becomes fact, print the legend."[3] Asked if he agreed that the statement applied also to *Fort Apache,* Ford said, "Yes—because I think it's good for the country to have heroes to look up to."[4] That defense, however, is itself a contradiction because Ford has not "printed the legend." He has "printed" an effective portrait of an egomaniac, with the "legend" merely tacked on at the end.

Those who defend the final scene of *Fort Apache* tend to ignore the narrative context. York's volunteered praise of Thursday—"They are better men now" and "Thursday did that"—cannot mean that Thursday improved recruitment or training while alive. The troopers he commands see him for what he is. "Aw, the madman," says Sergeant Major O'Rourke (Ward Bond) just before the fatal charge, yet the men obey, and they are slaughtered. York's praise can only mean (1) that he is telling a bald-faced lie, or (2) that the newspaper propaganda about Thursday is a successful lie and has attracted better recruits to the cavalry, which would mean that credit for the successful propaganda would go to journalists, not to the colonel.

Similarly, Thursday's repeated line—"Questions, gentlemen?"— may seem, when delivered by John Wayne as Colonel York, a practical and admirable bit of military efficiency. Colonel Thursday, however, uses the line to mean, Do you surrender your will and your military knowledge to my superior rank? His intent is clear enough in his badgering of Captain York, but it is unmistakable in the scene in which York has been ordered back to the supply wagons, and the charge is about to begin. Thursday demands of his remaining officers, "Are there any other questions?" Captain Collingwood (George O'Brien) answers, "No questions, Owen," and the rest are silent. Their acquiescence to Thursday is the final surrender, the knowing acceptance of a needless death, both for themselves and for the troopers.

What, then, has Thursday taught the replacements who serve, a few years later, under Colonel York?

But the ending is not the only cop-out in *Fort Apache*. The film as a whole—like other John Ford Westerns—is a series of flag-waving, down-home, contradictory signals designed to make a very un-American message seem American.

A brief but emblematic example of Ford's technique occurs early in the film. Colonel Thursday has just arrived at Fort Apache to take command. He is accompanied by his daughter, Philadelphia, played by the child star Shirley Temple, now grown up but convincing as a sixteen-year-old who is happy, good natured, trusting, spunky, and incredibly cute. A dance is in progress. The pompous colonel, forced to walk among inferiors, enters reluctantly, coldly refuses to shake the hand of an old comrade in arms, and arrogantly assumes the dance is in his honor.

York politely corrects the colonel: "It's a birthday dance, sir."

"Birthday whose birthday?" Thursday demands, suggesting that he is the only one present whose birthday is worth celebrating.

"General George Washington's, sir," York replies; and York, it should be noted, is first seen standing by the fireplace with a portrait of George Washington in the background to signal the association between our number one Western movie star and the father of our country.

Having won the exchange and done so in a way that cannot be called insubordinate, York changes from passive restraint to an aggressive courtesy. "Shall I show you to your quarters or will you remain?" Thursday's halting response ("Well, under the circumstances, I—") is overtaken as a decision to remain, and York quickly moves to the cutest teenager in America and gallantly asks for a dance. Phil, as she is called by her friends, is delighted with the handsome young captain and innocently adds to the embarrassment of her father by handing him her hat, purse, and cape, thus imposing a humble role on the pompous commanding officer of Fort Apache. Smiling happily, Captain York and Phil begin to dance.

Their brief dance is a more meaningful John Ford signature, I believe, than his oft-used Monument Valley. America's number one sweetheart, freshly blossomed into womanhood but as sweet and innocent as when she was a child, is dancing with John Wayne, our number one tough guy, bighearted, all-American Hollywood hero. Both are obviously superior, and yet, unlike the class-conscious Thursday, both are very democratic, being at ease with all classes and races, male and female. And the moment is also, of course, absolutely innocent. Phil is already smitten with the sergeant major's son, Lieutenant O'Rourke, played by John Agar. Captain York—taking the avuncular role—will encourage their romance on three separate occasions; and the original audience knew from the start that Phil would marry the lieutenant just as it knew that, in a widely publicized wedding, Shirley Temple was already married to John Agar.

But what is this deliciously American moment designed to sell? Why are Shirley Temple and John Wayne so suitable for the roles of Phil Thursday and Kirby York? The answer, I suggest, is that John Ford is brazenly using Hollywood images to sell a policy of cop-out and cover-up as necessary ingredients of the American dream. He can "print the truth" and tack the "legend" on at the end because good citizens must know that John Wayne and Shirley Temple are more American than scruples about accuracy. To graciously accept a little fanaticism here and there is to be a mature and realistic American. The cover-ups of the Kennedy assassination, Vietnam, Watergate, and Contragate are all justified if we understand and believe the insidious contradictions of *Fort Apache*. The American people, so the message goes, "need heroes to look up to." Since the type of hero desired by Ford is apparently in short supply, the people must be told lies. Heroes must be sold in marketplaces that include—insofar as the superior leadership can manage it—textbooks, newspapers, television, and movies. Thus John Wayne dances with Shirley Temple for the same reason that Ronald Reagan invoked George Gipp and the fighting Irish of Notre Dame. It's good salesmanship.

The effectiveness of the salesmanship, of course, is due in large part to Ford's rightly acknowledged mastery of cinematography. When Phil calls on Mrs. Collingwood (Anna Lee) for help in setting up quarters, for example, the name Mrs. O'Rourke (Irene Rich) is spoken three times, shouted down the veranda five times (finally in chorus), then used twice again by way of introduction. For those willing to judge the film by the standards of popular entertainment, the scene plays as effectively as the famous Jack Benny radio bit in which responsibility for a lost item is passed from one voice to another.

Or again, after Thursday has insulted Cochise and doomed any possibility of peace, there are twelve consecutive and very moving shots—individual and group—framing the charge against a backdrop of sky and clouds, thus relating the charge to something much larger than any single battle, to nature itself, perhaps, or to a suggested immortality for military heroes.

The first of these two examples, however, cheerfully shows women doing all they are allowed to do, domestic chores. Later, when Mrs. O'Rourke dares worry about her son, she is promptly put in her place. Sergeant Major O'Rourke gruffly orders his wife to go on "about her business." And the second example, the sky shots, glorifies an upcoming cavalry charge that is going to be a needless and pointless slaughter.

My position, I realize, may seem extremist to some moviegoers, but, to me, those of us who have argued that *Fort Apache* openly confesses its own hypocrisy are merely saying that the emperor is not wearing a stitch. The extremist position, I think, is the one taken by those who defend the ending. *Fort Apache,* after all, is a film in which a regiment is massacred because the commanding officer wants glory for himself and a more prestigious assignment. To say that the result constitutes "a recruiting picture for the Army, demonstrating its camaraderie and that a man never need be alone there"[5] is simply untenable. The cavalrymen do not die alone, true enough, but a photograph showing the camaraderie of dead bodies—dead for no purpose —would not make an effective recruiting poster. *reality*

Equally extremist is the position that Thursday is "valuable" because he was brave in a rich "event" ("event" being a euphemism for "pointless massacre") and therefore material around which effective lies could be told: "Though Colonel Thursday represents virtually every negative quality imaginable, still Ford shows him to be a valuable figure in an event that had legendary ingredients."[6]

Such extremist interpretations amount to buying and even promoting the extremist propaganda of the film. In the closing scene of *Fort Apache,* for example, when the reporter says it is too bad that we remember the great heroes but forget the rest, he then stumbles over a name and gets it wrong, thus illustrating the unfortunate neglect he has just described.

"You're wrong there," says York. "The faces may change, the names, but they're there. They're the regiment."

Note the logic: you are wrong to say the names are forgotten because the regiment goes on whatever their forgotten names may be. And note also that while triumphant music is played in the background, while ghost troopers appear on the screen, still living on "beans and hay" and riding off to battle even though they have died and gone to heaven, while our favorite American Western star raises his voice and rhetoric in homage to the ordinary soldier, the substantive remark is, "The faces may change, the names."

What does that mean? Obviously, it means the individual cavalryman, with his own face and own name, is not important. Faces and names are interchangeable. There will always be more cannon fodder. Thus the body count is of no consequence. The cause for which individual human beings die is of no consequence.

As the film admits, those who died fighting Cochise—that is, their replacements—may have to dine on "horse meat" in the upcoming fight against Geronimo. And Colonel Thursday did get his regiment massacred. And Captain York had just told him it was a trap and that charging into the canyon was suicide. But so what? Troopers with new faces and new names are mounted and ready. The originals, our good old alcoholic and supposedly funny but always able and brave stock-company troopers, are all dead now, killed on behalf of racism and egomania, but it's okay. Shirley Temple, as we see in the final scene, has given birth to one replacement, and there are plenty of anonymous faces maturing on the vine or fully ripe and eager to be used.

Of course it could be argued that John Ford is just doing bits, searching with the camera and with verbal humor for whatever plays, whatever entertains. That position could be supported by the silver-salver scene, the initial training of recruits, the "destroying" whiskey scene, and so on; but Ford's Western films reveal a studied preference for certain bits which, however theatrical or hokey they may be, have been promoted to ideological status.

Several critics, for example, contend that *Fort Apache* and other John Ford Westerns reveal a concern for western expansion and settlement. Though I would argue that Ford's cinematic comments on the West are, like John Wayne's brief dance with Shirley Temple, decorative rather than substantive, I believe implications do exist in the sense that many—most?—viewers would assume a westering context with little or no evidence from the film itself. One critic says that all of Ford's Westerns "in one way or another celebrate the settling of the American frontier. Among the most vibrant and patriotic films ever made, these works depict a mythological world of Manifest Destiny."[7] Ford's Westerns, however, offer no responsible portrayals of

Manifest Destiny or patriotism, and the most interesting implications, the subtexts, are, unfortunately, stillborn. In the making of *Fort Apache*, the real challenge is to include rather than omit the inevitable investigation that would follow the massacre. If Captain York covered up for the colonel (by saying that no one warned Thursday, that no dispute took place), then he would also be covering up for himself (by failing to mention that he challenged his commanding officer to a duel and was threatened with a court-martial). When asked why he was with the supply wagons instead of leading his own company into the battle, what would he say? If he told the truth, would a grateful army later promote him to colonel and make him the commanding officer?

Other potentially rich veins in the film are also ignored. Did Thursday order Lieutenant O'Rourke to lead the burying party—with only four men and with minimal ammunition—in hopes he would be killed and no longer be a possible mate for his daughter? And why did Thursday, just before the fatal charge, order Lieutenant O'Rourke to the rear? Did the adamant colonel repent of his sins at the peak moment of anger and ambition?

Omissions, however, are probably less important than the contradictions in *Fort Apache*. The tactics that mark Colonel Thursday as a martinet—and therefore as a flawed human being, completely lacking the combination of toughness and flexibility shown by the John Wayne hero—are actually picked up and imitated. Colonel York's imitation of Thursday's language, in the closing scene, echoes other scenes in which the language of Thursday is imitated by his victim.

On his first morning at headquarters, Thursday tells Sergeant Major O'Rourke to have officers' call sounded. The sergeant is astounded: "Officers' call?" And Colonel Thursday snaps him up: "How long have you been in the army? Then you've heard of officers' call; have it sounded."

Sergeant O'Rourke immediately uses the same verbal whip on the bugler. The trooper is as surprised as he was: "Now?" "No, next Christmas, you looney! How long have you been in the army? Then you've heard of officers' call. Sound it!"

Meanwhile, Phil is in despair. She is in the housekeeper's role for her father, and their quarters are a mess. The good ladies of Fort Apache come to the rescue, and, with the aid of Guadalupe, her Hispanic maid (Movita Castenada), Phil brings order to the living room and prepares the first meal in their new home. The colonel arrives. It is a proud moment. When duty calls and Colonel Thursday has to walk out on dinner, he consoles his daughter in a perfunctory manner and only after being nudged: "There'll be other dinners, Phil." The spunky Phil then consoles Guadalupe with more warmth but much the same words: "It's all right, Guadalupe. We'll cook other dinners together."

These quick but significant imitations of the colonel are matched by playful cover-ups on behalf of authority. Captain York, who knows all, knows that the recruits have been miraculously whipped into shape by the good sergeants; but when Colonel Thursday gives Lieutenant O'Rourke the credit, York smiles and says, "West Point training, sir." When Sergeant Mulcahey (Victor McLaglen) wants to make an acting corporal of any recruit from his home county in Ireland, or, barring that, anyone from a neighboring county, the audience is supposed to chuckle. When Sergeant Beaufort (Pedro Armendariz) shows the same prejudice for any recruit who served in the Confederate army, the sergeant who objects is immediately put down: "Aw, let them [i.e., former Confederates] have one." Rank has its privilege, and a little prejudice for the "right class" is supposed to be understandable, natural, and American.

For all his reputed resentment of authority, Ford was an authoritarian. His beloved lower classes are consistently hard-drinking brawlers who are consistently loyal to the upper class, and it is the combination that is supposed to make them lovable. Victor McLaglen is usually cast by Ford (and others) as a drinker or an alcoholic who loves a good fistfight; but that's funny because he is, after all, brave, obedient, and lower class. The drinking problem of Captain Sam Collingwood, however, is shown by discreet hints and never onstage because he is an officer and a gentleman. Lieutenant O'Rourke, our democratic breakthrough from the lower classes into the higher class, has been rebirthed at West Point and become such a fine gentleman that he is an absolute idiot when trying to drill the recruits. "That's no job for a gentleman," says Sergeant Mulcahy, meaning, We sergeants belong to an inferior class and thus are capable of doing low-level work (instructing other inferiors) that is too crude for the splendid sensibilities of a gentleman.

Apparent exceptions to Ford's authoritarianism are just that, apparent exceptions. Authority is supposedly violated on the basis of an appeal to a higher authority or an equivalent principle. When Colonel Thursday calls York a coward, the captain can move from one version of honor (courage in combat) to another version (no gentleman can permit himself to be called a coward) and thus be ordered to the rear without damage to his character or his military oath of obedience to authority. Another example is the destruction of whiskey and rifles secreted by the corrupt Indian agent, Silas Meacham (Grant Withers). Thursday has to play word games to justify his ordering the whiskey and rifles destroyed, but he is clearly acting in accordance with military and humanitarian principles that are higher than government regulations about the rights of Indian agents.

Likewise, at the end of *Rio Grande* (1950), Sergeant Tyree (Ben Johnson) steals General Sheridan's horse and flees from a sheriff who wants to arrest him for murder. Tyree, however, is innocent and will return home to prove it in court, but he wants to wait until after his sister has married and left the county because the trial would be an embarrassment to her even though she is also innocent. When the general (J. Carroll Naish) chuckles at Tyree's cleverness in picking the best horse available, John Ford is not showing disrespect for authority. Instead, he is dramatizing the belief that good authority can outwit bad authority, that wise leadership can bend the law because those who are superior to the majority are also superior to the law.

In *Fort Apache,* when the good sergeants welcome Lieutenant O'Rourke back from West Point, the lieutenant is respectfully saluted and—chuckle time again—spanked. In the end, the commanding officer gets the regiment massacred, but then comes the cover-up, and authority is confirmed even though it is horribly wrong. Authority may be teased, may relax at the right time, or it may be corrupt and dangerous; but authority, good or bad, is necessary for the inferior, just as heroes—genuine or bogus—are necessary for the country.

This message, though found in a Hollywood Western, is significant because of the remarkable persuasive powers of John Ford-John Wayne (and other) films. Critic Jon Tuska, for example, believes that Colonel Thursday's insane desire to slaughter Cochise—who is willing to live on the reservation as ordered if only the army will guarantee him an honest Indian agent—is an indication of his desire to restrain Indians so the West can be settled. Thursday, he says, "is a man convinced of his own importance and the manifest destiny the white man has in keeping the Indians in check."[8] The colonel, it seems to me, is concerned with his own destiny, and his main interest in Indians is the wish for opponents famous enough for their slaughter to earn him an assignment back east.

The message, of course, is not confined to movies. (How we respond to words and pictures out of Hollywood is directly related to how we respond to words and pictures out of Washington, D.C., or any other center of government.) Minds trained to admire Colonel York's cover-up are better prepared to buy the report of the Warren Commission, the official explanation of the war in Vietnam, Richard Nixon's version of Watergate, and Ronald Reagan's version of Contragate.

≈Oliver North et al.

Taking it a step further, if we ordinary citizens know we are being lied to and buy the false report anyway, buy the "legend," why that is obviously much better for the authoritarian leadership. They can lie, get caught, and become part of the "legend" anyway. Portraits of Colonels Kirby York and Oliver North can be hung side by side. George Bush can align himself with Hollywood tough guys and metamorphose from wimp to presidential caliber in one White House-winning performance. Dan Quayle, a wealthy man from a big city who wanted to be vice president, can associate himself with *Hoosiers,* a movie about poor, small-town people who win a basketball tournament, and thus he can be a winner too.

The relationship between Hollywood and American history is of course very self-conscious on the part of both filmmakers and politicians. In their study of the politics of Hollywood, Michael Ryan and Douglas Kellner treat the Western only briefly, and their subject is the contemporary film. Their conceptual basis, however, is relevant, also, to the films of John Wayne and John Ford: "The thematic conventions—heroic male adventure, romantic quest, female melodrama, redemptive violence, racial and criminal stereotyping, etc.—promote ideology by linking the effect of reality to social values and institutions in such a way that they come to seem natural or self-evident attributes of an unchanging world. The conventions habituate the audience to accept the basic premises of the social order, and to ignore their irrationality and injustice."[9]

The trick is to invoke history for the purposes of propaganda, to convince by association. John Ford's cavalry trilogy includes numerous historical signals, but they have no more narrative substance than Sergeant Major O'Rourke's referential pose over the Bible as his son returns from West Point.

In *She Wore a Yellow Ribbon* (1949) and *Rio Grande,* as in *Fort Apache* (the three films are well known as Ford's cavalry trilogy), Ford invokes the uniting of Indian tribes that took place at Little Big

Horn, but a widespread and effective unity was achieved only at Little Big Horn. Colonel Thursday is somewhat like George Custer, and General Ranald Mackenzie's raid into Mexico is vaguely suggested by Colonel York's raid in *Rio Grande*. Admittedly, *Fort Apache* need not be faulted because John Ford moves a river into the path of Captain York and Sergeant Beaufort so they can cross it, and York is certainly right when he explodes with a brief philippic against the Indian ring; but Ford's invocations of history in his cavalry trilogy are basically another version of the night John Wayne danced with Shirley Temple. History—like the wondrous shots of Monument Valley, appeals to family and community, folk dances, an Irish brand of vaudevillian fights and shenanigans, flashing sabers, and romance—is used to sell a white male economic exploitation called civilization.

In *Rio Grande* we see a cinematic example of the authoritarianism that occurred historically in Korea, Vietnam, and Nicaragua. General Sheridan denounces the government policy that forbids the military to cross the Mexican border in pursuit of Apaches who ford the Rio Grande to raid in Texas, then escape back into Mexico before the U.S. Cavalry can catch them. Calling the policy a game of "diplomatic hide and seek," the general gives Colonel York a verbal order to "cross the Rio Grande," to "hit the Apache and burn him out."

York grins, delighted with the order and understanding immediately: "Which of course I didn't hear."

"Course you didn't hear."

To have your favorite movie star enact a betrayal of the Constitution, however, is a tad uncomfortable. Whether or not the American cavalry should have been allowed to cross the border may be subject to debate; but the dramatized message in *Rio Grande*, if stated flat out, would be that the American military should determine foreign policy. So John Ford does one of his little dances. *After* Sheridan and York have agreed to disobey the Constitution, the Indians kidnap a wagon load of children and take them to Mexico. Now where is your armchair intellectual? Out in the cold, that's where he is, and the audience roots for John Wayne to break the law and go rescue those cute little children from those horrible Indians.

Easily forgotten during the brave rescue is the fact that, before the children are kidnapped, General Sheridan has promised to rig the jury. If the mission fails and there is a court-martial, the general explains, he will personally appoint Colonel York's comrades in arms as his judges. Meanwhile, according to their agreement, both would commit perjury and deny that the general had given the colonel a verbal order to cross the border into Mexico.

Even *Cheyenne Autumn* (1964), often called Ford's most realistic treatment of Indians, ends with a cop-out which says that the civilian authorities in Washington are humane, after all, in their treatment of Indians. The situation at the climax of the movie seems hopeless. Again an arrogant commanding officer is bent on slaughter. Instead of a cover-up, this time the "cavalry" comes to the rescue, just in the nick of time, in the form of Edward G. Robinson as deus ex bureaucracy. Individuals within the system may be wrong or villainous, as Custer, according to John Ford, was wrong at the Little Big Horn;[10] but the system itself is to be affirmed whatever the facts may be.

She Wore a Yellow Ribbon—featuring a slightly different cop-out—is the story of how sad it is for Captain Nathan Brittles (John Wayne) to be forced into retirement when the cavalry is the only home he has. John Wayne is very effective in the role of a much older man whose wife and children are dead and whose family is now the troopers he leads with skill and kindness. He loves them and they love him. As the movie ends, we see a very sad long-shot. The wonderful old captain is riding off alone into the sunset.

But wait! Here comes Sergeant Tyree galloping to overtake the old man with a message from Washington. Generals Grant, Sheridan, and Sherman have decided to rescue an obscure soldier from oblivion. The homeless and long-suffering old captain is magically promoted to lieutenant colonel and made chief of scouts. Three generals, however, are not enough for Sergeant Tyree, a former Confederate soldier who solemnly wishes that General Lee could also have signed the order.

Once again the story has denied itself, and what seems at first a narrative flaw turns out to be, upon examination, a sentimental invocation of history. By using the actual names of not one but three Civil War generals, and nostalgically invoking a fourth (unfortunately, the enemy, but nonetheless a hero of white America), the film has asserted the unanimous virtue of the military. Thus *Yellow Ribbon* is propaganda in praise of humble obedience to a distant authority that turns out to be omniscient and benevolent.

The overvoice at the end of *Yellow Ribbon*, going beyond sentimentality, is actually a shocking dance with history: "Wherever they rode and whatever they fought for, that place became the United States."[11]

The end justifies the means. That's America. And if the propaganda is hard to swallow, accept the cover-up and plunge on. That's the higher loyalty. If Colonels Kirby York and Oliver North get caught, there will always be heroes—the genuine and the manufactured—and there will be a plentiful supply of nameless soldiers to refill the empty ranks and ride to their death however insane, unjust, or illegal the cause may be.

According to the Declaration of Independence, it is the duty of all citizens to ask questions and require answers. According to John Ford, it is good for movies to supply the people with imaginary and pseudo-historical heroes even when heroism is marred by egomania, sentimentality, imperialism, and conspiracy to violate the Constitution.

Notes

1. *Fort Apache* (1948, Argosy Pictures-RKO Radio), directed by John Ford, produced by Ford and Merian C. Cooper, written by Frank S. Nugent, based on a story by James Warner Bellah called *Massacre*, filmed on locations in Utah and Monument Valley, 127 minutes.

2. For a clear, judicious, and perceptive presentation of arguments for and against the final scene, see William T. Pilkington, "*Fort Apache* (1948)," in *Western Movies*, ed. William T. Pilkington and Don Graham (Albuquerque: University of New Mexico Press, 1979), 40–49.

3. See, for example, William R. Meyers, *The Making of the Great Westerns* (New Rochelle, N.Y.: Arlington House, 1979), 173–83; Russell Campbell, "*Fort Apache*," *Velvet Light Trap* 17 (Winter 1977): 8–12; and Peter Stowell, *John Ford* (Boston: Twayne, 1986), 78–84.

4. Peter Bogdanovich, *John Ford* (Berkeley: University of California Press, 1968), 34, 86.

5. James Robert Parish and Michael R. Pitts, *The Great Western Pictures* (Metuchen, N.J.: Scarecrow Press, 1976), 102.

6. Stowell, *John Ford*, 78.

7. Kirk Ellis, "On the Warpath: John Ford and the Indians," *Journal of Popular Film and Television* 8, no. 2 (1980): 34.

8. Jon Tuska, *The Filming of the West* (Garden City, N.Y.: Doubleday, 1976), 516.

9. Michael Ryan and Douglas Kellner, *Camera Politica: The Politics and Ideology of Contemporary Hollywood Film* (Bloomington: Indiana University Press, 1988), 1.

10. Bogdanovich, *John Ford*, 86.

11. For an opposite reading see Stowell, *John Ford*, 84, who *honors* this statement by the overvoice. For an approach that is compatible with and yet different

from my own, see Ken Nolley, "Printing the Legend in the Age of MX: Reconsidering Ford's Military Trilogy," *Film Literature Quarterly* 14, no. 2 (1986): 82–88.

Bibliography

Bogdanovich, Peter. *John Ford*. Berkeley: University of California Press, 1968.

Campbell, Russell. *"Fort Apache." Velvet Light Trap* 17 (Winter 1977): 8–12.

Ellis, Kirk. "On the Warpath: John Ford and the Indians." *Journal of Popular Film and Television* 8, no. 2 (1980): 34–41.

Fort Apache (1948, Argosy Pictures-RKO Radio). Directed by John Ford.

Meyers, William R. *The Making of the Great Westerns*. New Rochelle, New York: Arlington House, 1979.

Nolley, Ken. "Printing the Legend in the Age of MX: Reconsidering Ford's Military Trilogy." *Film Literature Quarterly* 14, no. 2 (1986): 82–88.

Parish, James Robert, and Michael R. Pitts. *The Great Western Pictures*. Metuchen, N.J.: Scarecrow Press, 1976.

Pilkington, William T., and Don Graham, eds. *Western Movies*. Albuquerque: University of New Mexico Press, 1979.

Ryan, Michael, and Douglas Kellner. *Camera Politica: The Politics and Ideology of Contemporary Hollywood Film*. Bloomington: Indiana University Press, 1988.

Stowell, Peter. *John Ford*. Boston: Twayne, 1986.

Tuska, Jon. *The Filming of the West*. Garden City, N.Y.: Doubleday, 1976.

5. The New Historicism and the Old West

Forrest G. Robinson

It seems to me we are, at least on paper, supposed to be different from, or better than, we are. And that kind of irritation confronts us all the time and has from the very beginning. The Constitution was a precipitate of all the best Enlightenment thinking of Europe, and it's really quite a remarkable document. That we don't manage to live up to it is the source of all our self-analysis.
—E. L. Doctorow

1

The new historicism is notoriously difficult to define with any precision. "New Historicism has a portmanteau quality," observes H. Aram Veeser. "It brackets together literature, ethnography, anthropology, art history, and other disciplines and sciences, hard and soft." So broad is its base, and so intricate are the cultural negotiations that it explores, that "its politics, its novelty, its historicality, [and] its relationship to other prevailing ideologies all remain open questions."[1] Critics have seized upon this vagueness as the symptom of a concealed swerve from the approved political line. Versions of the new historicism are attacked for veering both toward and away from Marxism, for the failure to properly address political realities, for pessimism in matters of agency and the resistance to power, for secretly appropriating feminist ideas, for a lack of historical specificity, and for being "unselfconsciously sexist and racist."[2]

Catherine Gallagher, an avowed new historicist, grants that the politics of her methodology are "difficult to specify," but is puzzled at the "insistence on finding a single, unequivocal political meaning for this critical practice." Gallagher responds with what she regards as a leading tenet of the new historicist credo: "that no cultural or critical practice is simply a politics in disguise, that such practices are seldom intrinsically either liberatory or oppressive, that they seldom contain their politics as an essence but rather occupy particular historical situations from which they enter into various exchanges, or negotiations, with practices designated political."[3] Gallagher's reluctance to adopt a fixed political position is a characteristic new historical gesture. Such tentativeness is consistent with the view of history and culture as shifting, elusive constructions by variously interested and equally changeable men and women. The proper critical response to reality so construed is a principled flexibility, a sharp eye to the distortion in all perspectives, a cultivated pleasure in the discovery of doubleness and subversion in a world bound to have things both ways, and the genial refusal to claim an exemption from the general angling for position.

Stephen Greenblatt, a Renaissance scholar at the University of California, Berkeley, and a founding editor of *Representations,* is the person most often identified as the leader of the movement. Defining the new historicism as "a practice rather than a doctrine," Greenblatt is characteristically reluctant to adopt a fixed theoretical position. Still, he acknowledges "an openness to the theoretical ferment of the last few years." Foucault's impress has been especially marked, though the influence "of European (and especially French) anthropological and social theorists" has also been considerable. As to a more specific critical self-definition, Greenblatt locates himself at some midpoint along an axis with the American Marxist, Fredric Jameson, at one pole, and the French poststructuralist, Jean-Francois Lyotard, at the other. Jameson blames capitalism for perpetrating a false distinction between the public and the private, the aesthetic and the political; Lyotard, on the other hand, faults capitalism for its false integration of separate discursive domains. Greenblatt is fascinated by "the general question addressed by Jameson and Lyotard—what is the historical relation between art and society or between one institutionally demarcated discursive practice and another?"—but finds that neither of them offers a satisfactory answer. The problem, he argues, is that

[handwritten margin note: art is not special in relation to other social practices]

neither is willing to come to terms with the "apparently contradictory historical effects of capitalism." Both seize upon contradictions, but only to explain them away as the excrescences of "a unitary demonic principle." Theory, itself the servant of inflexible historical agendas, thus flattens the uneven topography of culture. Better, then, to move ahead tentatively, enabled by a certain "practice," but professing "no doctrine at all."[4]

The most conspicuous feature of the new historicism is an impulse to bring down the boundaries between what have been regarded as separate domains. On one side, this has involved the rejection of the new criticism, with its removal of art to a separate, timeless world, secure against social and ideological intrusions. True to its name, the new historicism insists on restoring the literary text to a place—alongside all other texts—in the material domain. Shakespearean theater, Greenblatt insists, "like all forms of art, indeed like all utterances," is "itself a *social event.* Artistic expression is never perfectly self-contained and abstract, nor can it be satisfactorily derived from the subjective consciousness of an isolated creator. Collective actions, ritual gestures, paradigms of relationship, and shared images of authority penetrate the work of art and shape it from within, while conversely the socially overdetermined work of art, along with a multitude of other institutions and utterances, contributes to the formation, realignment, and transmission of social practices." Art is in a dialectical relation to society. The artifact, the artist, and the audience are shaped by the social context that they in turn help to form and modify. Literature is at once socially produced and socially productive.

At the same time that it rehistoricizes the text, the new historicism retextualizes history. If it turns its back on the new criticism, and on all ahistorical formalism, it also rejects those traditional forms of literary historicism that construe the relations between the text and its context, its author, and its audience as more or less literal mirrorings or direct influences passing from one autonomous zone to another. Tudor history is framed, in this approach, as a "world picture" whose mirror image turns up in the canonical literature of the Elizabethan age; or, to offer an example closer to home, the Turner thesis is held up as historical background to countless fictional renderings of the solitary, even tragic, cowboy and gunfighter. Stephen Greenblatt is careful to distance himself from this "monological" brand of historicism, which is concerned to discover a "single political vision," to be treated as historical fact, assigned to a period, often aligned with Marxist or liberal master-narratives, and forming "a stable point of reference, beyond contingency," which literature may be said to mirror.[6]

The new historicism thus avoids all constructions of the literary field or frame of reference that suggest the direct, one-way traffic of images, ideas, and influences across the boundaries between separate domains. Instead, according to Louis Montrose, we have the constant interplay of "discursive *practices* in which versions of the Real are instantiated, deployed, reproduced—and also appropriated, contested, transformed."[7] The construction of history is an ongoing negotiation between shifting, changeable bases and variously interested parties. It is the business of the new historicist to scrutinize this dynamic process for its culture-specific manifestations—its versions of the real—as they surface in the complex circulation of information and impulse between author, text, context, and audience.[7] Nor is the critic exempt from implication in the cultural stew. The would-be new historicist is reminded that his or her critical practice is itself historically positioned, and therefore quite as partial and prone to contradiction as the texts selected for analysis. Just as there is no stable object of study, so there is no stable base from which to launch literary-historical inquiry.

The response to Greenblatt's critical "practice" has been voluminous and generally positive. Few would disagree that his work has advanced the scholarly understanding of English Renaissance literature and culture, and that his bridging of literature and history may serve as a valuable model in other areas of study. But the response has not been uniformly positive. The most forceful critique has centered on Greenblatt's analysis of the dynamics of power in his well-known essay, "Invisible Bullets: Renaissance Authority and Its Subversion." Observing that the imposition of the Christian order upon the "savages" of the New World had the effect of exposing the arbitrariness of that conquering faith, Greenblatt goes on to argue that the colonial power structure in fact produced this self-subversion that it might build upon it. "The radical undermining of the Christian order," he concludes, "is not the negative limit but the positive condition for the establishment of that order."[8] This analysis of containment is objectionable, according to Frank Lentricchia, because it implies "that radicalism is a representation of orthodoxy in its most politically cunning form and that all struggle against a dominant ideology is in vain."[9]

Carolyn Porter, identifying herself as one who values literary texts "as agents as well as effects of cultural change," is similarly critical of Greenblatt's tendency to exclude from the cultural conversation all voices save that of the dominant ideology.[10] There is evidence in Greenblatt's more recent work that he is alive to the questions that his critics have raised.[11] In what follows, meanwhile, it will be clear that my own notion of "containment" is much less final and hermetic than the one Lentricchia and Porter take so vigorously to task.

2

I was initially drawn to Greenblatt's work, and thereby to the new historicism, because his analysis of Renaissance texts helped me to better understand kindred patterns of doubleness, of self-subversion, in American literature. In the major works of Mark Twain, for example, I have detected a characteristic rift between a dominant and positive—comic, uplifting—if ultimately superficial "surface" narrative, and a submerged counternarrative that works to undermine the ostensible, and widely acknowledged, thrust of the book. The self-subversive split occurs, I have argued, because of competing impulses to reveal and to conceal what I define as "bad faith." My definition of bad faith takes rise from the close analysis of village social dynamics as they are represented in *Tom Sawyer*. I find that Mark Twain's characters are engaged in an elaborate form of social play whose dominant feature is the reciprocal deception of self and other in the denial of departures from leading public values. The term "bad faith" is also applied to the cognate pattern of denial that emerges in Mark Twain's handling of his materials, and that may be observed as well in the audience reception of his books. Thus the cultural dynamics observable in the action of the novel are repeated in the telling and in the response to the tale.

Bad-faith departures from leading public values, as Mark Twain represents them, are most frequently group phenomena, collaborative denials, and bear the clear implication that people will sometimes permit or acquiesce in what they cannot approve, so long as their complicity is submerged in a larger, tacit consensus. I should stress that bad faith is not always bad. In its benign and even beneficial phase, it enables a society to transcend the strict letter of its codes and the unanticipated limitations of its actors and circumstances. But it may also work to conceal problems of grave consequence. In either case, it is a telling feature of acts of bad faith that they incorporate silent prohibitions against the acknowledgment that they have occurred—denial is itself denied.

The recapitulating levels of bad faith witnessed in the complex, generally comical and benign world of *Tom Sawyer* reappear, now in a more pathological form, in *Huckleberry Finn*. Once again, bad faith is everywhere to be observed—in the behavior of people in towns along the river, but also in the young hero himself, in his author's management of the story, and in the novel's enduring popular reception. At the root of this pervasive malady is race-slavery, an institution whose maintenance in a Christian democracy requires extraordinary bad-faith denial, and whose existence over time fosters a wide range of kindred deceptions. The culminating episode in this darkly emergent cultural portrait is Tom's famous "evasion," the ostensibly humorous freeing of an already free man. Here as elsewhere in his writing, Mark Twain's approach to the tormented heart of his fictional enterprise intersects with a countering impulse toward distraction. The urge to tell the unbearable truth about Huck and Jim and their world arrives at a culturally revealing impasse with the urge to laugh it all off. This retreat from painful implication is also manifest in the history of the novel's halting composition, and in the enormous appetite for violent distraction among its leading actors. The same may be said of the enduring and widespread reader approval of *Huckleberry Finn*, a response arising out of pleasure that is itself the uncertain issue of Tom's evasion. At all these levels, then, *Huckleberry Finn* records or prompts a movement toward resolution, never completed, with nightmare. The dark implications of race-slavery press upward against the surface of the narrative, or of consciousness, only to be pressed down, and to rise and fall again and again in a repeating cycle of bad-faith denial.[12]

A somewhat broader notion of bad faith, geared to evasions in matters of race but alive as well to other varieties of social injustice, has been useful to me in efforts to understand some of America's most popular books. Classic Westerns such as *The Last of the Mohicans*, *The Virginian*, *The Sea-Wolf*, and *Shane* enjoy large, enduring audiences because of their emphasis on heroic action in colorful settings, and because they give dramatic endorsement to the virtues of courage, self-reliance, fair play, and the stoical indifference to pain. We come back to these books, and we urge them on our children, because they tell familiar and very gratifying stories about ourselves.

But they do more than this. If these books reinforce our sense of the heroic, they also challenge it. If they dramatize the triumph of traditional American values, they also explore the dark side of a dominant self-image. If they dwell on the exploits of white men, they are also attentive in less obvious ways to the grave injustices of the social order they portray, especially as those injustices bear on people of color, and on women. But while these texts feature sharp contrasts in shading and emphasis, none appears to do so in a fully controlled or premeditated way. Rather, each of the novels seems on its face to celebrate leading articles of the popular faith, yet each betrays an impulse, a self-subversive reflex, to undermine what it appears so clearly to approve.

The Last of the Mohicans was a great popular success because it addressed issues of race and gender that deeply troubled Americans in the mid-1820s, and because Cooper's management of those questions anticipated the habits of acknowledgment and denial, seeing and not seeing, of his audience.[13] The great popularity of *Shane* is geared in much the same way to a specific dynamic of revelation and concealment, advancing toward and then retreating from challenges to leading assumptions about family, self, sexuality, and society. The story is told by Bob Starrett, an adult who looks back on a dramatic childhood episode much of whose impact was no sooner felt than deflected, no sooner glimpsed than banished from sight and mind. The narrative is witness to complicating erotic strains between the adults. Bob's parents are both powerfully attracted to the magnetic cowboy, but even as they compete for his attention they subtly conspire to exploit his awesome power. Shane is hardly blind to signs of selfish manipulation and discord on the homestead; indeed, it seems clear that they confirm his suspicions of domesticity and hasten his departure. Bob sees all of this—sees it well enough, at any rate, to convey it to the attentive reader. But he resists his disenchantment even as he reveals it. Time and again Bob insists that the adult significance of his story eluded his boyish comprehension; and his conscious penetration is apparently not much deeper at the time of the story's telling.

Shane thus discloses its narrator's repressed disenchantment with father and mother and home. Bob must experience it all again precisely because he has failed since boyhood to face the heavy emotional burden that his narrative so clearly bears with it. He tells his story because he is compelled to. Readers return to Bob's story, I argue, for much the same reason. As the vast popular reception of *Shane* clearly indicates, readers accept fully into consciousness only those elements of the narrative that conform to a culturally preferred conception of home and heroism. The rest, the messiness and maneuvering, the self-ishness and sexual byplay, we are strongly inclined, following Bob, to repress. (Thus the impulse to deny may be said to tell the tale, though the denial in turn assures that we will pass this way again.)

This view of *Shane,* with its emphasis on the pattern of address and denial in the tale, the teller, and the audience, is cognate in a number of ways with the rather more indirect commentary set forth by E. L. Doctorow in another Western, *Welcome to Hard Times.* I like to think that Doctorow was reading *Shane* during the breaks he took from the composition of his own novel; in fact, he might have been reading, or watching on TV, any one of an endless procession of virtual replicas of the formula that *Shane* embodies.[14] In any case, *Welcome to Hard Times* offers itself as a comment on novels like *Shane,* and on their enormous popular audience. Doctorow makes his case by working within the formula, but by drawing it out to unusual extremes. Thus the violence-prone hero in *Welcome to Hard Times* is a tornado of ceaseless, motiveless, unrepentant destruction. The female protagonist, Molly, is an abused, degraded, ruthlessly grasping and manipulative prostitute. The two of them are locked in a marriage of blistering antipathy. It is an extreme variation on the submerged female/male thematics of the conventional heroic narrative. When the denying is finally over, and the truth is finally revealed, Doctorow seems to suggest, this is the way it is between the men and the women in our favorite stories.

The narrator of *Welcome to Hard Times,* a man named Blue, is by far the most fully developed of the novel's characters. Doctorow's emphasis on the teller is his way of underscoring the essential con-structedness of the very familiar, if very extreme, world that he sets before us. Blue is clearly akin to Bob Starrett. He is a narrator whose tale registers dark insights that never seem to surface fully in his consciousness. He is bland and matter-of-fact in describing a sordid, violent, doomed society. To the very end Blue keeps ledgers, written accounts of events as they unfold. The writing seems to provide a measure of control, distance, and hope. It reinforces Blue's sense of himself as an embattled innocent. But all of this, Doctorow makes clear, is false. The only things under control in the town of Hard Times are the narrator's carefully cultivated illusions. In fact, Blue is up to his writing hand in the hopeless world that he surveys. His innocence is a sham, a cover for spineless evasions and an imperfectly concealed fascination with the bloodletting. Thus his story, like Bob Starrett's, is a continuous and circular process of seeing and concealing, recording and denying, a recoil from experience into a consoling but utterly fabricated web of words.

Blue's self-deception is nowhere more extreme than in his attempt to join with Molly and a damaged orphan boy as the first new family in the town that the predatory outlaw has just destroyed. The parallels with the submerged domestic dynamics in *Shane* add up to a darkly ironic commentary on Schaefer's representation of the all-American family. This strange new Adam and Eve in their barren garden of ashes have their nucleus not in Blue, but in the Bad Man, who embodies the massive and finally uncontrolled violence and sexual energy that they have buried in themselves. The reminders of *Shane* are perhaps most irresistible in the boy, whose filial regard for the brutal rapist, and manifest calling as the next Bad Man, are the direct expression of an extreme oedipal urge. The family stays together only because its individual members wait together for the return, in the Bad Man, of repressed parts of themselves. When he arrives to destroy the town all over again, Blue, like Bob in *Shane*, retreats to his ledgers, and to yet another verbal reconstruction of a diminished reality.

"Fiction," E. L. Doctorow has observed, "is not an entirely rational means of discourse. It gives to the reader something more than information. Complex understandings, indirect, intuitive, and non-verbal, arise from the words of the story, and by a ritual transaction between reader and writer, instructive emotion is generated in the reader from the illusion of suffering an experience not his own. A novel is a printed circuit through which flows the force of a reader's own life."[15] This view of the essential collaboration of writer and reader in the fabrication of meaning clearly anticipates my own analysis of the dynamics of reader recapitulation in the popular response to books like *Shane*. As applied to *Welcome to Hard Times*, Doctorow's commentary finds its focus in Blue, whose ledgers are specimens of "fiction," and emphatically not an "entirely rational means of discourse." Blue is first and foremost a writer; and writers know, Doctorow insists, "that the world in which we live is still to be formed and that reality is amenable to any construction that is placed upon it. It is a world made for liars and we are born liars."[16] Quite as obviously, Blue exemplifies the grave perils of fictional world building. Here as elsewhere Doctorow seems strongly inclined to a psycho-sexual approach to history; for *Welcome to Hard Times* offers itself as a warning against the attempt, in civilization, to achieve stability by repressing powerful and potentially destructive energies and impulses. The construction of reality is here characterized as an activity dominated by omission, concealment, evasion, self-deception. But, Doctorow makes clear, the disposition to deny is broadly based. In its implied commentary on the authority of the Western formula story, *Welcome to Hard Times* implicates the reader in the culturally sanctioned, virtually obligatory refabrication of a fragile construction of reality. It is fragile because so much of the constructing involves conspicuous denial; it is obligatory because the repressed discordancies and contradictions are forever pressing against the surface of consciousness. "And now," Blue concludes, "I've put down what happened, everything that happened from one end to the other. And it scares me more than death scares me that it may show the truth."[17]

3

These novels by Twain, Schaefer, and Doctorow tell two stories, not just one; and the "parts" so divided work in a paradoxical and self-subversive way to reveal what they conceal, to affirm what they deny, to deny what they affirm. This is a complicated process—as complicated as Blue's deathly fear that his ledgers may somehow reveal the truth. On one side, his compulsion to inscribe obeys a mysterious, divided impulse to reveal some vaguely glimpsed truth, and, at the same time, a countering impulse to conceal it. On the other side, *Welcome to Hard Times* and Doctorow's observations on fiction bear the clear suggestion that the reader, like the teller of the tale—the born liar—will settle for a partial, incomplete construction of the truth on the page. I believe, as I think Doctorow does, that there is a discernible relationship in many of our favorite novels between the conscious, surface narrative and the submerged, subversive material that it conceals. The plausible, perfectly predictable surface of the tale answers the need to obscure yet once more a contrary, subversive perspective whose persistent resurgence on the margins of consciousness —and of the narrative—ensures that the tale will require repeating, and will thereby continue to enjoy popularity. There is here manifest an impulse to submerge discord and contradiction. But that impulse in turn points to a countering drive to address painful questions of value. Thus the evasive tendency is always found in combination with its opposite, and the negotiation of the tension between the opposed tendencies may be said to drive the narrative.

I want to stress that the contrary impulses to see and not see, to address painful issues and to turn away from them, are always delicately poised in these texts, and never fully "contained" or resolved. Indeed, it is the very essence of the appeal of books like *Shane* and *Huckleberry Finn* that they are the records of an unfinished cultural negotiation with failures in the moral order of America. The author and the novel contrive to have things both ways—to see and not see—in matters where we have fallen far short of our ideals. The reader, in turn, is initially drawn to the novel, and subsequently returns to it, because it forms the occasion for a similarly mingled experience. Let me emphasize that audience response, as I understand it, is not a merely passive surrender to ideological manipulation. If readers acquiesce in the false resolutions advanced on the face of novels like *Shane* and *Huckleberry Finn,* they do so in the active bad-faith denial of a resurgent, subversive challenge to the surface of the narrative. It is the repression of what we have glimpsed that keeps us coming back. These novels are popular because they enable movement toward a bearable angle of vision on matters that we can neither face for long nor fully forget.[18]

To offer this perspective on popular culture generally, and on western American literature in particular, is to obey what I take to be a new historicist impulse. It is to argue for the reintegration of the literary with the social and the historical. My texts at once derive from and substantially reinforce dominant constructions of reality. They cannot be understood in separation from the major social problems that they address, or from the cultural codes by which they represent them. This is not to suggest that they mirror a prior reality. Rather, they negotiate a compromise between competing impulses to reveal and to conceal what is often glimpsed, but less frequently confronted, in received constructions of the real. The history to which *Shane* "refers" is itself a text, a negotiated compromise requiring interpretation, just as the critical reading of the novel is susceptible to the very flaws that it seizes upon in its object of study.

Taken at its greatest latitude, bad faith, the retreat from unbearable truth, is what James Clifford, following Nietzsche, calls the "lie of culture." It is because the individual "learns to lie"—to acquiesce more or less completely in the "reality" of the world as given—that he or she is able "to communicate within the collective, partial fictions of cultural life."[19] I am inclined, as Clifford is, to make a potential virtue of this culture necessity, and to regard as extreme the view that the "lie of culture" leads directly to the slippery slope of nihilism and the abyss. Indeed, Peter L. Berger and Thomas Luckmann argue quite persuasively that our ability to confer legitimacy on humanly constructed "symbolic universes" is the key to such sanity as we possess, and perhaps to our survival. "All social reality," they insist, "is precarious. *All* societies are constructions in the face of chaos."[20] In this view, we have endured because we have denied the painful truth of our condition, accepted the sweeping "lie of culture," and then successfully concealed from ourselves that we have had any part in the construction of "reality."

The concealments performed and permitted by popular literature would appear to have a partial foundation in the dynamics of culture itself, which arises out of and builds upon the denial of its own constructedness. At the same time that they tell this "lie of culture" with extraordinary authority, popular texts also fill the space thus cleared with the more narrowly focused negotiations by which the members of a society or social subgroup accommodate themselves to the special conflicts and antinomies of their shared experience. For the majority of Americans, these special conflicts and antinomies have been racial prejudice, slavery, and varieties of sexual inequality. Time and again, it is to these issues, where contradiction and self-subversion gather, that we return. For it is in these areas, our fictions seem to declare, that we are most inclined to want to have things both ways.

In developing this variation on the new historicism, I have been especially attentive to Stephen Greenblatt's analysis of "the process whereby subversive insights are generated in the midst of apparently orthodox texts and simultaneously contained by those texts."[21] We are both interested in fictions that reveal, only to conceal, the same unsettling truths about the world. We agree that this distinctive feature is not the exclusive result of authorial intention, but figures instead as an essential ingredient in a collective, cultural undertaking.[22] Greenblatt does not align his analysis of literary doubleness, as I do, with a larger, informing "lie of culture." When it is framed in this way, power may be seen to express itself first in the authorization of meaning, in that denial of the denial of anomie that is the first step toward the construction of a world. Nor does Greenblatt stress the extent to which social and political power are an embarrassment in a Judeo-Christian cultural setting. To the very considerable degree that

they are Christian in origin, our notions of freedom and justice, and
our esteem for innocence, and for humility in the face of mystery, will
fall into some measure of conflict with virtually all manifestations of
social and political authority. The marked tendency toward self-
subversion in literature has a partial foundation, I believe, in deeply
divided affiliations along this conflicted border. And it is for this reason that literary self-subversion is likely to be "most intense"—in
Greenblatt's words—"when the moral value of a particular form of
power is not merely assumed but explained."[23]

This latter variation in emphasis brings us back to the place of
moral concerns in the dynamics of representation. Greenblatt recognizes such concerns, but he does not feature them centrally in his
analysis. In my readings, on the other hand, the preeminence of the
notion of bad faith is conspicuous. This separation of the ways has its
foundation in differences between the cultural contexts from which
our texts emerge. The pleasure of the Elizabethan audience, as described by Greenblatt, was to some extent the issue of the dramatic
subversion of authority. Pleasure came with a sigh of relief at the revelation that represented power was just that—represented, a fictional
construction. But the source of anxiety did not disappear; rather, it
was brought by the play into a temporarily softer, happier light.[24] The
modern audience, by contrast, takes its representations not so much
on the stage as in novels and on television. The point of vantage is
more remote, cooler, and power is represented, when it appears, either as a force for good on the side of the observer, or else as the possession of an evil or irrelevant other. But if represented power is not
the source of anxiety for most American readers or viewers, then
guilt—the emergent sense of individual moral responsibility for represented, socially, and politically authorized departures from public notions of the good and the just—is. Our anxiety is part and parcel with
a sense of complicity in the inherent inequities and abuses and tragic
miscarriages of power. Shane does not threaten us with punishment.
But his story may prompt us to reflect anxiously on the authorized violence in our world, a violence often rooted in varieties of inequality.
And in Shane's apparently fair-minded dealings with Marian Starrett,
we may also glimpse some of the inequities with which she must contend, and even the extent to which that injustice is bound up with the
ideal of male heroism embodied in the cowboy.

The popular American texts that I have studied were written for an audience of empowered participants in the social and political process. Most of the members in this audience, unlike the patrons of the Globe, perceive themselves as enfranchised, morally responsible actors in—and not merely passive subjects of—the world that unfolds before them. Thus their anxiety arises out of a feeling of inner complicity with power, and not from the spectacle of its threatening encroachment from without.[25] Concomitantly, their pleasure results not from the revelation that power is a kind of fiction, but from the concealment of its injustices. It is not what the audience sees, but what it sees and at that same time contrives not to see, that provides the relief; and it is relief from the anxiety arising out of guilt, and not out of fear, that contributes to the experience of pleasure. It follows that the Renaissance audience was relatively much less active than its modern counterpart in the actual construction of the meaning that it took away from its experience. Shakespeare's audience endured a happy subjection to the dramatic subversion of power; the audience that I have in mind participates with the text, and with its author/narrator, in the active evasion of departures from justice. Such containment, let me reiterate, is never complete. The impulse to conceal implies an accompanying revelation; evasions in literature, or in the literary response, are the correlative to the presence of something offensive to consciousness. In popular texts like *Shane* and *Huckleberry Finn*, I have argued, it is our moral equanimity that is upset, and then at least partially restored.

4

It is hardly my intention to propose that we ransack western American literature for texts that draw the reader into painful but psychologically obligatory encounters with repressed guilt. This would be to narrow the boundaries in a way that misses entirely the latitudinarian spirit of the new historicism. But I do want to suggest that our regional literature is characteristically American in its often complex, if frequently indirect, negotiation of difficult questions of value. Indeed, it strikes me that western American literature offers extraordinary opportunities for the study of what we may think of as the modern American ideology, that familiar array of ideals and aspirations that surfaced with especial urgency and clarity around the period of Jackson, and that has endured, with modifications along the way, right up to the present time. I am thinking here of the ideas of democracy, freedom, justice, equality, opportunity, brotherhood, progress, and of a unique, manifest, divinely sanctioned national destiny. The West has been the real and the symbolic place most closely identified with such ideas. Not surprisingly, therefore, the literature of the West has been largely concerned with the dramatization and evaluation of the American experience in these terms. The merest rehearsal of the names of leading (and for the most part very popular) regional writers—Abbey, Bierce, Brand, Cather, Clark, Cooper, DeVoto, Grey, Guthrie, Kerouac, Kesey, L'Amour, London, McMurtry, Momaday, Morris, Muir, Norris, Rølvaag, Sandoz, Schaefer, Silko, Stegner, Steinbeck, Twain, Welch, Wister—tends to bear this out.

The rendering of western history provided by these writers is hardly as extreme as some observers would have us believe. There is abundant attention here to the failures of the American experiment— to the play of greed, the surrender to self-serving illusions, the breakdown of institutions, the suffering of women and children, to racism, violence, and the tragic fate of indigenous peoples. To be sure, much of the story has to do with such darkly ironic departures from the familiar ideological scenario. But the literary record is also attentive to the fruition of high hopes and noble ideals in western places. There is freedom and abundance and fair play in these stories; they illustrate the human triumph over formidable obstacles, the transforming power of love and compassion, the achievement of continuity, and a yearning after redemption. This is a literature torn between powerfully competing versions of the same history. It is a literature that generally represents the American experience as a dramatic play of opposed moral energies; and it bears witness to a demand, by artists and audience alike, for the constant reassessment of the record, with an eye to the right and wrong of the thing, to the just apportionment of praise and blame.

If there is a tendency (as there certainly is in the stories that I have studied) to bend toward the positive side of the balance, there is also evidence (in those same stories) of a submerged but perceptible counter current, an unacknowledged and probably unconscious straining against the pull of the surface. I have drawn attention to this pattern in works by Cooper, Wister, London, Schaefer, and Twain. Consider, further, the cynicism that eddies from beneath the characteristically western humor of *Roughing It,* or the strangely muted strains of feminine protest in ostensibly affirmative pioneer narratives by Cather, Rølvaag, and Sandoz. Clark's *The Ox-Bow Incident* offers itself as a challenge to popular illusions. And Stegner's entire oeuvre may be read as a brilliant meditation on the new historical project that I am laboring to describe. Lyman Ward, the historian/narrator of *Angle of Repose,* learns only belatedly, and to his dismay, that his reconstruction of the family past is a distorted fabrication, driven by unacknowledged personal agendas, and most especially by an unwillingness to confront painful lapses from high ideals. As if to apply Lyman's hard lesson, Stegner is quite self-conscious in his mingling of history and fiction. In a prefatory note he declares that *Angle of Repose* "is a novel which utilizes selected facts from...real lives," but that he has "not hesitated to warp both personalities and events to fictional needs."[26] The misleading distinction between fiction and history is thus effectively collapsed, opening a new space in which the novelist/historian may conduct his or her own negotiations with the real.

"There is some history that I want not to have happened,"[27] Lyman is finally forced to admit. Toward the end of his career, the late Henry Nash Smith, distinguished scholar of western American literature and history, and—as it happens—a close friend of Stegner's, was brought to a similar reckoning with his own contributions to our understanding of the regional past. In an essay entitled "Symbol and Idea in *Virgin Land,*" published in 1986, Smith declares that "an American ideology" (quite similar to the one I have outlined above) "is constantly present in *Virgin Land,* but, so to speak, offstage, only occasionally given explicit recognition. The structure of the book, is basically a conflict between an assumed historical reality and the ideology, myths, and symbols generated in American culture by the contemplation of the moving frontier of settlement and the territory beyond." In rereading his book in the mid-1980s, however, Smith recognized that the attitudes that informed its original composition "were influenced by the basic myth or ideology of America to a greater extent" than he had realized. As the direct result, he failed in *Virgin Land* to give proper attention to Indians, to "the grimly ironic later history" of Manifest Destiny, to the national "cult of violence," and to regional legacies of racism and environmental abuse. "I took over from [Frederick Jackson] Turner," Smith admits, an attitude "characteristic of American culture, a refusal to acknowledge the guilt intrinsic to the national errand into the wilderness. Like my teachers and academic colleagues, I had in this fashion lost the capacity for facing up to the tragic dimensions of the Westward Movement."[28]

In effect, then, and by his own quite startling—and perfectly exemplary—acknowledgment, Smith offers his book as an example of what I have defined as bad faith, the deception of self and other in the denial of departures from leading public ideals. If his view is a correct one, then this habit of denial stretches backward in time through Turner, and forward through *Virgin Land* to those of us who came up as scholars under Smith's very considerable sway. To the extent that we were influenced by Smith, we adopted a view of the past that also served, in Sacvan Bercovitch's words, "to rationalize the worst aspects of the westward movement."[29] No doubt there is a measure of truth in this damning charge. Smith and his followers, it appears, were politically incorrect. But does Bercovitch's stern right-mindedness seem implicitly to proclaim itself exempt from vulnerability to the kinds of errors it condemns in others? This is not the place for a detailed comparison between the new historicism and what Frederick Crews has recently styled the new Americanism.[30] But such an undertaking might well begin with a close look at theoretical pronouncements by Greenblatt and Bercovitch, leading figures in their respective fields. Bercovitch's afterword to the volume of essays entitled *Ideology and Classic American Literature,* which he coedited with Myra Jehlen, would certainly figure prominently in the comparison. For it is here that Bercovitch defines the brand of "ideological analysis" practiced by the new Americanists whose work is represented in the volume. The afterword also includes Bercovitch's assessment of Henry Nash Smith's "Symbol and Idea in *Virgin Land,*" which is featured—rather as a hostage, it may appear—at the very beginning of *Ideology and Classic American Literature.*

I say "hostage" because Smith's essay serves Bercovitch primarily as an example of what critics should avoid—the complacent ideological sins of virtually all students in the field (Bancroft to Boorstin, Holmes to Hartz) whose misfortune it has been to labor without benefit of the new Americanism. Having declared *Virgin Land* "the single most influential book in American Studies," Bercovitch goes on to describe it as "an image of ideology in process—a mirror reflection of the way culture works, by imaginative and emotional appeal, to mask the effects of the ideas it promulgates, the unexamined (because internalized) values and beliefs that sustain the social order." Bercovitch defines ideology as "a system of ideas...through which a society, any society, elicits or enforces allegiance." The American ideology that has served to distort our cultural self-analysis for nearly two centuries has been especially crippling in this regard, for it has appeared to its deluded adherents "no less self-evident, no less true to sacred and natural law, than the once eternal truths of hierarchy, providence, and the Catholic Church." Thanks, however, to the kinds of insights afforded by Smith's timely apologia, the new Americanist "literary scholar can distance himself from cultural preconceptions, so as to make the study of myth a mode of cognitive criticism."[31]

The new historicism and the new Americanism—at least as it is represented by Bercovitch—share the view that culture and ideology have a key role to play in the concealment of resistance or dissent. But this similarity, though notable, is much less important than their very different conceptions of how this concealment occurs. For Bercovitch, ideology is first and foremost a mechanism of control; it is a virtually seamless "scheme" or dogma imposed from the outside on pliant, impressionable subjects (including past generations of Americanists) as a means of securing their "allegiance" to the dominant social and political order. For new historicists, on the other hand, ideology and culture are not generally spatialized as an outside somehow enclosing an inside. "Containment" is the changeable product of ceaseless negotiations involving multiple, shifting perspectives. Things ostensibly concealed make regular appearances along the unstable borders of the ideological veil. For the new historicist, and certainly for the new historicism that I profess, dissent is integral to ideology; resistance is a staple of culture. We are not simply seduced or coerced into compliance with society's "scheme." Rather, we are, in varying degrees, the schemers of the social order, constantly negotiating—both by what we accept and what we deny—our own compromises with the world as we find it.

It is one thing to admit that we have ignored or denied the presence of resistance within ideology; it is another to insist that the resistance is not there, and never has been. Bercovitch appears to take the latter view, and thus represents the new Americanism as the first party of dissent, rising as no previous generation of critics has risen into the clean, clear atmosphere above ideology. It is my understanding of the new historicism, on the other hand, that it assigns resistance a central place *in ideology*, but allows that culture-bearers, including critics, are not always able, or willing, to see it. Resistance is negotiable in the

new historicist model of culture; it's always there, though its presence
is frequently denied. For the new Americanist of Bercovitch's persua-
sion, however, resistance is a recent supplement to our ideology, and
it is the possession of a select, correct few. It is integral to the unstated
moral economy of this view that while it confers absolution on old
Americanists (for they could not have known), it claims broad legitimacy for the new (who enjoy, as Bercovitch says, a unique and saving
"distance...from blinding cultural preconceptions"). For the new
historicist, by contrast, and most especially for the *American* new historicist, the liability to blindness shared by all culture-bearers is relieved only to the extent that we are able to learn something from our
predecessors in the field. I prefer the atmosphere at this admittedly
lower elevation. From this altitude I am still able to admire Henry
Nash Smith, not only for his wonderful books, but also for his willingness to admit that he was wrong.

Smith confesses to an inability to look for long at the most painful
chapters of the western American story. I share that incapacity. What
Smith describes as "the tragic dimensions of the Westward Movement" are at once unbearable and unforgettable; we try to press them
from sight and mind, but they are always there, on the margins, ready
to spring back to view. The pain and the guilt are mine, just as surely
as the denial is. I am intermittently self-deceived, but never fully, finally blinded. That is why I come back to books like *The Last of the
Mohicans, Huckleberry Finn, Shane,* and the rest of them.

Notes

Special thanks to Jerome Frisk for his thoughtful attention to several earlier versions of this essay.

1. H. Aram Veeser, Introduction to *The New Historicism,* ed. H. Aram Veeser
(New York: Routledge, 1989), xi.

2. See the essays in *The New Historicism* by Vincent P. Pecora, Richard Ter-
diman, Judith Newton, and Frank Lentricchia. Also, see Edward Pechter, "The
New Historicism and Its Discontents: Politicizing Renaissance Drama," *PMLA*
102 (1987): 292–303; Marguerite Waller, "Academic Tootsie: The Denial of
Difference and the Difference It Makes," *Diacritics* 17 (1987): 2–20; and Carolyn Porter, "Are We Being Historical Yet?" *South Atlantic Quarterly* 87 (1988):
743–86. The direct quotation on racism and sexism is from Waller, "Academic
Tootsie," 3.

3. Catherine Gallagher, "Marxism and the New Historicism," in *The New Historicism*, 37.

4. Stephen Greenblatt, "Towards a Poetics of Culture," in *The New Historicism*, 1–6.

5. Stephen Greenblatt, "The Cultivation of Anxiety: King Lear and His Heirs," *Raritan* 2 (1982): 103.

6. Stephen Greenblatt, "The Forms of Power and the Power of Forms in the Renaissance: Introduction," *Genre* 15 (1982): 5.

7. Louis Montrose, "Renaissance Literary Studies and the Subject of History," *ELR* 16 (1986): 7.

8. Stephen Greenblatt, "Invisible Bullets: Renaissance Authority and Its Subversion," *Glyph* 8 (1981): 47–48.

9. Frank Lentricchia, "Foucault's Legacy—A New Historicism?" in *The New Historicism*, 239.

10. Carolyn Porter, "Are We Being Historical Yet?" 782.

11. This is especially clear in "The Circulation of Social Energy," the lead chapter in Greenblatt's *Shakespearean Negotiations: The Circulation of Social Energy in Renaissance England* (Berkeley: University of California Press, 1988). Greenblatt here allows that in his earlier work he "had tried to organize the mixed motives of Tudor and Stuart culture under the rubric *power*," adding that "that term implied a structural unity and stability of command belied by much of what I actually knew about the exercise of authority and force in the period" (2).

12. For the fuller development of these ideas, see my *In Bad Faith: The Dynamics of Deception in Mark Twain's America* (Cambridge: Harvard University Press, 1986).

13. My essay on Cooper, "Uncertain Borders: Race, Sex, and Civilization in *The Last of the Mohicans*," *Arizona Quarterly* 47 (1991): 2–18. On Wister, see "The Virginian and Molly in Paradise: How Sweet Is It?" *Western American Literature* 21 (1986): 27–38; on London, see "The Eyes Have It: An Essay on Jack London's *The Sea-Wolf*," *American Literary Realism* 18 (1985): 178–95. The commentary on Schaefer is much more fully elaborated in "Heroism, Home and the Telling of *Shane*," *Arizona Quarterly* 45 (1989): 72–100.

14. In a 1980 interview with Larry McCaffery, Doctorow recalls that he was working at a "film company and reading lousy screenplays" at the time that he wrote *Welcome to Hard Times* (*E. L. Doctorow: Essays and Conversations*, ed. Richard Trenner [Princeton, N.J.: Ontario Review Press, 1983], 33).

15. Doctorow, "False Documents," in *E. L. Doctorow: Essays and Conversations*, 16.

16. Ibid., 26.

17. E. L. Doctorow, *Welcome to Hard Times* (1960; reprint, New York: Bantam, 1975), 213.

18. In his very influential essay, "Reification and Utopia in Mass Culture," Fredric Jameson urges us to approach "mass culture not as empty distraction or 'mere' false consciousness, but rather as a transformational work on social and

political anxieties and fantasies which must then have some effective presence in the mass cultural text in order subsequently to be 'managed' or repressed" (*Social Text* 1 [1979]: 141). Despite obvious similarities in approach, Jameson and I differ in important ways. For example, he finds that the "inside" of the text contains a Utopian conception of life that the "outside" manages. In my texts, however, the "preferred" view of the world tends toward the surface, while a competing, subversive perspective is pressed downward, though never completely from sight. Jameson casts readers or viewers as active only to the extent that they penetrate briefly to a glimpse of Utopia; thereafter they are the passive subjects of "ideological manipulation." My audience, on the other hand, participates in an active evasion of the acknowledgment that their ideals have been compromised. Such ideals, I find, figure prominently in popular fiction. For Jameson, by contrast, the discovery of a socially redeeming dimension in texts otherwise dismissed as "degraded" is something of a scandal. "We cannot fully do justice to the ideological function of works like these," he writes, "unless we are *willing to concede* [my emphasis] the presence in them of a more positive function as well" (144).

19. James Clifford, "On Ethnographic Self-Fashioning: Conrad and Malinowski," in *Reconstructing Individualism*, ed. Thomas C. Heller et al. (Stanford: Stanford University Press, 1986), 147.

20. Peter L. Berger and Thomas Luckmann, *The Social Construction of Reality* (Garden City, N.Y.: Doubleday, 1966), 103.

21. Stephen Greenblatt, "Invisible Bullets," 41.

22. Greenblatt makes this point in several different places, but perhaps most directly in *Shakespearean Negotiations:* "Works of art, however intensely marked by the creative intelligence and private obsessions of individuals, are the products of collective negotiation and exchange" (vii). See also *Shakespearean Negotiations,* 12; and "The Cultivation of Anxiety: King Lear and His Heirs," 102.

23. Greenblatt, "Invisible Bullets," 51.

24. See Greenblatt, "Martial Law in the Land of Cockaigne," in *Shakespearean Negotiations,* 133–35.

25. It should be obvious that this is not always the case. Popular American texts sometimes represent social and political authority as a threat to the interests of the assumed audience, and they sometimes represent the injustices of power without inviting their evasion. This overt, relatively unequivocal subversiveness is perhaps more prevalent today than ever before in our history. In the wake of the civil rights movement, Vietnam, Watergate, and the advent of the new feminism, there is an increased audience readiness to acknowledge the injustices of the system, and an expanding constituency of audience members who regard themselves as un- or under-enfranchised.

26. Wallace Stegner, *Angle of Repose* (Garden City, N.Y.: Doubleday, 1971), 9.

27. Ibid., 512.

28. Henry Nash Smith, "Symbol and Idea in *Virgin Land*," in *Ideology and Classic American Literature*, ed. Sacvan Bercovitch and Myra Jehlen (London: Cambridge University Press, 1986), 23, 27–29.

29. Sacvan Bercovitch, Afterword to *Ideology and Classic American Literature,* 421.

30. Frederick Crews, "Whose American Renaissance?" *NYRB* 35 (1988): 68–81.

31. Bercovitch, Afterword to *Ideology and Classic American Literature,* 420–23.

Bibliography

Bercovitch, Sacvan. Afterword to *Ideology and Classic American Literature,* edited by Sacvan Bercovitch and Myra Jehlen. London: Cambridge University Press, 1986.

Berger, Peter L., and Thomas Luckmann. *The Social Construction of Reality.* Garden City, N.Y.: Doubleday, 1966.

Clifford, James. "On Ethnographic Self-Fashioning: Conrad and Malinowski." In *Reconstructing Individualism,* edited by Thomas C. Heller et al., 140–62. Stanford: Stanford University Press, 1986.

Crews, Frederick. "Whose American Renaissance?" *New York Review of Books* 35 (1988): 68–81.

Doctorow, E. L. *E. L. Doctorow: Essays and Conversations,* edited by Richard Trenner. Princeton, NJ: Ontario Review Press, 1983.

———. *Welcome to Hard Times.* 1960. Reprint. New York: Bantam, 1975.

Gallagher, Catherine. "Marxism and the New Historicism." In *The New Historicism,* edited by H. Aram Veeser. New York: Routledge, 1989.

Greenblatt, Stephen. "The Cultivation of Anxiety: King Lear and His Heirs." *Raritan* 2 (1982): 92–114.

———. "The Forms of Power and the Power of Forms in the Renaissance: Introduction," *Genre* 15 (1982): 3–6.

———. "Invisible Bullets: Renaissance Authority and Its Subversion." *Glyph* 8 (1981): 40–61.

———. *Shakespearean Negotiations: The Circulation of Social Energy in Renaissance England.* Berkeley: University of California Press, 1988.

———. "Towards a Poetics of Culture." In *The New Historicism,* edited by H. Aram Veeser. New York: Routledge, 1989.

Jameson, Fredric. "Reification and Utopia in Mass Culture." *Social Text* 1 (1979): 130–48.

Lentricchia, Frank. "Foucault's Legacy—A New Historicism?" In *The New Historicism,* edited by H. Aram Veeser. New York: Routledge, 1989.

Montrose, Louis. "Renaissance Literary Studies and the Subject of History." *English Literary Renaissance* 16 (1986): 5–12.

Pechter, Edward. "The New Historicism and Its Discontents: Politicizing Renaissance Drama." *PMLA* 102 (1987): 292–303.

Porter, Carolyn. "Are We Being Historical Yet?" *South Atlantic Quarterly* 87 (1988): 743–86.

Robinson, Forrest G. "The Eyes Have It: An Essay on Jack London's *The Sea-Wolf.*" *American Literary Realism* 18 (1985): 178–95.

——. "Heroism, Home and the Telling of *Shane.*" *Arizona Quarterly* 45 (1989): 72–100.

——. *In Bad Faith: The Dynamics of Deception in Mark Twain's America.* Cambridge: Harvard University Press, 1986.

——. "Uncertain Borders: Race, Sex, and Civilization in *The Last of the Mohicans.*" *Arizona Quarterly* 47 (1991): 1–28.

——. "The Virginian and Molly in Paradise: How Sweet Is It?" *Western American Literature* 21 (1986):27–38.

Smith, Henry Nash. "Symbol and Idea in *Virgin Land.*" In *Ideology and Classic American Literature,* edited by Sacvan Bercovitch and Myra Jehlen. London: Cambridge University Press, 1986.

Stegner, Wallace. *Angle of Repose.* Garden City, N.Y.: Doubleday, 1971.

Veeser, H. Aram. Introduction to *The New Historicism,* edited by H. Aram Veeser. New York: Routledge, 1989.

Waller, Marguerite. "Academic Tootsie: The Denial of Difference and the Difference It Makes." *Diacritics* 17 (1987): 2–20.

6. Battered Pioneers: The Problem of Male Violence against Women as Seen through Mari Sandoz's *Old Jules*

Betsy Downey

One of the most compelling aspects of Mari Sandoz's biography of her father, *Old Jules,* is the violence that Jules Sandoz inflicted upon his family. Jules Sandoz had left his native Switzerland in a fit of temper and ended up in northwestern Nebraska in 1884. Well educated and from a well-to-do professional family, he was nevertheless a character by any standards. He had a violent temper that was matched by unflagging paranoia and contentiousness. He was remarkable for personal filth and filthy stories. But he was also a gregarious center of community life, an outstanding horticulturalist, a voracious reader with cultivated musical tastes, and a tireless correspondent. He married four times: he deserted his first wife; the second and third left him. His fourth wife, Mary, bore him six children and stayed with him until his death in 1928. Jules physically abused at least three of his wives and the three oldest children. Mari, his eldest child, wrote *Old Jules* partly as a response to his deathbed request that she "write of his struggles as a locator, a builder of communities, a bringer of fruit to the Panhandle."[1] In writing that story she also wrote of the dark side of Jules Sandoz.

Jules Sandoz's abuse of his family represents a frontier characteristic that has been long overlooked. Until recently the frontier has been primarily male landscape presented by males. During the past two decades, however, an increasing number of historians, many of them women, have started to examine American frontierswomen more closely. They find the numbers and significance of the frontierswomen are great enough to constitute what Susan Armitage and Elizabeth Jameson call a "Woman's West," or what Glenda Riley calls "a 'female frontier'...shaped...by gender considerations." Many aspects of the male and the female frontiers overlapped, of course; one area of overlap was violence. Susan Armitage believes that this violence was not simply the public violence so often associated with the male frontier, but was part of the domestic life of the frontier wife, a private violence in need of further investigation.[2]

This chapter uses *Old Jules* as a case study of wife beating on the American frontier, putting Mari Sandoz's biography of her father in social and historical perspective. I argue that the factors that fostered Jules Sandoz's violence toward his wives are virtually identical to—and in some ways more intense than—those that fostered it in the eastern United States in Sandoz's time and across the United States today. I find evidence in *Old Jules* itself, in women's accounts of their western experiences, and in other records that such violence was not unique to the Sandoz household but was part of the pattern of family life in frontier settlements.[3]

Scholars identify numerous causes of wife beating. Underlying social attitudes that support the supremacy of males and the subordination of females are, according to many sociologists, at the root of the problem. Closely related is patriarchal organization of the family which (though challenged by an emerging pattern of companionate marriage) persisted into the twentieth century. The presence of violence in society and social attitudes that accept or even condone violence are also extremely important in contributing to violence in the home. Finally, several specific factors put men at risk to become wife beaters. The individual's psychological makeup, poverty, stress, status, and isolation are among the most significant.[4] All of these factors were present in the frontier settlements of late-nineteenth-century America.

The world of Jules Sandoz provided an ideal setting for factors conducive to family violence to intersect with a man already predisposed toward violence. Jules Sandoz brought strong attitudes of male superiority and patriarchal authority to his family. These attitudes were very likely a part of the cultural baggage he took with him from

Switzerland; they would not have been challenged in the Nebraska panhandle.⁵ Sandoz consistently belittled the worth of women. He was notorious for his "smutty" stories and his insistence that women's function was to serve men sexually, as well as in other ways. It is likely that he was guilty of repeated marital rape. He complained after Mary had banished him from her bed, "making him sleep alone," that "a man needs a woman as he needs the earth, for relief" (414). Late in life he lamented that "there is nobody to carry on my work. . . . If the Marie was a man she might—as a woman she is not worth a damn" (418). Sandoz romanticized his old girlfriend Rosalie, but the real women in his life were little more than objects to be used, as one would use a farm animal or tool. "Every man need a good woman," he told his neighbors—somebody to take care of him, do the chores, lend a strong back to the tasks that could not be done alone (24). Once, when Rosalie had written to say that again she would not come to America, "he cursed her, . . . all women, and spent a lurid night in Chadron with the worst one he could find. And then, because his need for a wife had become great, he asked her to marry him" (95).

If companionate marriage was a trend among some American families of his day, it was not for Jules Sandoz. Within his family he was to have complete authority and control. "Women who won't obey their husbands are worthless," he proclaimed (95). "I learn my kids to obey instantly or I lick hell out of them" (284). It was Jules alone who made the decisions in the family, without discussion and often without warning. He exacted a terrible price for disobedience, as his family was to learn again and again. "I learn the goddamn balky woman to obey me," he raged as he beat Mary with a wire whip. "I learn her to obey me if I got to kill her!" (230). The last time he beat Mari, he used "a chokecherry club, broke a bone in her hand" (382). When Jules's first wife, Estelle, had refused to obey him, he "closed her mouth with the flat of his long, muscular hand" and left her (5). He beat Henriette until she could stand it no longer; she retreated into silence and submission and finally fled. Rather than submit to his abuse, Emelia left at once. But Mary and the children suffered Jules's fists and feet and nearby objects repeatedly, until finally he was too old to exact their obedience and the children were old enough to fight back and to flee.

Violence was an integral part of life for the Sandoz family and their neighbors, especially in the early years. As Mari wrote, "war and wholesale bloodshed stalked very close to the Panhandle" (326). The pages of *Old Jules* and the newspaper accounts Mari Sandoz used as her sources are filled with episodes of violence. On Jules's first night in western Nebraska he witnessed a barroom murder. Someone once shot a lighted lamp out of his second wife's hands. His own brother was later murdered by a cattleman's hired killer. The introduction of sheep brought "war with the cattlemen . . . conflicts, lawsuits, destruction of property, and finally murder" (226–27). Guns were as much a part of Jules's normal attire as was the old overshoe he wore to protect his crippled foot. The rifle was, as Helen Stauffer has suggested, an important tool for backing up legal rights. There seems to have been as much use of violence as of law and litigation to settle quarrels in the panhandle.

Several factors in Jules's own character put him at risk to become a battering husband. His very presence in Nebraska was the result of an uncontrollable temper that raged so often that his daughter wondered if it was "peace he could not endure or was there something in him that made him destroy as he built?" (245). No one could work with him or hunt with him. He lacked even enough self-control to work well with horses. Jules was notorious for his sharp and abusive tongue; one old neighbor wrote that "since he never walked the street without his long barrel rifle ready for instant action, some saw him as a potential killer."[7] But Sandoz apparently never resorted to actual physical violence with them, preferring verbal abuse and warning or harassing shots, and withdrawing from public confrontation before it resulted in physical exchange or bodily harm. Only twice in Mari's account did he actually come close to pulling the trigger in anger; both times left him shaken and subdued. Jules seemed to have remarkable control over his public outbursts, knowing exactly where he must stop to keep his neighbors' reactions limited. It was as if he was playing a game whose object was to show how dangerous he could be if pushed. "I'd a thought they'd a shot you years ago," a settler once remarked. "They were afraid of me," Jules responded. He had achieved his goal, for, as Mari wrote: "It wasn't worth the risk to mix with the old crack shot" (297). Only within his family did he actually go over the edge and lose control. Even in his rages Jules, like so many batterers, realized that the costs of public damage or harm would be unacceptable; there were too many fists, too many guns, and too many matches in the panhandle. Even there, the law was near enough that it often—or at least sometimes—caught up with murderers.[8]

As well as a violent temper, Jules had problems of self-image and status. He was a cripple in a land that required a strong and able body. A crushed ankle shortly after his arrival in the panhandle left him "crippled Old Jules for all time now, hurt and defiant" (55). The accident and its results haunted him for the rest of his life. Mari emphasizes how much it scarred him emotionally and diminished his self-esteem. Although it gave him an excuse to avoid physical labor, it must also have contributed immeasurably to his rages, limiting his freedom of motion and constantly reminding him how little control he had over his fate or even his own body.

Though he was posthumously honored by the University of Nebraska for his achievements in horticulture, and was regarded ultimately by his neighbors as a "big man" (398), he was not successful in any usual sense. Poverty was a constant problem. He could not keep the post-office stations that the government awarded him. His attempts at politics were unsuccessful. The same neighbors who saw his importance thought he was "unconfinably crazy" (172). Charley O'Kieffe wrote that "to most of us who so frequently saw him striding down the middle of Main Street, he presented a figure both pathetic and formidable. To others he was only a freak."[9] He was notorious among his neighbors for his personal dirtiness; old friends from Switzerland seeing him were shocked. "Where then was the dandy who must maintain the style of a gentleman's son in Zurich? It was almost to laugh!... 'Must one then become so coarse as the land?' " the wife boldly asked (235). Frustrated he once roared at Mary: "You want me, an educated man, to work like a hired tramp!" And he "threw her against the wall" (199). He was "the patriarch of pioneers in the Northwest," but he was at the same time a misfit, one of the community cranks (312).

In addition to Jules Sandoz's personal makeup, many factors in the harsh circumstances of pioneer life in Nebraska contributed to the physical violence of the Sandoz homestead. Economic stress and poverty were continual problems for the Sandoz family and for most of their homesteading neighbors. In selecting the Niobrara area and the Sandhills of northwestern Nebraska to build a future based on a small farm and orchard, Jules virtually sentenced himself to a battle against the elements and poverty that he could neither control nor win. Even a man less paranoid would find there a host of formidable enemies: the ranchers and sheepmen who wanted the range to themselves; the law, often in the hands of the enemy, often powerless; the government, disinterested in the feuds of the panhandle; the railroads, which too often did not come where they were wanted; and the banks, quick to lend at high interest and quicker to foreclose when payments were missed. Always there was the weather, the least controllable of all.

Predictable only in its violence and its extremes, nature seemed as determined to prove its invincibility as Jules was determined to triumph over it. While winter blizzards took a recurring toll on his stock, the summers were probably a greater problem, for rain was a constant—and frequently absent—need. The drought cycles and Jules's violent cycles seemed to run parallel. When there was rain it was better, for Jules and for the whole household. But even when the rains came, the weather could be fickle. One spring the weather was mild and the orchards lush with young fruit and promise. Then came the hail, pounding the corn into the ground, stripping the trees of foliage and fruit, and even beating the bark off the trees. The panhandle was, in the last analysis, ill suited for the small farming to which Jules was committed. The area "for years had been looked upon as the Creator's waste material dumping ground," wrote one Nebraskan. Another, who had been "in the Farm and Ranch loan business for over 30 years," concluded that "the Sand Hill country of Neb. would be the *last* place in the world that I would go to, to make a living as a farmer."[10] In such a climate, there could be no certainty of success or reward. Stress and frustration were the only certainties in the Sandhills.

The pounding of the weather and Jules's poor business sense brought grinding poverty and increased the stress on the entire family. Though in later years the farm prospered, in the early years Mary could hope "for nothing more than that her children might have enough to eat and someday have shoes between their feet and the iron-hard ground of winter" (219). Such a hard worker that she made other women "seem lazy, impractical and irresponsible," she was back in the fields hoeing ten days after the birth of her sixth child (221). But Jules was an unwise and impulsive businessman and an unpredictable worker who was apt to be reading, hunting, or talking when there was work to be done. Worse yet, in his zeal to populate the West, he brought a constant stream of guests to the home to eat up their meager rations. Too often "there was no flour, no sugar, no kerosene for months. Then Jules revived the skunk-oil lamp of his batching days and Mary ground wheat in the hand gristmill until the perspiration streamed from her veining temples" (222). And she would nag in despair and he would hit her to shut her up.

The privacy of Jules's frontier homestead provided both dependents he could control and a setting where his violence could rage unchecked. In some homes, sociologists suggest, the presence of many children in close quarters provided enough of an audience to deter violence.[11] Such was not the case in the Sandoz household. Even with Mary's mother and sister living with them, and a growing number of children, Jules's violence was frequent and physical. Once he beat Mary with a four-foot wire whip, so badly that with face and hand streaming blood, she tried to poison herself. While her mother knocked the strychnine from her hand and mouth, "and hidden far under the bed the three children cowered like frightened little rabbits," Jules burst in again screaming "I learn her to obey me if I got to kill her!" (230). This audience was a powerless one, incapable of halting his violence. Jules Sandoz's nearest neighbors were usually a mile or more away, providing him all the privacy he needed to create a reign of terror in his household. It is not clear from Mari's account how much the neighbors knew of the violence in the Sandoz household. They certainly knew something of it, but Jules had little to fear from their intervention. While Mari reports some head shaking and mutterings among the neighbors, they not surprisingly hesitated to invade Jules Sandoz's privacy.

Jules's family could do little to raise the costs of his violence to unacceptable levels. His second and third wives had been able to leave him because they had borne him no children. Henriette, who "did not intend to become a burden-bearing woman," also had a little money of her own that she kept from him and used to establish her own land claim. "Henriette's place" provided her with a threat and then finally an escape when his treatment of her became unbearable (102). In June 1892, Henriette filed for divorce, charging that on four occasions Jules, without provocation, beat her and caused bodily injury. Once he beat her with his fists; three times he used other objects: a shoe, a club, and a horsewhip. The divorce was granted.[12] Emelia, the third wife, had no money; even so, within two weeks she escaped to work in a hotel in the nearest town. But Mary was not so lucky. "Brought up in the tradition of a lifetime of subordination to man," she had turned over all her money to him (187). "Now there was no escape. She had nothing" (190). Soon she was pregnant. "With a baby she could never leave Jules, not so long as she could stay at all, so that was settled" (212)>Like so many battered wives, she was trapped with a growing family in grinding poverty. She would live with him until he died.

Submission and obedience on the part of his family were Jules Sandoz's rewards for his violence. His wives had much to nag about: the drudgery, the poverty, his habits, the weather. Jules's fists and feet soon put a stop to the nagging. The second wife, Henriette, "was intelligent, quick to recognize the potency of silence" (102). "Trying very hard to live in peace," Mary, the fourth wife, learned to keep her comments to herself, to avoid "crossing him or bothering him for help in anything she could possibly do alone" (199, 230–31). The children, too, were helpless victims who had to endure his physical and verbal violence until they became old enough to move out. Young Jules was stubborn and was beaten repeatedly, but Mari said she "learned conformity early" (266). "When the little Marie was three months old and ill with summer complaint, her cries awakened Jules. Towering dark and bearded in the lamplight, he whipped the child until she lay blue and trembling as a terrorized small animal.... The night's work was never to be undone," she wrote, and she "hid away within herself" after that (215–16)>Trapped by their poverty and their remoteness from better circumstances, the family's survival lay in remaining silent and docile. Jules's violence brought him other rewards besides their silence. Family patterns were organized around him, and family members tried to cater to him as much as possible to avoid unleashing his wrath. There were few extras in his impoverished household, but he always got the best of what there was.

The hardships, and even the physical abuse, that Mary Sandoz had to endure were shared by many women on the frontier. Women coped with them, sometimes successfully and sometimes not, in a variety of ways. Glenda Riley has concluded that the key factors for successful adjustment were "their ability to create a rich social life from limited resources, the tremendous reward they derived from their roles as cultural conservators, and their willingness and ability to bond to each other."[13] While Mary Sandoz clearly emerges from the pages of her daughter's book as a survivor and as a silent hero, I think she is also portrayed as a victim who had virtually no control over her own life. Whatever networking resources Mary had were not so much the result of her own individuality and development as they were of

Jules's activities. Jules discouraged her from visiting off the homestead, discouraged her from activities that were not initiated by him
or that did not include him. He did not allow her to create a life of her
own outside her battered household, and this was part of her abuse.
Nor is there much evidence in Mari's account of the family that her
mother was able to play a significant role as a cultural conservator, a
role that Riley sees as one of the constructive responses of women to
their harsh frontier conditions. Jules apparently preempted this role
for himself with his books and his wide-ranging interests and
hobbies.[14]

Although she did not have a support network of female friends
outside her home, Mary did have some significant support from her
family and probably, also, from the wives of Jules's brothers and a
few of his closest friends. Her mother seems to have been most important to her, coming to live in a lean-to adjacent to Jules's house a year
or so after their marriage and staying there until her death some years
later. She could not stop Jules's violence, but she supported her
daughter against his rampages. When Jules beat Mary so badly with
the wire whip, it was the grandmother who cursed Jules: " 'You!' the
grandmother cried, shaking her fist against him. 'For you there is a
place in hell!' . . . Then she led Mary out of the house" to a secret
place in the brush that was her refuge (230–31).

Mary's children were a bittersweet experience. Pregnancy increased the physical discomforts of daily routine; six pregnancies
took their toll on her strength. But with a baby in her arms she was
generally safe from Jules's fists; with a baby at her breast she felt she
could share her bed with him and cheat the stork, for a while at least.
Although the children were an invaluable asset to farm life, they
added to Mary's problems. She must have suffered greatly to see them
verbally and physically abused by their father, knowing that intervention was not merely futile but actually provocative. As they began to
lash back at their father she was "caught between husband and children" (368). Soothing Jules after one outburst she complained: "Always I have to eat the dirt between you and the children" (382). She
stood up for them when she could, however. When young Jules ran
off and his father threatened to retrieve him and send him to reform
school, she had threats of her own: "I'll tell them how you treat them
and me! You'll see—" (397).

Mari Sandoz left home with an enormous and understandable
amount of anger at her father, and her mother as well. *Old Jules*

reflects her enduring ambivalence about her childhood. Though *Old Jules* is a biography, Mari was highly selective in it, focusing on those qualities of her father and her family life that were most important to her: his vision, his love of the land, his violence, her sense of rejection by both parents.[15] Despite this selectivity, *Old Jules* remains an important document for the study of the female frontier.[16] We have corroborating evidence for Jules's character, for the conditions of life, and many of the major incidents of the Sandoz family's life. One important source is the short memoir, *Son of Old Jules,* written by Mari's brother Jules. Their sister Caroline writes in the introduction that the book was "meant to supplement, not contradict, the book *Old Jules.*" While his father's temper and the beatings he inflicted on the family are less central to young Jules's account than to Mari's, they still are powerful. Old Jules "never considered" Mary's interests, wrote young Jules:

> She was to do what he said, and that was that. One day I heard a ruckus in the house and ran down from the barn to look. Papa had Mama by the throat up against the wall, choking her. She was blue in the face and shaking, limp like a rag doll. I screamed as loud as I could that he was killing my Mama, and it got his attention. I thought he was going to come after me next, but he let go, and she crumpled to the floor in a heap. . . . I vowed that if I ever got big enough, I'd give him such a threshing he'd never forget when he tried such a thing again, cripple or no cripple.[17]

Jules Sandoz, Jr., gives us no reason to question the truthfulness of his sister's account of their battering father.

The experiences of the Sandoz family were not unique. Across the frontier, notes Glenda Riley, "women's diaries and memoirs . . . [and] newspaper accounts . . . reflect the incidence of wife abuse," and the occasional arrests of the abusers.[18] The West was full of families sharing the same attitudes toward women and marriage, the same stress and poverty and frustrations, and the same isolation and privacy that we see in *Old Jules.* There were numerous individuals in the West who were as eccentric as Jules Sandoz. Many of them came with personality traits that put them, too, at risk for domestic violence. Mari Sandoz wrote, after a lifetime of studying the history of the plains states, that "the maladjusted, the misfits—economic, social or emotional, men and women—normally drifted to the frontier. Many of these were further unsettled by the hardship and isolation, to end in a mental or penal institution or a suicide's grave."[19]

Ill-equipped by nature and background to deal with the hardships that faced them, too many of these men became wife beaters, too many of their households became violent. David Lavender wrote of his Colorado boyhood that

> our homesteading neighbors were not intentionally brutal. But, ...they were helpless in the iron grip of poverty. Ill-educated and overworked, some of them were perilously close to mental deficiency. If the parents cuffed and swore at the children, if toward each other they used vile talk and fought fist and nail, it was because their raw nerves demanded these sharp releases; because, remembering their own childhood, they were quite without realization that there might be other methods of exacting obedience.[20]

Mari Sandoz remarks almost incidentally on the violence in other households: perhaps Jules's brother William; a Polish neighbor; Cousin Pete who "kicked his wife until she almost bled to death"; and Blaska, the man who murdered his wife. Blaska

> admitted that he had whipped her, as is every husband's right. She started to run away again and, handicapped by his crutch, he sent her sons to bring her back. They held her while he pounded her with a three-foot piece of wagon tug with a metal cockeye in the end. Was it his fault that she died?
>
>   He cried like a lonesome little dog when they took him away to the asylum, but the boys calmly watched him go and then started to the reformatory (412).

The story of Blaska was unusual in its tragic ending, but wife beating was so common among the frontier families that Mari would write of "the ultimate accolade of the Plains as a good husband: 'He never laid a hand on his wife.' "[21]

Although Mari Sandoz was criticized by some readers for an "undaughterly" portrait of a man they considered atypical, *Old Jules* elicited both painful recognition and gratitude from others. "For a long time," one woman wrote to Mari, "I have thought there was a need to tell the story, not only of the heroism of the frontier but of its dreadful and needless cruelty to women." Another woman described growing up in a similar setting. "I don't know of any of the men who were duplicates of your father in all respects, but there were so many of them who resembles [sic] him in some of the ways that it is not hard to vision him as you have pictured him." She remembered "wives who trembled at the approach of the man coming into the house and children cowering behind the stove or staying out of doors just as long as they dared, afraid to talk or make any noise when the man was in the house," and a German who "was inclined to knock his wife around, regardless of whether she was pregnant or not." Many others mentioned similar experiences in their families.[22]

However, though there are significant indicators that violence was an important part of the frontier experience for many American women, it is difficult to find documentation as thorough and moving as *Old Jules*. Frontier women seem to have been as reticent as many modern women in discussing this aspect of their lives. One woman wrote to Mari Sandoz after the publication of *Old Jules* that "what impressed me most was the candor with which you wrote of the things that most people, and especially a person as repressed as your Marie, wish to hide in their own families." And Pauline Neher Diede's *Homesteading on the Knife River Prairies* is brutally frank in depicting her family's terrible poverty and living conditions, but most circumspect in dealing with its domestic violence. She says only that some of the men "became severe and took out their anxieties on wives and children by rough treatment, often beating them" and that it "was common practice among most homesteaders of all nationalities" to be "too strict with children and women."[23]

Perhaps further exploration of unpublished manuscripts, letters, and diaries will yield more accounts of wife beating, although Carl Degler warns that these are not the sorts of things women committed to paper, even privately.[24] The work of Elizabeth Pleck, Robert Griswold, and Paula Petrick suggests a more productive direction for researchers to take: court records. Pleck's article on nineteenth-century wife beating relies heavily on the records of assault-and-battery cases in several states. Griswold has studied divorce cases, which were very often initiated by abused women on the grounds of physical cruelty, in San Jose and San Mateo counties in the late 1800s, and Petrick has done a similar study of Helena and Butte, Montana. Testimony and depositions in these kinds of cases provide a wealth of information on violence against women who, as Griswold says, "would not tolerate behavior that their parents and grandparents accepted as a normal part of marriage."[25]

Although there is much work yet to be done, it is clear from the evidence now available that physical violence was a part of women's frontier experience. Probably less frequent, and certainly more private, than the violence of the male frontier, the violence of the female frontier was just as devastating. Perhaps it was more so, for it struck in the place where women were supposed to be most safe and within relationships that were supposed to be most supportive and most sacred. Thus, as Mari Sandoz intended, *Old Jules* is more than the story of a unique settler. It is powerful evidence of a pattern of intimate abuse, evidence of a characteristic of the American frontier that has long been buried "in a dark, hidden place" in the nation's memory (191).

Notes

1. Mari Sandoz, *Old Jules* (Boston: Little, Brown, 1935; Lincoln: University of Nebraska Press, Bison Books, 1971), viii. Page numbers will follow subsequent quotes from *Old Jules*. Mari Sandoz was called Marie during childhood and refers to herself as Marie in *Old Jules*. I use Mari throughout this chapter, except in direct quotes.

2. Susan Armitage and Elizabeth Jameson, eds., *The Women's West* (Norman: University of Oklahoma Press, 1987), 3–5; Glenda Riley, *The Female Frontier* (Lawrence: University Press of Kansas, 1988), 1–2, and *Frontierswomen: The Iowa Experience* (Ames: Iowa State University Press, 1981), vii–xiii; Armitage, "Through Women's Eyes: A New View of the West," in *The Women's West*, 17.

3. I have limited my study to Caucasian married families. Except for letters to Mari Sandoz, my sources are almost entirely published works. I have examined most of the published women's diaries, journals, and letters and collections of their writings; see my discussion on the problems of source material at the conclusion of this chapter. There are several excellent historical studies of wife beating in the eastern United States in the late 1800's. See Elizabeth Pleck's *Domestic Tyranny: The Making of Social Policy against Family Violence from Colonial Times to the Present* (New York: Oxford University Press, Oxford Paperbacks, 1987). See also her "Wife Beating in Nineteenth-Century America," *Victimology* 4, no. 1 (1979): 60–74; and her "Feminist Responses to 'Crimes against Women,' " *Signs* 8, no. 3 (Spring 1983): 451–70; and Linda Gordon's *Heroes of Their Own Lives: The Politics and History of Family Violence: Boston, 1880–1960* (New York: Viking, 1988).

4. Feminist sociologists stress gender issues, viewing male supremacy and power as the fundamental causes of wife abuse. Other sociologists see wife abuse as part of a pattern of "family" violence that may be rooted in a number of factors besides gender. Demi Kurz has discussed both approaches in "Social Science Perspectives on Wife Abuse: Current Debates and Future Directions," *Gender & Society* 3, no. 4 (Dec. 1989): 489–505. Wini Breines and Linda Gordon, "The New Scholarship on Family Violence," *Signs* 8, no. 3 (Spring 1983): 440–531, is a useful review essay from a feminist perspective. For more "family violence" oriented studies, see David Levinson, *Family Violence in Cross Cultural Perspective* (Newbury Park, Calif.: Sage, 1989); Richard Gelles and Murray A. Straus, *Intimate Violence: The Causes and Consequences of Abuse in the American Family* (New York: Simon and Schuster, 1988); R. Emerson Dobash and Russell Dobash, *Violence against Wives: A Case against the Patriarchy* (New York: Free Press, 1979); William A. Stacey and Anson Shupe, *The Family Secret* (Boston: Beacon, 1983). Donald G. Dutton, *The Domestic Assault of Women: Psychological and Criminal Justice Perspectives* (Boston: Allyn and Bacon, 1988), has a valuable discussion of the interaction of gender, psychological, and social factors. I am indebted to Jane Rinehart of Gonzaga University's Sociology Department and to Eloise Buker, Director of Women's Studies at the University of Utah, for their help with this interpretative material. For the trend away from patriarchy toward companionate marriage, see especially Robert Griswold, *Family and Divorce in California, 1850–1890* (Albany: State University of New York Press, 1982), 1–23; Carl Degler, *At Odds: Women and the Family in America from the Revolution to the Present* (New York: Oxford University Press, 1980), 50–51 and 74ff; Gordon, *Heroes,* 250–64; and Elizabeth Pleck, "Challenges to Traditional Authority in Immigrant Families," in Michael Gordon, ed., *The American Family in Social-Historical Perspective* (New York: St. Martin's Press, 1983), 504–17, cited hereafter as "Immigrant Families."

5. See the two articles by Melody Graulich on *Old Jules:* "Every Husband's Right: Sex Roles in Mari Sandoz's *Old Jules,*" *Western American Literature* 18, no. 1 (Spring 1983): 3–20; and "Violence against Women: Power Dynamics in Literature of the Western Family," in Armitage and Jameson, *The Women's West,* 111–25. See also Gordon, *Heroes,* 250–64, 286–87; Riley, *The Female Frontier,* 96; Julie Roy Jeffrey, *Frontier Women: The Trans-Mississippi West, 1840–1880* (New York: Hill and Wang, 1979), 7, 30; Griswold, *Family and Divorce,* 1–23; Degler, *At Odds,* 50–51, 74ff. For the European roots see Gordon A. Craig, *The Triumph of Liberalism: Zurich in the Golden Age* (New York: Scribner, 1988), 156–57; Karin Hausen, "Family and Role Division," in Richard J. Evans and W. R. Lee, eds., *The German Family* (Totowa, N.J.: Barnes and Noble, 1981), 56–57; and Catherine Prelinger, *Charity, Challenge, and Change* (New York: Greenwood Press, 1987), 15–23. These German attitudes may well have been shared by the Sandoz family; historian Karen Offen from the Institute for Gender Studies at Stanford has described Jules Sandoz's Neuchâtel to me as a "Germanic outpost." For the linkage between immigration and wife abuse see Pleck, "Immigrant Families," and Gordon, *Heroes,* 8–16. The suffragist editor Henry Blackwell wrote that the majority of incidents of wife beating "are com-

mitted by foreigners—probably because women are less esteemed and respected in foreign countries than in our own"; *Woman's Journal*, May 15, 1875, 156.

6. Helen Winter Stauffer, *Mari Sandoz: Story Catcher of the Plains* (Lincoln: University of Nebraska Press, Bison Books, 1982), 15; I am indebted to Helen Stauffer for her suggestions and her encouragement. Mari Sandoz's notebooks contain references from local newspapers contemporary to Jules's early days that document the extent of violence in the panhandle. See the Old Jules Notebooks in the Mari Sandoz Papers, Manuscripts and Publications, Box 18, University of Nebraska Archives, Lincoln. All subsequent references to the Mari Sandoz papers refer to this collection.

7. Charley O'Kieffe, *Western Story: The Recollections of Charley O'Kieffe* (Lincoln: University of Nebraska Press, 1960), 132.

8. See Gelles and Straus, *Intimate Violence*, 20–25; and Dutton, *Domestic Assault*, 60–65, for a discussion of control and consequences.

9. O'Kieffe, *Western Story*, 132.

10. Stauffer, *Mari Sandoz*, 108–9; letter from W. M. Heckler to Mari Sandoz, Jan. 15, 1936, Mari Sandoz Papers, Personal Files (Xerox copies), Box 4; all the letters cited are from the Xerox files.

11. Gelles and Straus, *Intimate Violence*, 28–30.

12. Civil Case no. 694, Sheridan County, Nebraska. Jules divorced his first wife, Estelle, in 1886 on the grounds that *she* had abandoned *him*, apparently because she refused to follow him west after he left her in Knox County; he divorced his third wife, Emelia, in 1894 on the grounds that she had committed adultery; see Civil Case nos. 19, 996, Sheridan County. I am grateful to Eloise J. Kampbell, Clerk of the District Court, for her help in locating these documents.

13. Riley, *The Female Frontier*, 97; see also Jeffrey, *Frontier Women*.

14. Riley, *The Female Frontier*, 97–101. Helen Stauffer has modified Mari's portrayal of her mother's restricted life; though Jules "seldom allowed the women off the place for any reason," she thinks Mary "made a life for herself...in spite of Jules." *Mari Sandoz*, 37, 33. See also Jules Sandoz, Jr., *Son of Old Jules* (Crawford, Nebr.: Cottonwood Press, 1987; Lincoln: University of Nebraska Press, Bison Books, 1989). Christine Stansell, "Women on the Great Plains, 1865–1890," *Women's Studies* 4 (1976): 87–98, contrasts Mary's isolation on their homestead with Jules's and other frontiersmen's ability to "escape" to a variety of their own private or public activities off the homestead.

15. Sandoz defended her father in many of the letters she wrote in reply to comments from readers of *Old Jules*, insisting that although her father was stern and her childhood difficult, she would not change either. In *Mari Sandoz*, Helen Stauffer cites the letter to Katherine Dugan in which Mari Sandoz explained of Old Jules that "although it appeared that the women and children of his family had been sacrificed to his ego, they actually had been privileged to 'look upon the lightning' " (106). In her introduction to *Old Jules*, Sandoz wrote that she would not want to change any of the figures in her book. Even Jules himself she would not "have one whit different"; they were "a gallant race, and I salute them" (ix). It could be argued that the affection within the Sandoz family was a product of

the "traumatic bonding" that proponents of the Stockholm Syndrome find in battering households. For a valuable discussion of the Stockholm Syndrome see Dee R. Graham, Edna Rawlings, and Nelly Rimini, "Survivors of Terror: Battered Women, Hostages, and the Stockholm Syndrome," in Kersti Yllo and Michelle Bograd, eds., *Feminist Perspectives on Wife Abuse* (Newbury Park, Calif.: Sage, 1988), 217–33.

16. For a discussion of *Old Jules*'s proper literary genre see Stauffer, *Mari Sandoz*, 101–8.

17. Jules Sandoz, *Son of Old Jules*, vii, 1, 82.

18. Riley, *The Female Frontier*, 96–97.

19. Mari Sandoz, "Friendly Earth for Hoof and Plow," in *Love Song to the Plains* (New York: Harper and Row, 1961; Lincoln: University of Nebraska Press, Bison Books, 1966), 124–25.

20. David Lavender, *One Man's West* (New York: Doubleday, 1956), 208.

21. Sandoz, "Friendly Earth for Hoof and Plow," 125; see also "Ideas for Dunn article: S. Dak, homestead period," in Mari Sandoz Papers and "Pioneers" file in General Subject Files, Box 38.

22. Letters from Magdalene Craft Radke, Nov. 25, 1935; Edna M. Hornburg, May 25, 1936, in the Mari Sandoz Papers, Boxes 2, 5. I found nearly two dozen other letters in Mari Sandoz's correspondence from 1935 to 1938 from writers who said that they too had experienced or seen similar abuse of pioneer women. More than half of the writers specifically mentioned that their families were immigrants—mainly German or Swiss.

23. Katharine C. Gregg to Mari Sandoz, Dec. 14, 1935, Mari Sandoz Papers, Personal Files, 1935, Box 2; Pauline Neher Diede, *Homesteading on the Knife River Prairies*, ed. Elizabeth Hampsten (Bismarck, N.D.: Germans from Russian Heritage Society, 1983), 84, 86.

24. Degler, *At Odds*, 41. Mari Sandoz commented in a letter to a reviewer in 1936 that there was a general "drouth of source material" in pioneer history partly because so many of the first settlers were nonwriters, if not actually illiterate. See her letter to Glenn McFarland, Mari Sandoz Papers, Personal Files, Box 4 (photocopies), Feb. 1, 1936. See also Carol Fairbanks and Sara Brooks Sundberg, eds., *Farm Women on the Prairie Frontier* (Metuchen, N.J.: Scarecrow Press, 1983), 55–59, and Ruth B. Moynihan, Susan Armitage, and Christiane Fischer Dichamp, eds., *So Much to Be Done: Women Settlers on the Mining and Ranching Frontier* (Lincoln: University of Nebraska Press, 1990), xiii–xiv.

25. Griswold, *Family and Divorce*, 1. See also Paula Petrick's *No Step Backward: Women and Family on the Rocky Mountain Mining Frontier, Helena, Montana 1865–1900* (Helena: Montana Historical Society, 1987) and "If She Be Content: The Development of Montana Divorce Law, 1865–1907," *Western Historical Quarterly* 18, no. 3 (July 1987): 261–86.

Bibliography

Armitage, Susan. "Through Women's Eyes: A New View of the West." In *The Women's West*, edited by Susan Armitage and Elizabeth Jameson, 9–18. Norman: University of Oklahoma Press, 1987.

Armitage, Susan, and Elizabeth Jameson, eds. Introduction to *The Women's West*, 3–6. Norman: University of Oklahoma Press, 1987.

Breines, Wini, and Linda Gordon. "The New Scholarship on Family Violence." *Signs* 8, no. 3 (Spring 1983): 440–531.

Craig, Gordon A. *The Triumph of Liberalism: Zurich in the Golden Age*. New York: Scribner, 1988.

Degler, Carl. *At Odds: Women and the Family in America from the Revolution to the Present*. New York: Oxford University Press, 1980.

Diede, Pauline Neher. *Homesteading on the Knife River Prairies*. Edited by Elizabeth Hampsten. Bismarck, N.D.: Germans from Russian Heritage Society, 1983.

Dobash, R. Emerson, and Russell Dobash. *Violence against Wives: A Case against the Patriarchy*. New York: Free Press, 1979.

Dutton, Donald G. *The Domestic Assault of Women: Psychological and Criminal Justice Perspectives*. Boston: Allyn and Bacon, 1988.

Fairbanks, Carol, and Sara Brooks Sundberg, eds. *Farm Women on the Prairie Frontier*. Metuchen, N.J.: Scarecrow Press, 1983.

Gelles, Richard, and Murray A. Straus. *Intimate Violence: The Causes and Consequences of Abuse in the American Family*. New York: Simon and Schuster, 1988.

Gordon, Linda. *Heroes of Their Own Lives: The Politics and History of Family Violence: Boston, 1880–1960*. New York: Viking, 1988.

Graham, Dee R., Edna Rawlings, and Nelly Rimini. "Survivors of Terror: Battered Women, Hostages, and the Stockholm Syndrome." In *Feminist Perspectives on Wife Abuse*, edited by Kersti Yllo and Michelle Bograd, 217–33. Newbury Park, Calif.: Sage, 1988.

Graulich, Melody. "Every Husband's Right: Sex Roles in Mari Sandoz's *Old Jules*." *Western American Literature* 18, no. 1 (Spring 1983): 3–20.

———. "Violence against Women: Power Dynamics in Literature of the Western Family." In *The Women's West*, edited by Susan Armitage and Elizabeth Jameson, 111–25. Norman: University of Oklahoma Press, 1987.

Griswold, Robert. *Family and Divorce in California, 1850–1890*. Albany: State University of New York Press, 1982.

Hausen, Karin. "Family and Role Division." In *The German Family*, edited by Richard J. Evans and W. R. Lee, 51–83. Totowa, N.J.: Barnes and Noble, 1981.

Jeffrey, Julie Roy. *Frontier Women: The Trans-Mississippi West, 1840–1880*. New York: Hill and Wang, 1979.

Kurz, Demi. "Social Science Perspectives on Wife Abuse: Current Debates and Future Directions." *Gender & Society* 3, no. 4 (Dec., 1989): 489–505.

Lavender, David. *One Man's West*. New York: Doubleday, 1956.

Levinson, David. *Family Violence in Cross Cultural Perspective*. Newbury Park, Calif.: Sage, 1989.

Moynihan, Ruth B., Susan Armitage, and Christiane Fischer Dichamp, eds. *So Much to Be Done: Women Settlers on the Mining and Ranching Frontier.* Lincoln: University of Nebraska Press, 1990.

O'Kieffe, Charley. *Western Story: The Recollections of Charley O'Kieffe.* Lincoln: University of Nebraska Press, 1960.

Petrick, Paula. "If She Be Content: The Development of Montana Divorce Law, 1865–1907." *Western Historical Quarterly* 18, no. 3 (July 1987): 261–86.

———. *No Step Backward: Women and Family on the Rocky Mountain Mining Frontier, Helena, Montana, 1865–1900.* Helena: Montana Historical Society, 1987.

Pleck, Elizabeth. "Challenges to Traditional Authority in Immigrant Families." In *The American Family in Social-Historical Perspective,* edited by Michael Gordon, 504–17. New York: St. Martin's Press, 1983.

———. *Domestic Tyranny: The Making of Social Policy against Family Violence from Colonial Times to the Present.* New York: Oxford University Press, Oxford Paperbacks, 1987.

———. "Feminist Responses to 'Crimes against Women'." *Signs* 8, no. 3 (Spring 1983): 451–70.

———. "Wife Beating in Nineteenth-Century America." *Victimology* 4, no. 1 (1979): 60–74.

Prelinger, Catherine. *Charity, Challenge, and Change.* New York: Greenwood Press, 1987.

Riley, Glenda. *The Female Frontier.* Lawrence: University Press of Kansas, 1988.

———. *Frontierswomen: The Iowa Experience.* Ames: Iowa State University Press, 1981.

Sandoz, Jules, Jr. *Son of Old Jules.* Crawford, Nebr.: Cottonwood Press, 1987; Lincoln: University of Nebraska Press, Bison Books, 1989.

Sandoz, Mari. "Friendly Earth for Hoof and Plow." In *Love Song to the Plains,* 115–42. New York: Harper and Row, 1961; Lincoln: University of Nebraska Press, Bison Books, 1966.

———. *Old Jules.* Boston: Little, Brown, 1935; Lincoln: University of Nebraska Press, Bison Books, 1971.

———. Papers. University of Nebraska Archives, Lincoln.

Sheridan County, Nebraska. Civil Case nos. 19, 694, 996.

Stacey, William A., and Anson Shupe. *The Family Secret.* Boston: Beacon, 1983.

Stansell, Christine. "Women on the Great Plains, 1865–1890." *Women's Studies* 4 (1976): 87–98.

Stauffer, Helen Winter. *Mari Sandoz: Story Catcher of the Plains.* Lincoln: University of Nebraska Press, Bison Books, 1982.

7. Polygamous yet Monogamous: Cultural Conflict in the Writings of Mormon Polygamous Wives

Paula Kelly Harline

In response to the federal government's efforts to abolish polygamy in 1870, five thousand Mormon women held a "mass indignation meeting" in the Salt Lake Tabernacle, where they heard their female leader proclaim: "Were we the stupid, degraded, heartbroken beings that we have been represented to be, silence might better become us." High-profile polygamous wives were adamant about their right to live their religion as they pleased, and bristled at accusations that they might be in a "state of vassalage."[1] Outsiders, such as the historian Hubert Howe Bancroft,[2] and a Pennsylvania woman, Elizabeth Kane, who visited Utah during the later half of the nineteenth century,[3] for the most part backed up these outspoken feminists by suggesting that, despite what the general public thought, polygamy didn't appear to be scandalous.

During the past couple of decades, with new interest in women's history and the opening of archives in Utah, scholarship on the topic has centered on the thesis that nineteenth-century polygamous wives were often the strong women we endeavor to emulate in our currently feminist culture.[4] But lately, some scholars have begun to suggest that polygamous wives paid a very high price in personal suffering for the respect they get from us. Jill Mulvay Derr writes that the women who became plural wives created a powerful sisterhood based on their common "aspiration and commiseration"—for while some became well-known feminists and career women, all the while defending their life-style, their lives were strewn with emotional struggles because of polygamy.[5] Richard Van Wagoner's *Mormon Polygamy: A History* discusses several prominent women who "publicly" supported plural marriage while "privately suffering" and wishing they weren't involved in the practice.[6] And Jessie Embry's recent valuable work, *Mormon Polygamous Families: Life in the Principle,* documents numerous cases of conflict as well as satisfaction in a cross section of polygamous families. Although Embry readily records her findings of difficulties and misunderstandings in polygamous households, she concludes that "Mormon polygamous families were not much different than Mormon monogamous families and other non-Mormon families of the same era. The Mormons simply adapted Victorian ideology to fit their new polygamous life-style."[7] Embry's findings are problematic because they assume it is simple to shift gears from a monogamous life-style to a polygamous one, when it is actually quite complex.

The more than thirty-five autobiographies and diaries written by polygamous wives that I have studied usually contain both expressions of belief in polygamy as the will of God and lamentations about the life-style. There seemed to be no such thing as being "born again," or converted, to polygamy and never looking back. Polygamous wives who wrote are distressed and confused because they are caught in the whirlpool of a major cultural reversal—the attempt to leave monogamy for polygamy. Polygamy and monogamy could not (as Embry suggests) coexist. The two became intertwined, in part because polygamy needed monogamy to define the primary male/female relationship; monogamy was affected by the presence of polygamy, as well.[8] Although polygamy was publicly touted in Mormondom as the highest and holiest spiritual experience, the long-held Western standard of monogamy could not be immediately or sufficiently undone, which resulted—as the private writings of these women show—in a culture in conflict over the religious practice they stood united to defend. These women writers often undermine their own talk, illustrating how confusing it could be to both want, and not want, to live in polygamy—and to be living it. Overall, private writings show that polygamous wives, being tugged in different directions at various moments in their lives, rarely could thoroughly or comfortably incorporate polygamy into their lives.[9]

Polygamy among the Mormons was publicly acknowledged in

1852 in Utah when Brigham Young's spokesman announced that the new religion's doctrine embraced "celestial marriage" as one of the holiest laws of God. Not until 1890 would the federal government succeed in officially ending the practice,[10] and it would be many years later that secret polygamous marriages ceased.[11] In the meantime, historians estimate that between 25 percent and 50 percent of the Mormon population in Utah and scattered throughout the West contracted polygamous marriages.[12] The concept of polygamy was foreign to early Americans and Western European converts with Protestant backgrounds. Joseph Smith himself, the founder of the Mormon faith who originally privately introduced polygamy, worried about the relationship between adultery and polygamy and felt the need for a definition distinguishing between the two.[13] The general membership had similar hesitations. Within six months of the official announcement that polygamous marriage was sanctioned and encouraged by the church, 1,776 British converts to Mormonism abandoned their new-found religion.[14] Some who learned of the practice through hearsay were stunned and found the news unbelievable. While traveling in a wagon train to Salt Lake City in 1850, diarist Martha Heywood recorded her disbelief of a report from "the valley" that a man she knew had married another wife.[15]

After the initial shock, however, women who stayed in the church began the process of reconciling their "former" tradition with their "new" tradition. In the process, some tried to have faith and sought spiritual experiences to help them along. Johanna Nielsen wrote that while she sat "idly dreaming" one evening, a light appeared before her and she had a vision that convinced her to accept polygamy.[16] Lorena Larsen turned down several polygamous marriage propositions, but when one man proposed to her just the way she had seen it in a dream, she decided to become his second wife.[17] Another writer, Lucy Flake, wrote of her frustration in seeking an answer about polygamy through prayer: "I had great faith in prayer—but how could I know whether the feelings in my soul were answer to prayer or my own desires, they conflicted so."[18] Overall, most women somewhere in their writings echo the sentiments of Elizabeth MacDonald, who wrote late in life: "I bear testimony that the revelation on Celestial Marriage given through the Prophet Joseph Smith, is of God."[19] In a recent article, Jill Mulvay Derr casts doubt on some of these testimonials when she suggests that they became ritualized, conventional, and institutionalized,[20] but writers who were polygamous wives for the most part seem sincere and convinced of the importance of their life-style as a way to please God and learn through hard lessons in life.

In addition to spiritual rationale, some women attempted to see polygamy in relation to other social systems that embraced it. With a broader perspective, a woman might make progress in justifying her life-style. Mary Jane Tanner wrote that "if [polygamy] were immoral the Bible would not sustain it. It is at present practiced by four-fifths of the world." Because it makes her feel better, she goes on to say that the "crowned heads of Europe and the nobility practice it," but qualifies this by explaining that they don't do it in a manner pleasing to God as the Mormons do.[21] Lorena Larsen elaborates on a biblical theme by appropriating terminology from Abraham and Sarah's story of polygamy. A blessing she was given told her that she would be "heir to all the blessings of Sarah, and of all the daughters of Israel," and furthermore, "if [she] would obtain them, [she] must yield obedience to the law of Sarah," or the law of polygamous marriage.[22] By not only extending the bounds of polygamy to other nations and four-fifths of the world, as Mary Jane Tanner did, but by also reverting through time appropriating biblical references, as Lorena Larsen did, women could attempt to overcome the delimitations of their immediate cultural context and make strides in adapting a new worldview.

Perhaps unfortunately for them, spiritual and other cultural rationales helped the women only to a certain extent—sometimes temporarily to get them through chunks of time. Ideologically women could imagine polygamy, but in practice they were tripped up by inculcated standards that defined the family. Since monogamy had reigned firmly entrenched as the Western/Christian/Victorian/Puritan standard for centuries, redefining family positions such as "wife" and "husband" could be troublesome. Levi-Strauss explains that family positions "exceed the individuals who temporarily occupy them," because each person is "inserted" into an "already defined symbolic system."[23] In other words, simply calling a second wife "wife" did not erase the impressions already associated with the term. Being an additional wife could not be the same as being an only wife, just as being a husband to several wives could not be the same as being a husband to one wife, and the father of one family. While Derr argues that polygamous wives forged bonds among themselves that would not have been possible without the presence of polygamy,[24] she cannot argue that these sisterly bonds could often be found in the same family of wives with a living husband. Embry suggests that wives in a family, lacking co-wife models, defined one another as "mother" or "sister," drawing on cultural models familiar to them;[25] but such designations as these would deny sexual ties to the husband. Mormons tried to make polygamy coexistent with a monogamy-oriented culture, but this created havoc for polygamous wives. A husband's courtship of additional wives, for example, was highly complicated by the first wife's feeling that her husband's efforts resembled infidelity.[26]

Rooted in monogamy, the Mormons' religion demanded that they reconsider and reconstruct their tradition to incorporate polygamy. The religious rhetoric in support of this change came not only from high levels of authority and official sources, such as scripture and Brigham Young, but also from lay members, who often publicly sustained their leaders and bore testimony to the divine purposes of polygamy, which in turn bolstered the effect of the official message. For example, Emma Nielson described an enjoyable women's meeting, recalling that

> Coun[selor] E O Teitjen spoke upon her severe trials in this country; haveing been on the frontiers from its first settlement; she had been tried in poverty, polygamy, and being deprived of her husband..., but haveing passed through it all she was thankful she had remained firm and faithful to the cause she had espoused and still desired to progress in the Kingdom of God; spoke very effecting, and encourageing to the sisters.[27]

This type of encouragement and example from older, experienced women helped other women develop courage and faith in the polygamous system. Testimonial meetings were frequent among the Mormons, and no doubt helped create the feeling among women that although the system was difficult, it was worthwhile because of the character-building experience gained and for the reward one would have in heaven.

So, the official church would sanction, support, encourage, and laud polygamy, but the unofficial church could be more problematic. The unofficial church included attitudes of the Mormon community outside official church meetings and buildings, and these unofficial reactions to official policies illustrate conflicts in the ranks. For example, Martha Cox wrote of her dismay at the community's general disapproval of her decision to marry an older man who was poor and already had two wives. The unfavorable rumors made her stay at home and "like a porcupine," roll herself "into a ball whenever [her enemies] approached." Martha wrote that some of her friends "cold-shouldered" her and made "uncomplimentary remarks."[28] This reaction particularly surprised Martha, young and perhaps naive, because, as she wrote, "It had always seemed to me that plural marriage was the leading principle among the L.D.S. and when I came to know how generally my action in going into it was denounced, especially the fact I had married into poverty, I was saddened as well as surprised."[29] In another autobiography, the story is told of a group of women who broke up the engagement of a couple who were on their way to be married. The bride-to-be was to become the man's fifth wife, but when she heard from women during a tea party at the house where they were staying what a poor reputation her fiancé had in caring for his wives, she broke off her engagement, much to the delight of the tea party women.[30]

Almost all parents had opinions to give their daughters about marrying into polygamy, and these parental leanings and urgings represent but a more focused view of what the Mormon community really thought about polygamy. Olive Potter's parents were "very much opposed" to the attention she received from a man more than twice her age.[31] Johanna Nielsen's parents butted heads over her future: her father "was determined" that she live the law of plural marriage, but her mother couldn't match his forthrightness. According to Johanna "Father was very serious about it and as the [church] authorities continued to preach it he felt we should not treat it lightly. The saints had always suffered when trying to keep the laws of God. A commandment of God was life itself to father." Johanna remembers that "Mother and I wept together but nothing changed fathers mind," and she eventually gave up the boyfriend her father didn't approve of and became the third wife of a young doctor.[32]

Although no other parents seem to have been as determined as Johanna's father, some didn't mind if their daughters considered marrying into a polygamous situation. Ruth Rogers's parents hoped that she would seek out Samuel Rogers, who had been a missionary in their native New Jersey, and didn't seem daunted by the knowledge that he already had a wife and several children.[33] Lorena Larsen's parents gave their approval for their daughter to marry an older, respectable church leader.[34] On the other hand, many parents seemed hesitant, like Johanna Nielsen's mother, who wept over her husband's insistence that their daughter become a polygamous wife. Martha Cox's autobiography suggests that her parents were angry with her decision to become an older man's third wife, primarily because they perceived no romantic feeling in the relationship. "It was not a marriage of love," her parents claimed, and their anger "broke" a "storm" on her head.[35] In another example, Annie Clark Tanner's father, a polygamist himself, tried to discourage Annie from becoming the second wife of one of her college professors. Annie's father told her, "Yes, . . . it is easy to win the affections of a girl; but it is not, in polygamy, an easy task to keep her affections."[36] When she overlooked her father's hesitations and married the already-married professor anyway, her father once again asserted his skepticism. To her response that the marriage ceremony wasn't "half bad," her father said, "You haven't half begun yet."[37]

Mothers of women who were first wives and whose husbands wanted to marry another wife reacted, as well. Lucy Flake, a first wife, wrote that after her husband asked for her permission to marry a second wife, she went to have a private conversation with her mother about polygamy. Her mother "said gently, 'My daughter, that is something you and Heavenly Father have to decide. That is one thing I cannot advise you about.' "[38] By refusing to give her opinion, Lucy's mother suggests that personally she can't endorse it, but feels her opinion weak in comparison to God's. In another example, Rachel Simmons's autobiography relates how her husband's flirtations with another woman annoyed her mother. When Rachel's husband started courting another young lady, Rachel's mother began to ask questions and "scold Joe" to her.[39]

Private writings are full of examples of hovering monogamous expectations and the simultaneous desire to be converted to new polygamous expectations. While writing of how polygamy came to find her, Lydia Brinkerhoff attempts to exonerate her husband from the negative connotations she admitted into existence when she suggests that he wouldn't have wanted to marry another wife if he weren't pressured into it. She wrote, "In those days a man was hardly considered eligible to be a bishop until he had more than one wife,"[40] as though it was his position as bishop that required it. Ordinarily he would have respected the standard most people felt more comfortable with—being exclusively focused on one woman after marriage. Similarly, Lucy Flake apologized for her husband by insinuating that it was not the general pulpit preaching about polygamy that opened a floodgate for him, but that he was personally asked by church authorities to consider entering polygamy.[41]

The ideal of monogamous fidelity in marriage did not easily go away. Lorena Larsen lovingly described how she furnished and decorated the little house that her polygamous husband could rarely visit, and concluded her description by quoting a salesman who often stopped by to rest. According to Lorena, "He always looked around the house, and sometimes heaved a sigh, and said, 'Oh what solid comfort a man could take reading the paper in a home like this.' "[42] To her, this seemed the ultimate compliment, yet, as a polygamous wife, she could never live in her house the way that she envisioned living. In another diary, Elvira Day wrote that her husband told her while they were walking one day that she was "selfish" because she wanted to caress him. To his reaction she wrote, "but I could not see it."[43] She was confused and hurt about why she could not be affectionate with her husband until he later told her that he wanted her "affectionate expressions" when they were "alone."[44] Elvira saw her husband as though there was no other wife, as though they were living by monogamous standards for a husband and wife, while her husband was attempting to negotiate a new standard in order not to displease his first wife. Another husband, "Pa" McAllister, sent letters to both wives in the same envelope while he was in prison for "cohabitation." His second wife, Aggie, wrote that she didn't want her letters "to come that way any more," and she was "so happy" when she received "the loveliest love letter" that the other wife didn't know about.[45] For Aggie, having a husband to herself was her greatest desire.

Marital fidelity was so crucial to Lucy Flake that when her husband asked her permission to marry a second wife, she said yes in order to find out in whom he was interested. During the grueling week that followed, Lucy reflected on her husband's request: "I tried to picture in my mind what young lady had won a place in my husband's affections. I hadn't seen anything in his actions that he had a thought for anyone but me. He was kind and courteous to all but had shown no preference as far as I could see."[46] Lucy phrased her answer to her husband in such a way that he had to tell her *who* he had in mind for another wife, and at the same time acknowledge that Lucy was still central in his life. She asked, "Will, who is the young lady *we* are going to marry?" (italics mine). When he hesitated to tell her, she wrote that at that moment she "loved him" as "never . . . before because," as she wrote, "I knew that he had been true to me." Curiously, she wrote this despite the later revelation that he did indeed have a young woman in mind.[47] Tortured by the revelation that he wanted to marry an eighteen-year-old girl whom they had watched grow up, she "slipped out of bed" after her husband fell asleep that night "and went over and sat down on the floor by babies cradle, and cried until [she] was tired."[48] Lucy undermines much of her story by insisting on portraying her relationship with her husband as two people thoroughly devoted to each other, embarking on the journey of polygamy together, when she doesn't feel that way at all. Her story suggests instead that she feels beaten because she has lost monogamy and can't understand where she fits into polygamy.

Another monogamous standard that caused difficulties in polygamous relationships was the notion that a husband should be a provider and protector. Annie Tanner's husband eventually requested a separation from her, probably in great part because she refused to give up her house and come to live with him in Canada with his other wives. Annie agonized about the decision to keep her own house because she felt that she should follow her husband; she reasoned, however, "am I justified in robbing my children of an ideal home, situated among all my people, and where they have the opportunities for an education."[49] Annie found that she could not conveniently fit her situation into a monogamous or polygamous pattern, and yet her independent mindset was not simple, either. In another example, Johanna Nielsen left her husband when she was finally struck by the severity of her poverty. When she had tried to talk with him about the unfair way in which the other wife gave out provisions, he refused to listen to criticism and she received a "reprimand" from him. Frustrated by not being able to depend on her husband to provide for her, yet exiled to an isolated home, she couldn't provide for herself, either. She prayed and "cried until [she] was weak" before deciding to leave her husband and the isolated place where she was living and get work to provide for herself and her children.[50]

Other husbands also had problems providing for all of their wives and families, and although many wives became resourceful to make ends meet, the confusion they might feel over not being able to depend on a man, as their mothers and grandmothers did, could be difficult. Ruth Rogers was a new bride and deeply in love when her husband asked her if she could return to live with her parents, presumably because he hadn't enough money to care for her in addition to his other burgeoning family. According to Ruth, "He said he thought it would be better for me to stay with them if they were willing...this made me feel as if my heart was most broke but I governed my feelings...I saw by his countenance that he was in trouble."[51]

Being left alone as a married woman could cause some resentment, as it did in Isabell Nixon's case. Isabell was left with her children at one of the family's isolated cabins during a troublesome time with some Indians but the Indians came to her place several times demanding flour and other things, and she sent word to her husband and her husband's family to come to her rescue because she "didn't know what [the Indians] might do."[52] When her husband didn't respond, she sent word to her father, who had to go to her husband's house and demand that his daughter be looked after.[53]

Living without a husband for long periods of time was usually part of the polygamous experience and not necessarily pleasant for the polygamous wife. Without exception, the women writers in my collection wrote of the constant adjustments of living without their husbands, and of the anticipation they felt in awaiting their visits. Polygamous wives seemed to be forced to construct a middle space where they existed by straddling polygamy and monogamy, a foot in each camp. Emma Nielson wondered often about the inconvenience polygamy caused her and the necessity of giving up what she had previously come to depend on as an only wife:

After getting my precious little ones in bed I took a walk in the moonlight all the while wondering where my precious FG [her husband] was and a sweet response would be, he is in Arizona doing his duty [to his other family], and then I often wonder if he is doing his duty to his family [here]. How pleased I would be if he would step in [and] administer to our wants, soothe the cries of my four little ones and do a fathers part; how their little hearts would leap with joy at first site; they have looked forward to the time (so long) that they would see their Pa that they begin to think they have no Pa. I feel heart broken myself my heart is so sore and who in all this world can heal it except my dear F.G....one word from his precious lips at this moment could do it; I love him as I do my own life; and when can I linger by his side as I once use to.[54]

She concludes this excerpt by stating that she's "thankful" to be a polygamous wife so that she can be "tried even to the very core" of her heart, but these sentiments seem undermined by the powerful longing she has just expressed to have her husband back. In another example, Jane Hindley feels defensive when her aunt and uncle visit and criticize polygamy,[55] and yet much in her diaries criticizes her own polygamous experience. At Christmastime and while she was nine months pregnant, her husband brought home two new wives. She wrote, "The house is full of company music and dancing but there is a void in my Heart; and my eyes are full of tears. Oh! I am very unhappy, and my pride will not suffer me to appear so."[56] She goes on to detail her misery and jealousy, and then reprimands herself for not learning "the lesson of selfdenial better."[57]

These many examples illustrate the complexity of living the back-and-forth, in-and-out nature of polygamy in a culture attempting to create polygamous patterns within the monogamous context. Joan Iverson concludes that during this stretch of time "the only model that was understood was that of monogamy," and this despite attempts by many to overthrow much of its influence.[58] For example, Brigham Young encouraged women to cope by toppling old notions of what they deserved from a husband in marriage. Once he asked some women, "Are you tormenting yourselves by thinking your husbands do not love you? I would not care whether they loved a particle or not; but I would cry out, like one of old, in joy of my heart, 'I have got a man from the Lord! Hallelujah! I am a mother! I have borne an image of God.' "[59] Some women attempted to convince skeptics that polygamy was liberating by arguing that it held many advantages over the traditional monogamous system: shared child care and shared work; increased opportunities in education, careers, and charitable service; greater independence, greater spacing of children, and closer friendships among women; the availability of marriage and families for all women, freedom from sexual relations during pregnancy and lactation, and alleviation of prostitution. These brave attempts to destroy old expectations and showcase new ones are admirable; their logic was perhaps not flawed, but rather unsuccessful in practice.

On one level the polygamous wife obviously wanted to accept the new culture, but what could she do with residual gut-level feelings? Sifting through her catalog of responses, on every side she was faced

with voices suggesting actions and reactions, and how to frame them in writing: voices reminding her of traditions about the family, and of her religious duty to the strange-made-to-seem-ordinary, and of what it meant to be a woman in the nineteenth century—all of this complicated her responses and her writing. New messages about the changing roles of women in the West, a new land, and a new religion forced women to attempt this complex shifting and altering. On the surface all seemed calm and unified among the Mormons; but in private writings we find evidence of struggle beneath the surface.

For polygamous wives, the switch from a monogamous culture to a polygamous one could be described as a sudden, midstream change that especially caught the polygamous wife, who was the new player, the extra, the additional, and yet the essential. Not only was she caught in this whirlpool, but she also *was* the whirlpool. As Ellen Parkinson wrote in later life, "But for the trial of polygamy, life would have been very good. I see of late years how foolish I was. I could not escape it so should not have grieved, but caught all the happiness I could." She went on to say that she was "hurried into it" and not "prepared."[60] In retrospect, with husbands and other wives dead, many polygamous women autobiographers thought that they could see more clearly what forces they were up against, and as a result sometimes wanted to revise their lives. But while they traveled through it, they could not escape the foggy mist that rose up from the whirlpools they stood in.

Notes

My thanks to the John Calhoun Smith Fund at the University of Idaho for the generous grants that supported this research, and to the English department at the University of Idaho for a Grace V. Nixon Thesis Fellowship to write the thesis from which this essay evolved.

1. Leonard J. Arrington, *Brigham Young: American Moses* (New York: Knopf, 1985), 364.

2. Hubert Howe Bancroft, *History of Utah, 1540–1886*, vol. 26 of *The Works of Hubert Howe Bancroft* (San Francisco: The History Company, 1889), 385–96. Mormon polygamy, explains the author, is not as offensive as bigamy or adultery, and should not be considered criminal, although "an intelligent and well-balanced mind . . . cannot look upon polygamy as conducive to the highest culture."

3. Elizabeth Dennison Kane, *Twelve Mormon Homes Visited in Succession on a Journey through Utah to Arizona* (Philadelphia, 1874), 53, 67. At one point, Kane finds one polygamous wife's explanation of her life-style "insane," but, overall, she is sympathetic toward Mormon polygamous wives, who she finds are as charitable as any other Christian women.

4. See, for example, Joan Iverson, "Feminist Implications of Mormon Polygyny," *Feminist Studies* 10 (Fall 1984): 507–22; Julie Dunfey, " 'Living the Principle' of Plural Marriage: Mormon Women, Utopia, and Female Sexuality in the Nineteenth Century," *Feminist Studies* 10 (Fall 1984): 523–36; Stephanie Smith Goodson, "Plural Wives," in *Mormon Sisters: Women in Early Utah*, ed. Claudia Bushman (Salt Lake City: Olympus, 1976), 89–111; Carol Lynn Pearson, *The Flight and the Nest* (Salt Lake City: Bookcraft, 1975); Kenneth W. Godfrey, Audrey M. Godfrey, and Jill Mulvay Derr, *Women's Voices: An Untold History of the Latter-day Saints, 1830–1900* (Salt Lake City: Deseret Book, 1982).

5. Jill Mulvay Derr, " 'Strength in Our Union': The Making of Mormon Sisterhood," in *Sisters in Spirit: Mormon Women in Historical and Cultural Perspective*, edited by Maureen Ursenbach Beecher and Lavina Fielding Anderson (Urbana: University of Illinois Press, 1987), 165.

6. Richard S. Van Wagoner, *Mormon Polygamy: A History* (Salt Lake City: Signature, 1986), 94.

7. Jessie L. Embry, *Mormon Polygamous Families: Life in the Principle* (Salt Lake City: University of Utah Press, 1987), xvi.

8. Over one hundred years later, some in Mormondom are still concerned that the ghost presence of polygamy negatively affects Mormon monogamy by breaking down its ultimate of fidelity. See, for example, Eugene England, "On Fidelity, Polygamy, and Celestial Marriage," *Dialogue* 20, no. 4 (Winter 1987): 139–40.

9. The John Calhoun Smith Fund at the University of Idaho funded my travel and expenses to collect documents from Oboler Library at Idaho State University, Pocatello; Utah State Historical Society, Salt Lake City; Historical Department of the Church of Jesus Christ of Latter-day Saints, Salt Lake City; Harold B. Lee Library at Brigham Young University, Provo, Utah; Genealogical Society of the Church of Jesus Christ of Latter-day Saints, Salt Lake City; LDS Institute of Religion, University of Idaho; and personal collections. This study is based on approximately thirty-five autobiographies and diaries chosen according to the following criteria: (1) the obscurity of the writer—in other words, women who have been little studied and who were not prominent during their lifetimes; (2) the writer's apparent willingness to write about or mention her relationship with her husband and other wives in the family, as determined by leafing through archive catalogs, *The Guide to Mormon Diaries and Autobiographies*, by Davis Bitton, and skimming holographs; (3) the date of the woman's polygamous marriage (sometime between 1850 and 1890); and (4) the length of the document (usually not more than 250–300 pages), to make the research manageable. In all cases, I have kept original spelling, grammar, and punctuation.

10. James B. Allen and Glen M. Leonard, *The Story of the Latter-day Saints* (Salt Lake City: Deseret Book, 1976), 278–79.

11. Martha S. Bradley, "Changed Faces: The Official LDS Position on Polygamy, 1890–1990," *Sunstone* 14 (Feb. 1990): 26–33.

12. Derr, "Strength in Our Union," 166.

13. *Doctrine and Covenants* (Salt Lake City: Church of Jesus Christ of Latter-day Saints, 1981), 270–71.

14. Van Wagoner, *Mormon Polygamy,* 84.

15. Martha Spence Heywood, Journal, ts. MAN B 137, Utah State Historical Society Library, Salt Lake City, 25.

16. Johanna Catherine Nielsen, "Life of Johanna Catherine Nielsen," ed. Robert Merrill Harrison, 1983 (from family collection of Delia Davison Madsen, Pullman, Wash.), 14.

17. Lorena Larsen, *Autobiography of Lorena Eugenia Washburn Larsen* (Provo, Utah: Brigham Young University Press, 1962), 36.

18. Lucy Hannah White Flake, Autobiography, compiled from diary, ts. MAN A 284, Utah State Historical Society Library, Salt Lake City, 58.

19. Elizabeth Graham MacDonald, Autobiography, ts. MAN A 2554, Utah State Historical Society Library, Salt Lake City, 12.

20. Derr, "Strength in Our Union," 165.

21. Mary Jane Mount Tanner, *A Fragment: The Autobiography of Mary Jane Mount Tanner,* ed. Margery W. Ward (Salt Lake City: Tanner Trust Fund, University of Utah, 1980), 188.

22. Larsen, *Autobiography,* 36.

23. Kaja Silverman, *The Subject of Semiotics* (New York: Oxford University Press, 1984), 180.

24. Derr, "Strength in Our Union," 163.

25. Embry, *Mormon Polygamous Families,* 137.

26. See, for example, Lydia Ann Nelson Brinkerhoff, Autobiography, ts. MAN A 1945, Utah State Historical Society Library, Salt Lake City, 4.

27. Emma Nielson, Diary, ts., Utah State Historical Society Library, Salt Lake City, 16.

28. Martha Cragun Cox, Autobiography, ts. MAN A 146–3, Utah State Historical Society, Salt Lake City, 93.

29. Ibid., 92.

30. Larsen, *Autobiography,* 15.

31. Olive Andelin Potter, Autobiography, ms. MSS 690, Brigham Young University, Provo, Utah, 2.

32. Nielsen, "Life," 14.

33. Ruth Page Rogers, Autobiography, from Diary and Letters, ts. MS d 1854, Historical Department of the Church of Jesus Christ of Latter-day Saints, Salt Lake City, 16.

34. Larsen, *Autobiography,* 33.

35. Cox, Autobiography, 90.

36. Annie Clark Tanner, *A Mormon Mother* (Salt Lake City: Tanner Trust Fund, University of Utah, 1983), 51.

37. Ibid., 67.

38. Flake, Autobiography, 58.

39. Rachel Emma Wooley Simmons, "Rachel Emma Wooley Simmons [Autobiography]," *Heart Throbs of the West* 11 (1950): 167.

40. Brinkerhoff, Autobiography, 4.

41. Flake, Autobiography, 57.

42. Larsen, *Autobiography,* 59.

43. Elvira E. Day, Diary, ms. Ms f 31 item 3, Historical Department of the Church of Jesus Christ of Latter-day Saints, Salt Lake City, entry dated Jan. 23, 1891.

44. Ibid., entry dated May 30, 1891.

45. Agatha Walker McAllister, Autobiography, ts. MAN A 723, Utah State Historical Society Library, Salt Lake City, 11.

46. Flake, Autobiography, 59.

47. Ibid.

48. Ibid., 60.

49. Tanner, *A Mormon Mother,* 172.

50. Nielsen, "Life," 20.

51. Rogers, Autobiography, 19.

52. Hannah Isabell Fawcett Nixon, Autobiography, ts. MAN A 760, Utah State Historical Society Library, Salt Lake City, 16.

53. According to Nixon's autobiography, her husband never got her first message because he was sick, and his other wives, who were caring for him, decided not to worry him with the news from Hannah. This story is important because it illustrates Nixon's reliance on her husband for protection.

54. Nielson, Diary, 6.

55. Jane Charter Robinson Hindley, Diary, ms. Ms d 1764, Historical Department of the Church of Jesus Christ of Latter-day Saints, Salt Lake City, entry dated Oct. 19, 1879.

56. Ibid., entry dated Dec. 29, 1862.

57. Ibid., entry dated Jan. 6, 1863.

58. Iverson, "Feminist Implications of Mormon Polygyny," 512.

59. Goodson, "Plural Wives," 101.

60. Ellen Elvira Nash Parkinson, "Ellen Elvira Nash Parkinson [Autobiography]," *Our Pioneer Heritage* 8 (1965): 209.

Bibliography

Allen, James B., and Glen M. Leonard. *The Story of the Latter-day Saints*. Salt Lake City: Deseret Book, 1976.

Armitage, Susan. "Women's Literature and the American Frontier: A New Perspective on the Frontier Myth." In *Women, Women Writers, and the West*, edited by L. L. Lee and Merrill Lewis, 5–13. Troy, N.Y.: Whitston, 1980.

Arrington, Leonard J. *Brigham Young: American Moses*. New York: Knopf, 1985.

Auerbach, Nina. *Communities of Women: An Idea in Fiction*. Cambridge, Mass.: Harvard University Press, 1978.

Bancroft, Hubert Howe. *History of Utah, 1540–1886*. Vol. 26, *The Works of Hubert Howe Bancroft*. San Francisco: The History Company, 1889.

Baym, Nina. *Women's Fiction: A Guide to Novels by and about Women in America, 1820–1870*. Ithaca: Cornell University Press, 1978.

Bennett, Dana. "Mormon Polygamy in Early Southeastern Idaho." *Idaho Yesterdays* 28, no. 1 (Spring 1984): 24–30.

Benstock, Shari, ed. *Feminist Issues in Literary Scholarship*. Bloomington: Indiana University Press, 1987.

Bernhard, Kathleen Fullerton. *Jealousy: Its Nature and Treatment*. Springfield, Ill: Charles C. Thomas, 1986.

Bitton, Davis. *Guide to Mormon Diaries and Autobiographies*. Provo, Utah: Brigham Young University Press, 1977.

Bradley, Martha S. "Changed Faces: The Official LDS Position on Polygamy, 1890–1990." *Sunstone* 14 (Feb. 1990): 26–33.

Brinkerhoff, Lydia Ann Nelson. Autobiography, ts. MAN A 1945. Utah State Historical Society Library, Salt Lake City.

Cox, Martha Cragun. Autobiography, ts. MAN A 146–3. Utah State Historical Society Library, Salt Lake City.

Day, Elvira E. Diary, ms. Ms f 31, item 3. Historical Department of the Church of Jesus Christ of Latter-day Saints, Salt Lake City.

Dean, Florence Ridges. Diary, ms. Ms d 1530. Historical Department of the Church of Jesus Christ of Latter-day Saints, Salt Lake City.

Derr, Jill Mulvay. " 'Strength in Our Union': The Making of Mormon Sisterhood." In *Sisters in Spirit: Mormon Women in Historical and Cultural Perspective*, edited by Maureen Ursenbach Beecher and Lavina Fielding Anderson, pp. 153–207. Urbana: University of Illinois Press, 1987.

Doctrine and Covenants. Salt Lake City: Church of Jesus Christ of Latter-day Saints, 1981.

Dunfey, Julie. " 'Living the Principle' of Plural Marriage: Mormon Women, Utopia, and Female Sexuality in the Nineteenth Century." *Feminist Studies* 10 (Fall 1984): 523–36.

Eagleton, Terry. *Literary Theory: An Introduction*. Minneapolis: University of Minnesota Press, 1983.

Embry, Jessie L. *Mormon Polygamous Families: Life in the Principle*. Salt Lake City: University of Utah Press, 1987.

England, Eugene. "On Fidelity, Polygamy, and Celestial Marriage." *Dialogue* 20, no. 4 (Winter 1987): 138–54.

Farley, Angelina. Diary, ms. Ms f 262, item 2. Historical Department of the Church of Jesus Christ of Latter-day Saints, Salt Lake City.

Felman, Shoshana. "The Originality of Jacques Lacan." *Poetics Today* 2 (1980–81): 45–57.

Flake, Lucy Hannah White. Autobiography, compiled from diary, ts. MAN A 284. Utah State Historical Society Library, Salt Lake City.

Foster, Lawrence. *Religion and Sexuality: Three American Communal Experiments of the Nineteenth Century.* New York: Oxford University Press, 1981.

Freeze, Mary Ann Burnham. Diaries, ms. MSS 993. Brigham Young University, Provo, Utah.

Godfrey, Kenneth W., Audrey M. Godfrey, and Jill Mulvay Derr. *Women's Voices: An Untold History of The Latter-day Saints, 1830–1900.* Salt Lake City: Deseret Book, 1982.

Goodson, Stephanie Smith. "Plural Wives." In *Mormon Sisters: Women in Early Utah,* edited by Claudia Bushman, 89–111. Salt Lake City: Olympus, 1976.

Greene, Gayle, and Coppelia Kahn. *Making a Difference: Feminist Literary Criticism.* London: Methuen, 1985.

Heywood, Martha Spence. Journal, ts. MAN B 137. Utah State Historical Society Library, Salt Lake City.

Hindley, Jane Charter Robinson. Diary, ms. Ms d 1764. Historical Department of the Church of Jesus Christ of Latter-day Saints, Salt Lake City.

Iverson, Joan. "Feminist Implications of Mormon Polygyny." *Feminist Studies* 10 (Fall 1984): 507–22.

Jelinek, Estelle C., ed. *Women's Autobiography: Essays in Criticism.* Bloomington: Indiana University Press, 1980.

Kane, Elizabeth Dennison. *Twelve Mormon Homes Visited in Succession on a Journey through Utah to Arizona.* Philadelphia: 1874. Reprint. Salt Lake City: Tanner Trust Fund University of Utah, 1974.

Larsen, Lorena. *Autobiography of Lorena Eugenia Washburn Larsen.* Provo, Utah: Brigham Young University Press, 1962.

McAllister, Agatha Walker. Autobiography, ts. MAN A 723. Utah State Historical Society, Salt Lake City.

MacDonald, Elizabeth Graham. Autobiography, ts. MAN A 2554. Utah State Historical Society, Salt Lake City.

McKnight, Jeannie. "American Dream, Nightmare Underside: Diaries, Letters, and Fiction of Women on the American Frontier." In *Women, Women Writers, and the West,* edited by L. L. Lee and Merrill Lewis, 25–44. Troy, N.Y.: Whitston, 1980.

Nielsen, Johanna Catherine. "Life of Johanna Catherine Nielsen," edited by Robert Merrill Harrison, 1983. From family collection of Delia Davison Madsen, Pullman, Wash.

Nielson, Emma. Diary, ts. Utah State Historical Society, Salt Lake City.

Nixon, Hannah Isabell Fawcett. Autobiography, ts. MAN A 760. Utah State Historical Society, Salt Lake City.

Parkinson, Ellen Elvira Nash. "Ellen Elvira Nash Parkinson [Autobiography]." *Our Pioneer Heritage* 8 (1965): 202–18.

Pearson, Carol Lynn. *The Flight and the Nest.* Salt Lake City: Bookcraft, 1975.

Potter, Olive Andelin. Autobiography, ms. MSS 690. Brigham Young University, Provo, Utah.

Rogers, Ruth Page. Autobiography, from diary and letters ts. Ms d 1854. Historical Department of the Church of Jesus Christ of Latter-day Saints, Salt Lake City.

Showalter, Elaine. "Feminist Criticism in the Wilderness." *Critical Inquiry* 8 (1981): 179–205.

Silverman, Kaja. *The Subject of Semiotics.* New York: Oxford University Press, 1984.

Simmons, Rachel Emma Wooley. "Rachel Emma Wooley Simmons [Autobiography]." *Heart Throbs of the West* 11 (1950): 153–208.

Smith, Sidonie. *A Poetics of Women's Autobiography: Marginality and the Fictions of Self-Representation.* Bloomington: Indiana University Press, 1987.

Smith-Rosenberg, Carroll. "The Female World of Love and Ritual: Relations between Women in Nineteenth-Century America." *Signs: Journal of Women in Culture and Society* 1 (1975): 1–29.

Tanner, Annie Clark. *A Mormon Mother.* Salt Lake City: Tanner Trust Fund, University of Utah, 1983.

Tanner, Mary Jane Mount. *A Fragment: The Autobiography of Mary Jane Mount Tanner,* edited by Margery W. Ward. Salt Lake City: Tanner Trust Fund, University of Utah, 1980.

Thurber, Laura Ann Keeler. Diary, ms. ms f 4745. Historical Department of the Church of Jesus Christ of Latter-day Saints, Salt Lake City.

Van Wagoner, Richard S. *Mormon Polygamy: A History.* Salt Lake City: Signature, 1986.

Wells, Merle W. *Anti-Mormonism in Idaho, 1872–92.* Provo, Utah: Brigham Young University Press, 1978.

8. The Journals of Lewis and Clark: An American Epic

Frank Bergon

West of the Mississippi, the names appear: Lewis and Clark Pass, Lewis and Clark Caverns, Lewis and Clark College. You can stop in Lewis and Clark State Park—in Missouri, or Iowa, or Montana, or Washington, or even Illinois. You can visit rivers named after each of the famous explorers, and towns, like Lewiston, Idaho, and Clarkston, Washington. Landmarks still bear names the explorers left 185 years ago in honor of their friends and political leaders, like Mount Jefferson and Rivers Gallatin and Dearborn. The ghosts of their loves grace other rivers: the Marias River named for Meriwether Lewis's young cousin, Maria Wood—"that lovely fair one,"[1] he wrote in his journal; and the Judith River, named for Julia (Judy) Hancock of Virginia, who later became William Clark's wife. In Iowa you can visit Council Bluffs, where the explorers held, under an awning of sailcloth, the first of many councils with Native Americans. Like epic heroes, Lewis and Clark have given names and meaning to a national landscape.

Today, even western birds bear the explorers' names, like Lewis's woodpecker—"black as a crow," Lewis wrote, "the belly and breast is a curious mixture of white and blood red,"—and Clark's nutcracker, a delightfully impish bird with "a loud squawking note something like the mewing of a cat." Grass and plants at your feet, like Lewis flax or Lewis and Clark synthyris, and blooming flowers, like the beautiful blue *Clarkia pulchella,* and the bitterroot, or *Lewisia rediviva*—now Montana's state flower—remind you how deeply these men explored what one naturalist called the "other nations" of the planet: the animals, trees, birds, mountains, rivers, swamps, flowers, fishes, reptiles, and other minorities among today's marginal and disenfranchised in American life.

It is through the exploration of this so-called fifth world that the Lewis and Clark expedition reached truly epic proportions. From the hindsight of 185 years, it might even be suggested that through their particular fusion of scientific and literary concerns, Lewis and Clark's firsthand encounters with the land, animals, and native peoples of the West give expression—after the founding of this nation—to our first American literary epic.

"Epic" is a word frequently used to describe Lewis and Clark's remarkable journey across the continent from 1804 to 1806.[2] In its scale, that journey certainly exhibits something in common with acknowledged epics like *The Odyssey,* or even Hollywood's latest version of heroic feats. It was the largest and longest U.S. expedition into terra incognita. It was also the first. Now seen as the most skillfully managed journey in the history of North American exploration, the one against which all others are measured, the expedition lasted two years, four months, and ten days. It covered 7,689 miles between the mouth of the Missouri River and the Pacific outlet of the Columbia River. It was called the Voyage of Discovery, and like the adventures in *Beowulf* and *Gilgamesh,* it was a journey into an unknown wilderness.

To a young nation—the United States was barely a dozen years old at the time—Lewis and Clark brought back maps of previously uncharted rivers and mountains, specimens of previously unknown plants and animals, amazing artifacts, and even representatives of previously unseen peoples of the West. But their most valuable contribution came in elkskin-bound field books and red morocco-bound journals, stored in tin boxes. To a nation with no commonly sung mystique of the state or of the race or of the empire, no national literature—no *Iliad* or *Chanson de Roland* or *Cantar de Mio Cid*— these uneven, fragmented, and unpolished journals offered the equivalent of a national poem, a magnificent epic for an unfinished nation.

With their detailed logs of temperature and weather, astronomical observations, tabulations of longitude and latitude, descriptions of flora and fauna, anthropological data, misspellings, and neologisms, these journals tell a heroic story of a people's struggles through a wilderness and the return home. Better than more artfully constructed poems or novels or plays, they embody with the directness and plainness of an oral epic the mythic history of a nation, a compressed story of who we are as a people. Like ancient epics they tell the story of the tribe, in this case the story of a people moving west. It is not the story of an individual frontiersman but of a pluralistic, fluctuating community of thirty-five to forty-five people, including soldiers, woodsmen, blacksmiths, carpenters, cooks, French *engagés,* a black slave, a Lemhi Shoshone woman, and a newborn baby of mixed race, all heading west. In retrospect that story portrays the fall of one civilization and the rise of another. It dramatizes the relationship of a people to the natural world and the design of a nation committed to the belief that—as William Gilpin expressed it seventy years later—"the *untransacted* destiny of the American people is to subdue the continent."

Just to get about forty-odd people through the wilderness and to keep them fed was a feat of epic proportions. The expedition's fifty-five-foot masted keelboat and two pirogues entered the Missouri River with more than seven tons of food, but the wilderness itself became the main source of provisions. Clark noted that his hunters had shot 1,001 deer, Lewis in one day with ten men "cought upwards of 800 fine fish," and when provisions were low the captains purchased 190 dogs from Indians. On the Pacific coast they set up a camp on the beach, where fires burned twenty-four hours a day for almost three months while men boiled seawater to make salt for the return trip. Gifts for Indians included 2,800 fishhooks, 4,600 assorted needles, and 130 twisted rolls of tobacco. Among medicines were 3,500 pills to counter sweats, 1,100 doses of emetics to induce vomiting, and over 600 "Bilious Pills," partially composed of a poisonous compound of mercury. Created by the country's leading physician, Dr. Benjamin Rush, to counteract constipation, they were suitably called "Rush's Thunderbolts."

The expedition passed through "scenes of visionary enchantment" and "curious adventures" that Lewis "thought might be a dream." Their boats entered a floating mass of white feathers seventy yards wide and three miles long through which they passed to an island covered with thousands of pelicans. On a bluff they found the petrified backbone of an ancient fish 45 feet long, and on the Pacific coast they found the carcass of a recently beached whale, a "monstrous fish," 110 feet long. In July the ground thundered with hail measuring seven inches in circumference and bouncing 12 feet into the air. On the

Great Plains wolves were "fat and extreemly gentle," a buffalo calf followed Lewis like a pet, and elk and buffalo extended for miles, forcing the expedition to stop and watch as the herds crossed the river. Wounded grizzly bears with more than eight rifle balls through their lungs and stomach continued to charge their attackers. The formidable Rocky Mountains almost defeated the expedition; "their fatiegues are incredible," Lewis wrote about his men; "some are limping from the soreness of their feet, others faint and unable to stand for a few minutes, with heat and fatiegue, yet no one complains, all go with cheerfullness." In the evening, with the mountains conquered, a one-eyed French boatman named Cruzatte played the fiddle and the men danced by firelight. "Ocian in view!" Clark wrote, "O! the joy."

As the heroes of this epic adventure, Captain Meriwether Lewis and Captain William Clark were first of all, like the heroes of ancient epics, men of demonstrated military leadership and physical courage. William Clark had experience in actual battle against the Creek and Cherokee Indians, but both men were archetypal American frontiersmen whose characters had been forged in confrontation with the wilderness. Meriwether Lewis, appointed by the president to lead the expedition, had served in the militia during the Whiskey Rebellion before joining the regular army and rising to the rank of captain in the First U.S. Infantry. As an ensign, Lewis had served briefly in a rifle company under the command of Captain William Clark, who became his immediate choice as cocommander of the expedition. At the time of his appointment, Clark had resigned his army commission as a captain in the infantry, and despite Lewis's promise and President Jefferson's approval of his reappointment as a captain, the Department of War's bureaucratic machinations led to Clark's reappointment as a second lieutenant in the artillery, a subordinate to Lewis. Defying military red tape, Lewis made it clear that his former commanding officer was to be his equal on the expedition and that the men under their authority would never know them as other than Captain Clark and Captain Lewis, cocommanders of the Corps of Discovery.

The effectiveness of this strange alliance, a sharing of command that defies military hierarchy, is unique to military history. But Lewis and Clark seemed to command as one, effortlessly and without conflict, remaining friends to the end. At the start of the trip Lewis was twenty-nine and Clark thirty-three. While Lewis enjoyed eating dog meat and Clark hated it, and Lewis craved salt and Clark dismissed it as a luxury, and Lewis liked eating black currants and Clark favored yellow ones, the two leaders otherwise formed a perfectly harmonious relationship. A moving aspect of their journals is how much they cared for each other.

It is now a commonplace to present the personalities of the two men as polar opposites: Lewis as a brooding, romantic introvert, Clark as an even-tempered, sociable extrovert. Charles Willson Peale's famous portraits of the two explorers, now hanging in the Independence National Historical Park in Philadelphia, seem to emphasize these contrasting images of their personalities. William Clark, a large, husky man with a high forehead and shock of red hair, looks boldly from the canvas directly at the viewer, while Meriwether Lewis, tall and slender with sensitive bow lips and an aquiline nose, gazes dreamily toward the side of the canvas. The contrasting careers of the two men after their renowned expedition also reinforce the image of Clark as a gregarious public official and Lewis as a moody loner. In 1807, the year after the return of the expedition, President Jefferson appointed William Clark as brigadier general of militia and principal Indian agent for the Louisiana Territory. In 1813 Clark became governor of the Missouri Territory, a position he kept until Missouri became a state in 1820. From 1822 until his death in 1838, Clark served in St. Louis as U.S. superintendent of Indian affairs. Respected and trustworthy, he was the man Indian delegations from the West sought for reconciliation of their conflicts with white trappers and traders. Married to Julia Hancock, for whom he'd named the Judith River, he had five children, and later, after her death, he remarried and had two more sons. Every exploring and trading party venturing into the West stopped in St. Louis to consult with the knowledgeable William Clark. With new information from traders and trappers he continually updated his master map of the West. Assuming responsibility for the publication of the journals, he helped see the first official version of the journals into print in 1814, eight years after the return of the Corps of Discovery.

Meriwether Lewis, in contrast, became a public failure. During the year following the expedition he spent four months in Philadelphia arranging with naturalists, artists, and printers for the publication of the journals in three volumes, along with "Lewis and Clark's Map of North America." Three years later, he still had not supplied a word to the publisher. He had a falling out with President Jefferson and was spurned by the woman he wished to marry. He was drinking heavily, the "habit into which he had fallen," Jefferson later wrote. Appointed governor of Upper Louisiana after his return from the West, he governed in absentia for over a year before finally arriving in St. Louis in 1808. There he fell into a turbulent frontier world of petty commerce, greed, and political intrigue. While in a power struggle with the secretary (equivalent to a lieutenant governor) of the territory, he became indebted to land speculators. A new administration in Washington stopped honoring even his legitimate vouchers for governing expenses. His political and financial affairs in a mess, he set out for the national capital, apparently to keep himself from bankruptcy and political ruin. Arriving at Fort Pickering (now Memphis) by boat, he was reported to have tried to kill himself twice during the trip. On October 11, 1809, just three years after his triumphant return from the West, at a remote tavern on the wilderness road in Tennessee called the Natchez Trace, seventy miles southwest of Nashville, Lewis was found alone in his room, shot, a probable suicide, although a strong folk tradition maintains that he was murdered.

These sad extremes of personality are not evident in the journals, where both men are leaders of imposing stature and skill.[3] Like earlier epic heroes, they both show cunning, intelligence, and dignity in their leadership of others. But they are always men, not gods. In them we see the flip side of heroism, the human dimension that gives rise to excesses and weakness, as well as to doubts and concerns about day-to-day details we all share. They sometimes reverse roles. At times it is Clark who seems the melancholy loner depressed by bad weather and bugs, while it is Lewis who retains his joie de vivre amid misfortune and who longs for the companionship of friends and civil society. It is as if this division of the classical hero into two men allows Lewis and Clark to embody the heroic virtues and antiheroic impulses of the classical hero in believable ways. They are heroes cut down to credible size, eighteenth-century men who merge into a composite hero acceptable to the cynicism of a rational, modern era. When the explorers copy from each other's field notes or journals, original authorship, as in oral narratives, sometimes becomes blurred or lost. The "I" of some entries becomes that composite hero and author whom Clark seemed to honor, after his cocaptain's death, when he named his son Meriwether Lewis Clark.

It is the composite character of these leaders—their pervasive outpouring of intellectual and moral energy—that sustained the expedition and guaranteed its success. That composite character manifested itself in the thousands of right decisions the leaders jointly made to avert disaster. It was only when Lewis and Clark were apart on the return journey that tragedy struck and two Blackfeet Indians were killed. While they were still apart, Lewis himself was almost killed when accidentally shot by one of his own hunters. Reunited, the men successfully concluded their journey without incident. The unfortunate skirmish with the Blackfeet was the only eruption of violence during the hundreds of meetings with native peoples across the continent. Equally remarkable is that only one member of the expedition died despite numerous accidents and incessant illnesses during the long trip. Sergeant Floyd suffered what was most likely a ruptured appendix early in the trip. His death, it has been noted, would have probably been unavoidable even in the best hospital of the time, since the first appendectomy was not performed in the U.S. until over eighty years later.

In chronicling their trials and achievements, the heroes of this epic adventure sing of themselves, becoming—in a modern literary twist—their own bards. Just as the success of the expedition is unimaginable without the joint leadership of the two captains, so too is the contemporary appeal of the journals without their coauthorship. Where modesty commends one to silence about his own achievement, history compels the other to document the worthiness of the event. A small moment, flatly reported, becomes heroic. "My friend Capt. Clark was very sick," Lewis writes, "with a high fever on him and much fatiegued and exhausted. after a short respite he resumed his march."

The Muse to these journals was the president of the United States, Thomas Jefferson. His influence informs them like a third presence. The Voyage of Discovery was his dream, and the journals were his inspiration. "Westward the course of Empire makes its way" was the eighteenth-century sentiment that seemingly became reality when Napoleon, abandoning his own imperial designs in North America and trying to frustrate Britain's, surprisingly sold the vast Louisiana Territory to the United States for three cents an acre. Scarcely six months after congressional ratification of the sale in October 1803, Lewis and Clark were on their way across the continent and the United States was on its way to becoming a world power. The political design of Jefferson's expedition was imperial, to make way for American expansion from sea to shining sea.

The success of the expedition as a "literary pursuit"—a report in natural history on the lands, animals, and native peoples of the

American West—was also much to Jefferson's credit.[4] A fine naturalist, with a particular interest in phenology (the study of relationships between climate and periodic biological phenomena), Jefferson gave Lewis and Clark careful instructions for observing and recording in detail the natural world. They recorded the first descriptions of hundreds of new animals and plants, including the cutthroat trout, mountain quail, western meadowlark, pack rats, kit foxes, and *Ursus horribilis,* the "tremendious" grizzly bear. No sooner had they embarked on their journey than Clark noted that "Capt. Lewis went out to the woods & found many curious Plants & S[h]rubs." More scientifically competent than often assumed, Lewis made use of no fewer than two hundred technical botanical terms in his descriptions of over 170 new plants.

While Lewis served as the expedition's botanist and zoologist, Clark was the cartographer and geographer of the strange landforms and new watercourses encountered in the West. His maps record the longitude and latitude of all important geographical features as well as compass readings of each twist and turn in the streams and rivers he explored. As he sailed up the Missouri he estimated distances by eyesight, recording, for instance, that the expedition had traveled between the mouth of the Missouri and the Platte River a distance of 600 miles. A surveying team several years later concluded from their instruments that the distance was actually 611 miles.

Today, at the University of Portland, a monument marks the site where Clark led a small exploring party to what is commonly thought to be the southernmost point the men reached on the Pacific coast. A 6' 9" bronze statue of Captain Clark is flanked by equivalent statues of a black man and an Indian, all three "united," according to the brochure at the monument, "in a common experience—the sighting of the snowy tip of Mt. Jefferson along the horizon." The monument worthily reminds us that Lewis and Clark were not alone in their achievement. The black man is York, who began the journey as Clark's slave and helpmate and ended as a free man, released from bondage when the men returned to Virginia. During the expedition York carried a gun, although it was illegal for a slave to do so, and he cast his vote along with other members of the corps when they all voted on a place for winter quarters on the West Coast. To the right of Clark in this monument stands a member of the Cushook tribe that inhabited the Willamette River Valley. This statue of an unnamed Native American beside the explorer reminds us that without the instruction and abundant assistance of Indians across the continent, Lewis and Clark would not be remembered today. In turn, the journals constitute the most valuable ethnographic record of Indian people in the literature of exploration, especially of the Lemhi Shoshone, whose meeting with the expedition marked their first encounter with whites.

The most famous Native American associated with the expedition was, of course, a young woman. Memorialized at the Sacajawea State Park in Washington and at Sakakawea State Park in North Dakota, this Lemhi Shoshone teenager is now more correctly known, according to scholars and the Bureau of American Ethnology, as Sacagawea, commonly translated as "Bird Woman" and pronounced to rhyme loosely with "Chicago-wee-a." Captured as a child by a Hidatsa raiding party, she was sold to a French trader, Toussaint Charbonneau, who became her husband and who was hired by the expedition as a translator at the Hidatsa and Mandan villages north of present Bismarck, North Dakota. Pregnant at the time, Sacagawea went into labor during a cold February; "her labor was tedious and the pain violent." Captain Lewis, who had honed his skills as a physician that winter by amputating frostbitten toes, reports how a visiting fur trader came to his aid with a prescription for crushed rattlesnake rings; "having the rattle of a snake by me I gave it to him and he administered of it to the woman broken in small pieces with the fingers and added a small quantity of water," Lewis wrote. "I was informed that she had not taken it more than ten minutes before she brought forth."

No American woman, it is often said, has more statues erected to her than Sacagawea, usually for the wrong reason. Recent scholars have mocked the Sacagawea legend as overblown. Known to most schoolchildren as the woman who guided Lewis and Clark across the continent, she really contributed to the expedition more serviceably as a translator. Most of the country on the trip was unfamiliar to her, but with her baby she "reconciles all the Indians to our friendly intentions," Clark wrote in his journal. "A woman with a party of men is a token of peace." While Sacagawea did not blaze the trail across the continent for the captains, she did help Clark on his separate return through her home turf and what is now Bozeman Pass in Montana. "The Indian woman," Clark acknowledged, "has been of great service to me as a pilot through this country." She added her own quiet heroism to that of the expedition, as when the pirogue in which she sailed overturned in a rapid current. Her husband, according to Lewis, was "crying to his God for mercy" because he could not swim, while Sacagawea, "equal [in] fortitude and resolution with any person onboard at the time of the accident, caught and preserved most of the light articles which were washed overboard."

Of all the heroic moments recorded in the journals, however, none surpasses the recording of the journals themselves. Under the unbearably difficult circumstances of the journals' composition, the writing of carefully detailed and fully documented accounts of the expedition was the most heroic of acts. Anyone who has tried to keep a diary at the end of a day of hiking along modern trails with the guidance of modern maps can only marvel at the fortitude of the captains as they continued to record their experiences despite exhaustion and illness while forging through an uncharted wilderness in all extremes of heat and cold. The journals offer an understated catalog of trials by mosquitoes, floods, hunger, storms, and grizzlies. In a touching moment, Meriwether Lewis notes in his journal that "the ink friezes in my pen," and he continues to write. The journals appropriately end with Clark's last brief entry on September 25, 1806, "a fine morning we commenced wrighting &tc."

It is appropriate that the statue in Portland shows Clark holding a journal in his left hand, as do similar statues of Lewis and Clark two thousand miles away in the Missouri State Museum. What other explorers and epic heroes are honored in statues for their writings? Despite their inventive spelling and punctuation, both men were extremely effective writers. In fact, their phonetic spelling created a special language characteristic of epics. Through their fragmented, colloquial style we can hear their voices with an immediacy and intensity that is lost in more polished writing. Even mosquitoes become epically menacing in the rolling "rr" of Clark's spelling: "Musquetors verry troblesom."

Conventional rhetoric and cultural assumptions break down as the facts of the actual country, animals, and native peoples of the West give shape to new forms of perception. We sense the urgency, the struggle in the prose, as language itself had to be altered to give expression to a new country and its native inhabitants; words coined and twisted and adapted to the occasion in the journals produced the addition of over fifteen hundred new words to the American language, many adapted from Native American languages and frontier

French, others jammed into new linguistic hybrids, like "mule deer" and "prairie dog."

Today the journals offer contemporary readers a sense of a bygone era as Lewis and Clark begin their journey up the snag-infested Missouri River with its banks dangerously caving into the muddy water. There is nothing else like it in our literature. No other exploratory report of North America is as vivid, no other evokes such a sense of immediacy. As the explorers leave the fringes of white civilization and move into the West, they seem to move back in time. At the Mandan villages they abandon their masted keelboat and paddle toward the headwaters of the Missouri in two pirogues and six small canoes. At Great Falls of the Missouri Lewis watches as his portable iron-framed boat, designed and built in the East, sinks uselessly into a western river. In the Rockies they abandon their canoes and depend on Indian horses to cross the Bitterroots to where they can chop and carve native cottonwoods into dugouts for the final run down the Snake and Columbia Rivers to the sea.

In gradually abandoning attempts to present their experience through conventional aesthetic forms and expressions, the explorers seem to let the wonder of the country and its incredible wildlife speak more and more through plain fact and events. The explorers do seem like new men in a new Eden walking peacefully among hundreds of animals that will not scare: "the whole face of the country," Lewis writes, "was covered with herds of Buffaloe, Elk & Antelopes; deer are also abundant, but keep themselves more concealed in the woodland. the buffaloe Elk and Antelope are so gentel that we pass near them while feeding, without appearing to excite any alarm among them and when we attract their attention, they frequently approach us more nearly to discover what we are."

Horror shatters this Edenic world in the form of enraged grizzly bears, charging buffalo, violent storms, smashed boats, horses rolling down hillsides, feet torn and bleeding from cactus needles, incessant rain, fleas, and mosquitoes. The journals often become a story of epic confrontations with monsters and dark powers. But the real snake in the garden hideously accompanies the explorers themselves. In the wanton smashing of a wolf's skull with a spontoon, the slaughtering of animals, and the proprietary, exploitative attitudes toward the land and native peoples, we get sad glimpses of the coming dark side of American imperialism. As an expedition of American expansionism, the Voyage of Discovery made way for others seemingly bent on transforming the land of plenty into a land of waste.

Hard as it may be to read the journals without a sense of what we have lost, without nostalgia, they still offer a vision for the future. In their timeless struggle through a dominating wilderness, Lewis and Clark present a counterimage to the mythical frontiersman alone in a western landscape. They are not alone in this wilderness. They are not the self-sufficient, independent, gunslinging western loners so popular in American fiction and film. They are dependent on each other, on the other members of the expedition, on the native peoples of the West, and especially on the natural world through which they pass. Their story is not one of individualism but of communalism.

When the expedition finally reaches the Pacific at the mouth of the Columbia River, we see that moment when the whole community—including a black man and an Indian woman—votes on where it wishes to encamp for the winter. Rather than striving to conquer the wilderness, these people learn to make a home within it. It is an epic moment in the story of a westering people. What they have learned is not independence but interdependence in its largest sense. In a moment of cooperation among people of differing races, they have recognized their ties to a greater natural world. It is still an important moment as an epic vision for this nation's unfinished story. In our age of oil spills and environmental politics, such a moment reminds us: human beings are not the measure of all things.

Notes

1. All quotations from the journals are from *The Journals of Lewis and Clark*, edited by Frank Bergon (New York: Viking Penguin, 1989).

2. For example, see Marius Bewley, "The Heroic and the Romantic West," *Masks and Mirrors: Essays in Criticism* (New York: Atheneum, 1974), 214: "The community that existed between Lewis and Clark and the forty-three men of the first American expedition to the upper Mississippi [*sic*] and across to the Pacific was very much of that character we find described in heroic poetry."

3. For the opposite view, see Robert Lawson-Peebles, *Landscape and Written Expression in Revolutionary America* (New York: Cambridge University Press, 1988), 213–21.

4. For a study of the journals as a "literary problem," see Robert Edson Lee, *From West to East: Studies in the Literature of the American West* (Urbana: University of Illinois Press, 1966), 11–38.

Bibliography

Allen, John Logan. *Passage through the Garden: Lewis and Clark and the Image of the American Northwest*. Chicago: University of Illinois Press, 1975.

Bergon, Frank, ed. *The Journals of Lewis and Clark*. New York: Viking Penguin, 1989.

Bewley, Marius. "The Heroic and the Romantic West." *Masks and Mirrors: Essays in Criticism*. New York: Atheneum, 1974.

Burroughs, Raymond Darwin. *The Natural History of the Lewis and Clark Expedition*. East Lansing: Michigan State University Press, 1961.

Chuinard, E. G. *Only One Man Died: The Medical Aspects of the Lewis and Clark Expedition*. Glendale, Calif.: Arthur H. Clark, 1979.

Cutright, Paul Russell. *Lewis and Clark: Pioneering Naturalists*. Urbana: University of Illinois Press, 1969.

————. *A History of the Lewis and Clark Journals*. Norman: University of Oklahoma Press, 1979.

DeVoto, Bernard. *The Journals of Lewis and Clark*. Boston: Houghton Mifflin, 1953.

Dillon, Richard. *Meriwether Lewis*. New York: Coward McCann, 1965.

Jackson, Donald Dean, ed. *Letters of the Lewis and Clark Expedition*. 2d ed. 2 vols. Urbana: University of Illinois Press, 1978.

Lawson-Peebles, Robert. *Landscape and Written Expression in Revolutionary America*. New York: Cambridge University Press, 1988.

Lee, Robert Edson. *From West to East: Studies in the Literature of the American West*. Urbana: University of Illinois Press, 1966.

Moulton, Gary E., ed. *The Journals of the Lewis and Clark Expedition*. 11 vols. projected. Lincoln: University of Nebraska Press, 1986–.

Ronda, James P. *Lewis and Clark among the Indians*. Lincoln: University of Nebraska Press, 1961.

Steffen, Jerome O. *William Clark: Jeffersonian Man on the Frontier*. Norman: University of Oklahoma Press, 1977.

Thwaites, Reuben Gold, ed. *The Original Journals of the Lewis and Clark Expedition*. 8 vols. New York: Dodd, Mead, 1904–5.

9. A Bridging of Two Cultures: Frances Hodgson Burnett and the Wild West

Susan Naramore Maher

In 1886, Frances Hodgson Burnett published a runaway bestseller that eventually eclipsed the considerable achievement of her adult fiction and unfairly earned her notoriety as the "feminizer" of the American boy. Mention *Little Lord Fauntleroy* and our collective memory instantly recalls what writers in the 1920s referred to as the Fauntleroy "plague": velveteen suits, lace collars, and a mother named "Dearest."[1] What possible connection could this rarefied, dandified little boy have with the American West, let alone his creator, who never traveled west of Chicago,[2] preferring instead to flee across the Atlantic whenever the restlessness of her adopted American homeland proved too stressful. Indeed, Hodgson Burnett crossed the Atlantic thirty-three times in her seventy-five years, dividing her life between the Old and New World, desiring but never achieving a synthesis between the two.[3] Though she won kudos for her portrayal of regional America—most notably for a short piece, "Seth" (1877), an examination of a Tennessee mining district; for *Louisiana* (1880), a satiric look at a North Carolina resort community; and for *Through One Administration* (1883), an accomplished Washington novel— Hodgson Burnett made most of her money providing her devoted transatlantic audience with critical evaluations of British culture. In other words, though informed by her American experience, the bulk of her oeuvre owes much to her childhood in Manchester, England,

146

and to her early reading of Dickens, Thackeray, Gaskell, and the Brontës. In the popular imagination, then, Hodgson Burnett is as disconnected from the American West as one can get.

But, of course, the popular imagination is wrong. At the height of her writing powers, when she was ranked in the forefront of American literature and considered the equal of William Dean Howells, Henry James, George Washington Cable, and Constance Fenimore Woolson,[4] Hodgson Burnett reworked the contemporary mythology of the American West—as a land of vigorous action and renewal—and used this myth as an effective counterpoise to the ennui of Anglo-American culture. Both her masterwork, *Through One Administration*, and her clever satire, *A Fair Barbarian* (1880), the subject of this essay, glorify the moral energy of the West and suggest that its very crudeness might be a necessary antidote to a civilized world's malaise. Through this explored difference Hodgson Burnett discovered the outline of her immortal children's tale, *Little Lord Fauntleroy* (1886)—one could argue *A Fair Barbarian* is, in a sense, the first draft of *Fauntleroy*—and provided the first articulation of her favorite theme: a millennial bridging of the Old and New World.

When *A Fair Barbarian* began serialization in *Peterson's* magazine (1880), some critics lauded the novel as a healthier portrayal of the American girl than that in Henry James's *Daisy Miller* (1879), though Hodgson Burnett's son Vivian insists that it "was probably not at all in [her] mind to 'answer' Mr. James."[5] The similarities are intriguing: both heroines are freshly pretty, overdressed, coolly disarming in their frankness and simplicity. The novels together made a fashion of "internationalism." But James's doomed Daisy is an easterner, from a part of America that Hodgson Burnett, from her vantage point in Washington, D.C., already perceived as tainted. She looked farther afield for her heroine's origins and found them in Bloody Gulch, Nevada.

It is here that Martin Bassett, an expatriate British gentleman, finally drops his bags, settles down with his infant daughter, and through hard work and sheer luck makes, loses, and then remakes his fortune in silver mining. It is here, in the West, that motherless Octavia Bassett receives her unorthodox rearing, "where she had been the only female member of the somewhat reckless community."[6] Hodgson Burnett, who apprenticed in the leading feminine journals of the day, was well versed in what Annette Kolodny calls "westernized domestics."[7] Her West, in the conventions of such novels, is an "undiminished" space removed from the "blighted garden" of the East, in this case Britain. Here, too, western lands "rehabilitate" male characters, enabling them to achieve their full potential. Yet her novel differs in significant ways from the conventional female Western. Octavia is no "domesticating Eve," dressed in calico and eager to create a new garden; she shares her father's love of adventure, travel, and gambling. She is a lone female, and an unconventional one, whose accounts of life in the West nearly reduce her British Aunt Belinda to apoplexy. "They were pretty good-natured, and made a pet of me," Octavia, describing her all-male community, informs her aunt. "They made me a present of a set of jewelry made out of gold they had got themselves. There is a breastplate, and a necklace like a dog-collar: the bracelets tire my arms, and the ear-rings pull my ears; but I wear them sometimes—gold girdle and all" (25). From her imperial name, Octavia, to her war-goddess jewelry, then, Hodgson Burnett's heroine is meant to be a conqueror, a leveler, "a fair barbarian." Her Wild West upbringing has prepared her to meet all at eye level, from the dirtiest and meanest to the wealthiest miner, for in Bloody Gulch it is only luck that divides the classes.

The West, in its excesses and boundlessness, does not nurture in Octavia the requisite domestic virtues. Her father sends her across the Atlantic to his forsaken England for "polishing" within the feminine bosom of Slowbridge, a village culture antithetical to the one Octavia has left behind. When she arrives in this sleepy village, her overwhelming jewels, showy *toilette*, and indiscriminate manners "shake" the village "to its foundations" (5). Her American origins immediately disqualify her as a gentlewoman, for "[in] Slowbridge, America was not approved of—in fact, was almost entirely ignored as a country where . . . 'the laws were loose, and the prevailing sentiments revolutionary.' . . . It was not considered in good taste to know Americans" (6, 8). As the sole female member of a Nevada mining community and the daughter of a San Francisco actress, she is doubly damned. When Aunt Belinda listens to Octavia's calm, free, and unembarrassed announcements, her "faith in her own identity" is rattled: "[To] find herself sitting in her own genteel little parlor, behind her own tea-service, with her hand upon her own teapot, hearing that [Martin's] wife had been a young person who had been 'a great favorite' upon the stage, in a region peopled, as she had been led to suppose, by gold-diggers and escaped convicts, was almost too much for her to support herself under" (22).

Hodgson Burnett uses Octavia, then, as a comic foil. It is as if Annie Oakley has entered the world of Elizabeth Gaskell's *Cranford*, though, admittedly, Octavia does not wear men's clothing and draw six-shooters. Though all of Slowbridge is ruffled, shaken, excited, including its stern matriarchal head, Lady Theobald, Octavia remains undisturbed by their disapproval. She, unlike the class-fettered, unassertive maidens of the village, has been raised as a free agent. When Lady Theobald first greets Octavia with a withering comment—"You don't look like an English girl"—Octavia coolly remarks, "I suppose I ought to be sorry for that... I dare say I shall be in time—when I have been away longer from Nevada" (35). Lady Theobald attempts to put her in her place once more with the reply, "I must confess that I don't know where Nevada is," to which Octavia humorously responds, "It isn't in Europe" (35). Unable to bring this ignorant Nevadan to her knees, Lady Theobald attempts one last barrage in this interchange, asserting that "it is not so necessary for English people to know America as it is for Americans to know England." Octavia's simple question—"Isn't it?"—leaves Lady Theobald groping to answer her own bigotry (35). Clearly Hodgson Burnett is deflating the English predilection toward cultural hegemony. It is not hegemony that needs to be established but a bridging, a mutually strengthening bond between old and new. The need to resolve the tension between these cultures propels her narrative to its comic conclusion.

Class bigotry is the rotten center of Slowbridge. It is a malady that has weakened the already weak and prevented much happiness in the village. The two champions of bigotry, Lady Theobald and her privileged, haughty nephew, Francis Barold, are the two most powerful members of Slowbridge society. Their weaker counterparts, most notably Belinda Bassett and Lady Theobald's own granddaughter, Lucia Gaston, are timid souls in need of rescue. Belinda's life, as a "genteel Slowbridge entertainer," has been an uneventful fifty years of rising at seven, breakfasting at eight, dining at two, taking tea at five, and going to bed at ten—a pattern repeated in every Slowbridge cottage. Lucia's life threatens to continue this deadening routine. "Lady Theobald," Hodgson Burnett comments, "had her granddaughter under excellent control... At nineteen she was simple, sensitive, shy. She had been permitted to have no companions, and the greatest excitements of her life had been the Slowbridge tea-parties" (48).

Only marriage, a rare event in Slowbridge, can lift a woman from such passivity, yet even nuptials are arranged pro forma. Wealth,

social standing, and family connections make desirable a marriage between cousins, Barold and Lucia. It matters not that he dislikes his
quiet relation nor that she loves another, a gentleman mill owner
named Burmistone. When the odiousness of her fate dawns on her,
Lucia tells Octavia, "I am to run after a man who does not care for
me, and make myself attractive, in the hope that he will condescend
to marry me because Mr. Binnie [a wealthy family connection] may
leave me his money" (222).

Needless to say, Bloody Gulch, Nevada, remains free of such con-
voluted arrangements. In the West, an English-born gentleman can
marry an actress and not risk the condemnation of a community.
Convention plays little part in the lives of Martin and Octavia Bassett; self-determination is key to their happiness. Because she has not
been reared to be a compliant ornament, an attractive catch in a cold-
blooded marriage market, Octavia cannot, to the horror of Slowbridge society, play an instrument, sing prettily, or speak French. In
America, Octavia sees whomever she pleases, even drives by moonlight unchaperoned. To Slowbridge society she appears "fast and
loud" (138). But as Belinda and Lucia become better acquainted with
her open ways, they learn to appreciate her forthrightness and independence. To her aunt's perennial question, "What will people
think?" Octavia replies: "Isn't it queer how often you say that!...I
think I should perish if I had to pull myself up that way as you do. I
just go right on, and never worry. I don't mean to do any thing queer,
and I don't see why any one should think I do" (142). Lady Theobald
hopes Lucia's contact with "the free-and-easy manners of young
women from Nevada might lead to some good result." She views
Octavia as a negative example, in whose bold shadow the quiet, well-
bred Lucia will appear doubly alluring to her eligible cousin. Instead,
Barold finds himself increasingly attracted to the unconventional
Octavia, and Lucia resolves to remake herself in the image of her
American friend. In this way, the two cultures begin their slow
synthesis.

Octavia never intentionally subverts long-standing Slowbridge tradition. And though the top of the social pyramid, Lady Theobald, dis-
dains her, the broad base of Slowbridge's poor adores her. Octavia's
charity to them stems from pure joy and compassion; "duty" is not
part of her vocabulary. The privileged prophesy that "Lady Theobald
will put a stop to it" (166); but a ground swell of admiration toward
the young Nevadan prevents any effective countermeasure on Lady

Theobald's part. Increasingly, Lady Theobald's own set defects, start-ing with the Reverend Poppleton and ending with Barold, Lucia, even the wealthy Mr. Binnie himself. Lucia, emulating Octavia's direct-ness, admits that in the American's presence she feels "old-fashioned and badly dressed" (162). More startlingly, she declares, "I have always thought her lucky." "You have thought her lucky!" retorts her provoked grandmother. "You have envied a Nevada young woman, who dresses like an actress, and loads herself with jewels like a barbarian?" (163). Then Lucia courageously admits she admires Octavia, an admission that nearly silences Lady Theobald.

So what is the legacy of cool, frank, independent Octavia Bassett? Can a fair barbarian from Nevada thwart stultifying Slowbridge con-vention and rejuvenate its people? The tally is mixed. Her example in-spires Lucia to reject an arranged and mercenary marriage with the snobbish Barold in return for a less socially advantageous marriage to Burmistone, the mill owner. Timid Aunt Belinda agrees to cross the Atlantic and visit Bloody Gulch, "horribly frightened" though she is at the prospect, a voyage that promises much in the way of self-discovery. The poor, who have benefited from Octavia's generous hand, live in improved circumstances. But the reigning snobs are nei-ther toppled nor changed. Lady Theobald accepts Lucia's marriage to a mill owner only because Mr. Binnie bestows a fortune on the couple (much to his credit, Mr. Binnie dislikes Barold). Barold departs from Slowbridge undisturbed, an unchanged man, save in one respect. All along he has tried to appropriate Octavia, to possess her as he would want to possess any desirable property. Vexed by her acceptance of all as equals, he has attempted—and failed—to make her aware of "social hierarchies." Finally, against his very will, Barold, one of England's prized bachelors, condescends to ask uncultivated Octavia to marry him. To his chagrin, she rejects his offer. In her eyes such a husband is no prize: "You were going to give me a great deal, I suppose—looking at it in your way...but if I *wasn't* exactly what you wanted, I had something to give, too. I'm young enough to have a good many years to live; and I should have to live them with you, if I married you" (249). Having glimpsed himself in such a telling way, Barold leaves Slowbridge hurriedly. Octavia, having repulsed an En-glish gentleman's embraces, then accepts the hand of "the finest fel-low in the West," one Jack Belasys, an American silver miner from Bloody Gulch. By novel's end, England's best appears shopworn.

Earlier in the novel, Lady Theobald ironically pronounces that

"Miss Octavia Bassett... has come from Nevada to teach our young people a great many things,—new fashions in duty, and demeanor, and respect for their elders" (199). She does not know she speaks the truth—for the New World *has* much to teach the Old. Octavia is not cowed by appearance or social standing. Her life does not conform to precut patterns. In rejecting an English gentleman's marriage bid, she rejects all that such privileges stand for: unearned regard, hollow manners, and greed. Octavia's example is as sterling as the silver her father mines. Indeed, her frontier upbringing is a moral force to be reckoned with in Hodgson Burnett's novel: it is what empowers Octavia and enables her to reject the decided opinion of her social "betters" and create her own happy ending. In this way, *A Fair Barbarian* shares the concern of contemporaneous American fiction that civilization faces decline if not countered by the redeeming virtues of the West. James K. Folsom has recently argued that the Gilded Age was preoccupied "with the frontier and literature about it."[8] "The presence of the frontier represents a force," Folsom concludes, "which constantly rejuvenates an American society that, left to itself, would become constantly more over-refined and decadent." Hodgson Burnett replaced the American East with an even more settled society: Britain. But the message is the same: Octavia's surprise visit to her father's homeland proves necessary medicine to an ailing culture.

Six years after the publication of *A Fair Barbarian*, Hodgson Burnett returned to the same cultural dialectic, but with a new cast: the bold Octavia becomes the forthright little boy, Cedric Erroll; Lady Theobald is replaced by the imperious Earl of Dorincourt; Slowbridge is now Erleboro. In the Wild West as well as the tame East, *Little Lord Fauntleroy* raised laughter and wrung tears from its audience. If Hodgson Burnett never traveled west, her young hero did, first in book form and then in a road show that by century's end rivaled the enormously popular *Uncle Tom's Cabin* and *Ben Hur*.[9] Fauntleroy toys, playing cards, writing paper, chocolates, and dark velvet suits undoubtedly found their way west, too, for then, as now, spin-offs proved profitable. But Hodgson Burnett's true gift to the West was more important than the pleasure both *A Fair Barbarian* and *Little Lord Fauntleroy* bestowed: her potent articulation of a young country's mythology, her glorification of its energy and moral might, helped define an America emerging from the wings not as a bit but as a principal player.

Notes

1. Francis J. Molson, "Frances Hodgson Burnett (1848–1924)," *American Literary Realism* 8 (Winter 1975): 39.

2. Ann Thwaite, *Waiting for the Party: The Life of Frances Hodgson Burnett, 1849–1924* (New York: Charles Scribner's Sons, 1974), 149.

3. Ibid., 150.

4. Phyllis Bixler, *Frances Hodgson Burnett* (Boston: Twayne, 1984), 7.

5. Vivian Burnett, *The Romantick Lady (Frances Hodgson Burnett): The Story of an Imagination* (New York: Charles Scribner's Sons, 1927), 106.

6. Frances Hodgson Burnett, *A Fair Barbarian* (Boston: James R. Osgood, 1881), 25. Subsequent page references included in the text are to this edition.

7. Annette Kolodny, *The Land before Her: Fantasy and Experience of the American Frontiers, 1630–1860* (Chapel Hill: University of North Carolina Press, 1984), 240. Quotations in the next two sentences are from Kolodny, 202, 223, where she discusses "westernized domestics" without including Hodgson Burnett.

8. James K. Folsom, "Imaginative Safety Valves: Frontier Themes in the Literature of the Gilded Age," in *The Frontier Experience and the American Dream*, ed. David Mogen, Mark Busby, and Paul Bryant (College Station: Texas A&M University Press, 1989), 87. The following quotation is from Folsom, 92.

9. Bixler, *Frances Hodgson Burnett*, 9.

Bibliography

Bixler, Phyllis. *Frances Hodgson Burnett*. Boston: Twayne, 1984.

Burnett, Frances Hodgson. *A Fair Barbarian*. Boston: James R. Osgood, 1881.

Burnett, Vivian. *The Romantick Lady (Frances Hodgson Burnett): The Story of an Imagination*. New York: Charles Scribner's Sons, 1927.

Folsom, James K. "Imaginative Safety Valves: Frontier Themes in the Literature of the Gilded Age." In *The Frontier Experience and the American Dream*, edited by David Mogen, Mark Busby, and Paul Bryant, 87–94. College Station: Texas A&M University Press, 1989.

Kolodny, Annette. *The Land before Her: Fantasy and Experience of the American Frontiers, 1630–1860*. Chapel Hill: University of North Carolina Press, 1984.

Molson, Francis J. "Frances Hodgson Burnett (1848–1924)." *American Literary Realism* 8 (Winter 1975): 35–41.

Thwaite, Ann. *Waiting for the Party: The Life of Frances Hodgson Burnett, 1849–1924*. New York: Charles Scribner's Sons, 1974.

10. Making an Aristocratic Frontier: Selective History in Willa Cather's *Shadows on the Rock*

Gary Brienzo

Willa Cather describes Oswald Henshawe in *My Mortal Enemy* as a man whose "life had not suited him . . . [who] possessed some kind of courage and force which slept, which in another sort of world might have asserted themselves brilliantly. . . . he ought to have been a soldier or an explorer."[1] She similarly depicts Claude Wheeler in *One of Ours* as an unhappy dreamer who stares at a statue of Kit Carson and thinks, "but there was no West, in that sense, any more. There was still South America; perhaps he could find something below the Isthmus. Here the sky was like a lid shut down over the world."[2]

Both of these characters, created after 1922, the year Cather named as her time of great disillusionment,[3] reflect a closing of the western frontier as the Nebraska author had celebrated it in such novels as *My Ántonia* and *O Pioneers!* From this time on, like her own disappointed characters, Cather looked elsewhere for the transplanted frontiers of her fiction, often to the past in novels like *Death Comes for the Archbishop* or *Shadows on the Rock*. A study of Cather's writing of *Shadows*, her novel of late-seventeenth-century New France, offers insights into how she selected her materials to transform the past into a frontier of meaning for herself and her readers.

In his introduction to *Count Frontenac and New France Under Louis XIV*, Francis Parkman describes French Canada's history in terms that could only have appealed most strongly to Cather. This history, Parkman writes, "is a great and significant drama, enacted among untamed forests, with a distant gleam of courtly splendors and the regal pomp of Versailles."[4] In her fascination with the past, with all aspects of French culture, and with Parkman himself, Cather found a way to fuse all of her interests in the novel that she would describe as her only refuge during the difficult time surrounding the deaths of her parents.[5] Quebec's history also provided Cather with two characters who perfectly fit her conception of the pioneer spirit, the governor general, Count Frontenac, French Canada's greatest civil leader, and Francois de Montmorency-Laval, its first bishop. Both Laval and Frontenac, men of noble French ancestry, are the material of which frontier legends, particularly to Cather, are made. As Stephen Vincent Benét wrote in an interview with Cather, "She has always had a deep feeling for the frontier, for its freshness and strength, for the wild beauty of new land. At the same time she has liked to put a highly cultivated person against that setting."[6] In French Canada under Louis XIV, she found such a land and such people.

Her fictional treatment of Laval and Frontenac illustrates both her technique for transforming history into fiction and her need to transplant the noble pioneer she so admired to a time and place she believed free of the corruption that was destroying her own world. Cather, for example, a great admirer of Parkman, borrowed heavily, but selectively, from the historian's portrait of Bishop Laval. Parkman writes: "A drooping nose of portentous size; a well-formed forehead; a brow strongly arched; a bright, clear eye; scanty hair, half hidden by a black skullcap; thin lips, compressed and rigid, betraying a spirit not easy to move or convince . . . such is Laval, as he looks grimly down on us from the dingy canvas of two centuries ago."[7] To complement his unflattering physical depiction of Laval, Parkman paints his temperament in equally dark tones. Parkman's Laval is a prelate who possesses "an arbitrary and domineering temper . . . one of those who by nature lean always to the side of authority. . . . Austerities and mortifications, playing at beggar, sleeping in beds full of fleas, or performing prodigies of gratuitous dirtiness in hospitals, however fatal to self-respect, could avail little against influences working so powerfully and so insidiously to stimulate the most subtle of human vices [pride]."[8]

Cather's bishop, by contrast, though he physically resembles Parkman's subject, is totally unlike him in disposition. To Cather,

Laval is as generous as he is dignified and selfless, and this spiritual distinction comes to undercut the obvious physical similarity between Parkman's cleric and her own. Her first full-length portrait of "Monsieur L'Ancien" comes in book two of *Shadows on the Rock*, as the two children, Cécile and Jacques, meet him in Quebec's Notre Dame de la Victoire church, where they have gone to pray. It is a striking portrait of "a very heavy, tall old man with wide, stooping shoulders and a head hanging forward...[wearing a] shovel hat and...a black skullcap over his scanty locks"; with eyes "large and full, but set deep back under his forehead," and with "such a very large, drooping nose, and such a grim, bitter mouth, that he might well have frightened a child who didn't know him."[9]

The final words quoted above suggest Cather's divergence from her historical source; that is, while the austerity and rigidity of the man Parkman describes are calculated to frighten, Cather makes it clear that her fictional Laval is not a source of terror, especially to innocents like Jacques and Cécile. Temperamentally Cather's Laval, in keeping with her desire "to put a highly cultivated person" against the frontier setting and with her positive Catholic feelings remaining, as Edith Lewis said, from the writing of *Death Comes for the Archbishop*,[10] little resembles Parkman's cleric. Finding Parkman's interpretations too limited, Cather turned to the more favorable historical renderings of Abbé Henri Scott and of A. Leblond de Brumath in their contributions to the *Makers of Canada* series.

De Brumath describes Laval as a man known for "his ardent piety, and his tender respect for the house of God"[11] from his youth, and maturing into a leader with a beneficent influence over men's minds, "over which he had a great ascendancy by reason of his character and his reputation for sanctity."[12] De Brumath, like Scott, praises Laval's unstinting selflessness, describing his wearing of hair shirts and eating of only the scantiest food, and finally asserting that "Few saints carried mortification and renunciation of terrestrial good as far as he."[13] Laval's aim in living in such poverty, de Brumath concludes, was to have more to give the poor, "a storehouse full of garments, shoes and blankets, which he distributed gratuitously, with paternal kindness and prudence.... The charity of the prelate was boundless."[14]

Scott concurs with de Brumath's assessment, adding still more details of Laval's generosity, including the kernel of a story that Cather transformed into the bishop's first encounter with Jacques in *Shadows on the Rock*. Scott writes: "Once he met on the street in winter

time a poor child halfnaked and shivering with cold; he led him to the
priest-house, washed and kissed his feet, gave him shoes, stockings, a
complete suit of clothes and sent him home as content as himself."[15]
When Cather came to her own telling of the prelate's rescue of the
child, she first recast the story into Jacques's earliest recollection from
near-infancy and then enhanced the episode by creating background
details of the bishop's ensuing meeting with Jacques's profligate
mother and his continuing interest in the child. It is a skillful transformation of her materials, blending the thoughts of Jacques, his mother
'Toinette, and the bishop with direct narrative statements and description and so turning the historical footnote into an eight-page
passage.

As important as this selection in expanding her historical materials
is Cather's ability to refrain from borrowing what would weaken the
dignified image of Laval she wished to present. In the same passage in
which Scott describes the bishop's kindness to the boy, he also illustrates the old prelate's austerity to a degree that Cather chose not to
convey to her own readers. "His bed was a simple mattress on hard
boards without sheets, and he did not suffer fleas to be shaken from
his poor woolen blankets," Scott writes. "Under pretence that his
teeth could not afford to chew fresh meat, or his stomach digest it, he
ate some that had been cooked eight days before and was at times
swarming with worms. And so he mortified all natural inclinations
and deprived himself of all bodily comfort."[16] In her renderings of
such renunciations, Cather includes only enough to make Laval appear selfless, as when she tells of his rising at four each morning and
dressing without a fire, to summon his congregation to early mass, or
relates how he lived on meager food and "in naked poverty" so that
he would have more to give to his people.[17]

Cather practiced such selection in her portrayals of many of the religious who constituted Quebec society of the late seventeenth century, again and again expanding sympathetic images and anecdotes to
enhance the atmosphere of her novel and muting material that would
be ambiguous or contrary to her design. With her depiction of the
great magistrate Count Frontenac she relied more closely on historical sources, finding in the actual count's life a figure as full-blown as
any that fiction could create. One historian describes him as "the
most distinguished of the governors of New France" and tells how
Frontenac "at the head of affairs promptly assumed the aggressive...and French prestige in America was in consequence much

the [?]
western
hero

enhanced."[18] About him Parkman also says, "He was an excellent soldier, and more besides. He was a man of vigorous and cultivated mind, penetrating observation, and ample travel and experience."[19] And like the Frontenac of Cather's novel, befriender of the weaker Auclair and his daughter, Parkman's count is a friend to those beneath him: "It was not his instinct to clash with the humbler classes," the historian writes, "and he generally reserved his anger for those who could retort it." Parkman praises him in the same passage for his "air of distinction" and "surprising moderation and patience" with those he governed.[20]

Both Parkman and Cather also have much to say of Frontenac's amazingly proud spirit. When at age seventy he was sent to govern Canada for the second time, according to Parkman, and was to rescue the "prostrate colony" from both the English and the Iroquois, to "fight two enemies with a force that had proved no match for one of them alone" under other governors, "the audacious count trusted himself, and undertook the task."[21] Later, when Frontenac returns to Quebec from Montreal to repel the British forces under General Phips, Parkman tells us that "fear and doubt seemed banished by his presence."[22] And in a final summation of what well may make Frontenac the epitome of the frontier hero to Cather, Parkman writes: "From the moment when the Canadians found a chief whom they could trust, and the firm old hand of Frontenac grasped the reins of their destiny, a spirit of hardihood and energy grew up in all this rugged population; and they faced their stern fortunes with a stubborn daring and endurance that merit respect and admiration."[23]

natural authority over others

Cather, too, acknowledges Frontenac's fierce pride, but in carefully chosen words that enhance the nobility of her character even more than do Parkman's accounts. The fictional count is no less the savior of Canada than the historical one and is the man who "had accomplished his task...chastised the Indians, restored peace and order, secured the safety of trade," ruling into his seventy-eighth year.[24] And it is, Cather reflects through the thoughts of Euclide Auclair, just the man's pride that gives him his strength: "The Count had the bearing of a fencer when he takes up the foil; from his shoulders to his heels there was intention and direction. His carriage was his unconscious idea of himself,—it was an armour he put on when he took off his night-cap in the morning, and he wore it all day, at early mass, at his desk, on the march, at the Council, at his dinner-table. Even his enemies relied upon his strength."[25] In the same way that Cather provides such subjective reflections, she also transcends history in providing the aging count's thoughts as he approaches death, reconciling the proud, dying soul with the church, whose representatives he had opposed so many times during his life. "He would die here, in this room, and his spirit would go before God to be judged," Cather writes. "He believed this because he had been taught it in childhood, and because he knew there was something in himself and in other men that this world did not explain. In spiritual matters the Count had always accepted the authority of the Church; in governmental and military matters he stoutly refused to recognize it."[26]

In *Shadows on the Rock,* Cather dealt with many other historically based figures, and her treatment of them all, whether secular or religious, fits the patterns established in the development of these two great men. Cather's Mother Marie-Catherine de Saint-Augustin, for example, another important religious leader in the book, is "that remarkable girl who had braved the terrors of the ocean and the wilderness and come out to Canada when she was barely sixteen,"[27] and not the historical religious who believed herself, according to her biographer, as so tormented by demons to atone for the sins of the colonists that at times

> she became like a prison to several thousand demons, who were constrained, despite all their resistance, to enter this truly sainted girl, of whom they had greater horror than of hell itself.... No matter how they vented their rage against her, by subjecting her to all sorts of temptations, these evil spirits from hell always found themselves vanquished by [her]...[s]o that so far from possessing her, they themselves became captives in her... and often the number was so great, that this poor young girl was forced to combat entire armies of demons.[28]

Similarly, the "coureur de bois," Pierre Charron, Cather's greatest secular hero in the novel perhaps not even excluding Frontenac, is based upon the bush rangers described by Parkman as "a huge evil, baneful to the growth and morals of Canada" and "forest outlaws."[29] For Cather, however, Charron symbolizes "the romantic picture of the free Frenchman of the great forests... with the good manners of the Old World, the dash and daring of the New."[30] Cather makes Charron an even more important symbol of the noble pioneer, painting him, through Cécile's eyes, as "a friend, devoted and fearless... [who] had not a throne behind him...[but] authority, and a power which came from knowledge of the country and its people; from knowledge, and from a kind of passion. His daring and his pride seemed to her even more splendid than Count Frontenac's."[31]

Cultivated individuals set against a new land, Frontenac, Charron, Laval, Marie-Catherine de Saint-Augustin, and the many other inhabitants of seventeenth-century Quebec whose histories Cather embellished, all exemplify her search for ideals and values she feared were gone from the world. An examination of Cather's selection in developing these characters suggests that her fictional touches were carefully applied to create an overlying impression of immutability in this most symbolic of her works. Viewed in this way, the transformation of historical materials in *Shadows on the Rock* tells much not only about Cather's fictive techniques, but also about the permanence and strength she saw embodied in the rock of Quebec, her last, most unassailable frontier.

Notes

1. Willa Cather, *My Mortal Enemy* (1926; reprint, New York: Vintage Books, 1971), 52.

2. Willa Cather, *One of Ours* (1922; reprint, New York: Vintage Books, 1971), 104.

3. Willa Cather, *Not Under Forty* (New York: Alfred A. Knopf, 1936), v.

4. Francis Parkman, *Count Frontenac and New France Under Louis XIV* (Boston: Little, Brown, 1877), 1:vi.

5. James Woodress, *Willa Cather: A Literary Life* (Lincoln: University of Nebraska Press, 1987), 423.

6. L. Brent Bohlke, ed., *Willa Cather in Person* (Lincoln: University of Nebraska Press, 1986), 137.

7. Francis Parkman, *The Struggle for a Continent*, ed. Pelham Edgar (Boston: Little, Brown, 1902), 224.

8. Ibid., 225.

9. Willa Cather, *Shadows on the Rock* (1931; reprint, New York: Vintage Books, 1971), 68–69.

10. Edith Lewis, *Willa Cather Living* (New York: Alfred A. Knopf, 1953), 155.

11. Adrien Leblond de Brumath, *Bishop Laval*, Makers of Canada Series (Toronto: Morang, 1910), 19.

12. Ibid., 213.

13. Ibid., 253.

14. Ibid., 257.

15. Abbé H. A. Scott, *Bishop Laval,* Makers of Canada Series, Anniversary Edition (Toronto: Oxford University Press, 1926), 316.

16. Ibid., 315–16.

17. Cather, *Shadows,* 73–74.

18. Parkman, *The Struggle for a Continent,* 233.

19. Parkman, *Count Frontenac,* 1:24.

20. Ibid., 1:73.

21. Ibid., 1:195–96.

22. Ibid., 2:28.

23. Ibid., 2:82.

24. Cather, *Shadows,* 23.

25. Ibid., 23.

26. Ibid., 247.

27. Ibid., 40.

28. Paul Ragueneau, *La Vie de la Mère Catherine de Saint Augustin* (1671; reprint, Québec: Hôtel-Dieu de Québec, 1923), 109. My translation. Ragueneau's original text is as follows: "Elle était comme une prison à plusieurs milliers de démons, qui se voyaient contraints, malgré toutes leurs resistances, d'entrer dans cette fille vrayement Sainte, dont ils avaient plus d'horreur que de l'enfer même: Car plus ils exercaient contr'elle toute leur rage, par toutes sortes de tentations dont les impressions étaient extremes; toujours ces maudits esprits d'enfer se voyaient vaincus par cette ame. . . . En sorte que bien loin de la posseder ils étaient eux-memes captifs en elle . . . et souvent le nombre en a été si grand et si excessif, dont elle sentait les impressions, que cette pauvre fille avait à combattre des armées entières de démons." Original punctuation retained.

29. Parkman, *The Struggle for a Continent,* 180.

30. Cather, *Shadows,* 171–72.

31. Ibid., 268.

Bibliography

Bohlke, L. Brent, ed. *Willa Cather in Person.* Lincoln: University of Nebraska Press, 1986.

Cather, Willa. *My Mortal Enemy.* 1926. Reprint. New York: Vintage Books, 1971.

———. *Not Under Forty.* New York: Alfred A. Knopf, 1936.

———. *One of Ours.* 1922. Reprint. New York: Vintage Books, 1971.

———. *Shadows on the Rock.* 1931. Reprint. New York: Vintage Books, 1971.

Leblond de Brumath, Adrien. *Bishop Laval.* Makers of Canada Series. Toronto: Morang, Limited, 1910.

Lewis, Edith. *Willa Cather Living*. New York: Alfred A. Knopf, 1953.

Parkman, Francis. *Count Frontenac and New France Under Louis XIV*. 2 vols. Pt. 5 of *France and England in North America*. Boston: Little, Brown, 1877.

———. *The Struggle for a Continent*. Edited by Pelham Edgar. Boston: Little, Brown, & Company, 1902.

Ragueneau, Paul. *La Vie de la Mère Catherine de Saint Augustin*. 1671. Reprint. Québec: Hôtel-Dieu de Québec, 1923.

Scott, Abbé H. A. *Bishop Laval*. Makers of Canada Series, Anniversary Edition. Toronto: Oxford University Press, 1926.

Woodress, James. *Willa Cather: A Literary Life*. Lincoln: University of Nebraska Press, 1987.

Part 3

Writing in the New West

11. My Western Roots

Marilynne Robinson

When I was a child I read books. My reading was not indiscriminate. I preferred books that were old and thick and dull and hard. I made vocabulary lists.

Surprising as it may seem, I had friends, some of whom read more than I did. I knew a good deal about Constantinople and the Cromwell revolution and chivalry. There was little here that was relevant to my experience, but the shelves of northern Idaho groaned with just the sort of old dull books I craved, so I cannot have been alone in these enthusiasms.

Relevance was precisely not an issue for me. I looked to Galilee for meaning and to Spokane for orthodonture, and beyond that the world where I was I found entirely sufficient.

It may seem strange to begin a talk about the West in terms of old books that had nothing western about them, and of naive fabrications of stodgily fantastical, authoritative worlds, which answered only to my own forming notions of meaning and importance. But I think it was in fact peculiarly western to feel no tie of particularity to any one past or history, to experience that much underrated thing called deracination, the meditative, free appreciation of whatever comes under one's eye, without any need to make such tedious judgments as "mine" and "not mine."

I went to college in New England and I have lived in Massachusetts for twenty years, and I find that the hardest work in the world—it may in fact be impossible—is to persuade easterners that growing up in the West is not intellectually crippling. On learning that I am from

165

Idaho, people have not infrequently asked, "Then how were you able to write a book?"

Once or twice, when I felt cynical or lazy, I have replied, "I went to Brown," thinking that might appease them—only to be asked, "How did you manage to get into Brown?" One woman, on learning of my origins, said, "But there *has* to be talent in the family *some*where."

In a way *Housekeeping* is meant as a sort of demonstration of the intellectual culture of my childhood. It was my intention to make only those allusions that would have been available to my narrator, Ruth, if she were me at her age, more or less. The classical allusions, Carthage sown with salt and the sowing of dragon's teeth which sprouted into armed men, stories that Ruthie combines, were both in the Latin textbook we used at Coeur d'Alene High School. My brother David brought home the fact that God is a sphere whose center is everywhere and whose circumference is nowhere. I never thought to ask him where he found it. Emily Dickinson and the Bible were blessedly unavoidable. There are not many references in *Housekeeping* to sources other than these few, though it is a very allusive book, because the narrator deploys every resource she has to try to make the world comprehensible. What she knows, she uses, as she does her eyes and her hands. She appropriates the ruin of Carthage for the purposes of her own speculation.

I thought the lore my teachers urged on me must have some such use. Idaho society at that time at least seemed to lack the sense of social class which elsewhere makes culture a system of signs and passwords, more or less entirely without meaning except as it identifies groups and subgroups. I think it is indifference to these codes in westerners that makes easterners think they are without culture. These are relative differences, of course, and wherever accident grants a little reprieve from some human folly it must be assumed that time is running out and the immunity is about to disappear. As an aspect of my own intellectual life as a bookish child in the Far West, I was given odds and ends—Dido pining on her flaming couch, Lewis and Clark mapping the wilderness—without one being set apart from the other as especially likely to impress or satisfy anyone. We were simply given these things with the assurance that they were valuable and important in no specific way. I imagine a pearl diver finding a piece of statuary under the Mediterranean, a figure all immune to the crush of depth though up to its waist in sand and blue with cold, in tatters of seaweed, its eyes blank with astonishment, its lips parted to make a sound in some lost dialect, its hand lifted to arouse a city long since lost beyond indifference. The diver might feel pity at finding so human a thing in so cold a place. It might be his privilege to react with a sharper recognition than anyone in the living world could do, though he had never heard the name of Phidias or Myron. The things we learned were, in the same way, merely given, for us to make what meaning we could of them.

This extended metaphor comes to you courtesy of Mrs. Bloomsburg, my high school Latin teacher, who led five or six of us through Horace and Virgil, and taught us patience with that strange contraption called the epic simile, which, to compare great things with small, appears fairly constantly in my own prose, modified for my own purposes. It was Mrs. Bloomsburg also who trudged us through Cicero's vast sentences, clause depending from clause, the whole cantilevered with subjunctives and weighted with a culminating irony. It was all over our heads. We were bored but dogged. And at the end of it all, I think anyone can see that my style is considerably more in debt to Cicero than to Hemingway.

I admire Hemingway. It is simply an amusing accident that it should be Cicero, of all people, whose influence I must resist. This befell me because I was educated at a certain time in a certain place. When I went to college in New England I found that only I and a handful of boys prepared by Jesuits shared these quaint advantages. In giving them to Ruth I used her to record the intellectual culture of the West as I experienced it myself.

The peculiarities of my early education are one way in which being from the West has set me apart. A man in Alabama asked me how I felt the West was different from the East and the South, and I replied, in the West "lonesome" is a word with strongly positive connotations. I must have phrased my answer better at the time, because both he and I were struck by the aptness of the remark, and people in Alabama are far too sensitive to language to be pleased with a phrase like "strongly positive connotations." For the moment it will have to serve, however.

I remember when I was a child at Coolin or Sagle or Talache, walking into the woods by myself and feeling the solitude around me build like electricity and pass through my body with a jolt that made my hair prickle. I remember kneeling by a creek that spilled and pooled among rocks and among fallen trees with the unspeakably tender growth of small trees already sprouting from their backs, and thinking, there is only one thing wrong here, which is my own presence, and that is the slightest imaginable intrusion—feeling that my solitude, my loneliness made me almost acceptable in so sacred a place.

I remember the evenings at my grandparents' ranch, at Sagle, and how in the daytime we chased the barn cats and swung on the front gate and set off pitchy, bruising avalanches in the woodshed, and watched my grandmother scatter chicken feed from an apron with huge pockets in it, suffering the fractious contentment of town children rusticated. And then the cows came home and the wind came up and Venus burned through what little remained of atmosphere, and the dark and the emptiness stood over the old house like some unsought revelation.

It must have been at evening that I heard the word "lonesome" spoken in tones that let me know privilege attached to it, the kind of democratic privilege that comes with the simplest deserving. I think it is correct to regard the West as a moment in a history much larger than its own. My grandparents and people like them had a picture in their houses of a stag on a cliff, admiring a radiant moon, or a maiden in classical draperies, on the same cliff, admiring the same moon. It was a specimen of decayed Victorianism. In that period mourning, melancholy, regret, and loneliness were high sentiments, as they were for the psalmist and for Sophocles, for the Anglo-Saxon poets and for Shakespeare.

In modern culture these are seen as pathologies—alienation and inauthenticity in Europe, maladjustment and depression in the United States. At present they seem to flourish only in vernacular forms, country-and-western music being one of these. The moon has gone behind a cloud, and I'm so lonesome I could die.

It seems to me that, within limits the Victorians routinely transgressed, the exercise of finding the ingratiating qualities of grave or fearful experience is very wholesome and stabilizing. I am vehemently grateful that, by whatever means, I learned to assume that loneliness should be in great part pleasure, sensitizing and clarifying, and that it is even a truer bond among people than any kind of proximity. It may be mere historical conditioning, but when I see a man or a woman alone, he or she looks mysterious to me, which is only to say that for a moment I see another human being clearly.

I am praising that famous individualism associated with western and American myth. When I praise anything, I proceed from the assumption that the distinctions available to us in this world are not arrayed between good and bad but between bad and worse. Tightly knit communities in which members look to one another for identity, and to establish meaning and value, are disabled and often dangerous, however polished their veneer. The opposition frequently made between individualism on one hand and responsibility to society on the other is a false opposition as we all know. Those who look at things from a little distance can never be valued sufficiently.

But arguments from utility will never produce true individualism. The cult of the individual that, to the best of my belief, enlisted me here was aesthetic and religious. The significance of every human destiny is absolute and equal. The transactions of conscience, doubt, acceptance, rebellion, are privileged, secret, and unknowable. Insofar as such ideas are accessible to proof, I have proved the truth of this view of things to my entire satisfaction. Of course, they are not accessible to proof.

Only lonesomeness allows one to experience this sort of radical singularity, one's greatest dignity and privilege. Understanding this permits one to understand the sacred poetry in strangeness, silence and otherness. The vernacular form of this idea is the western hero, the man of whom nothing can ever really be known.

By this oblique route I have arrived at the matter of the frontier, which, I would propose, was neither a place nor a thing, neither a time nor a historical condition. At the simplest level, it amounted to no more than the movement of European-origin people into a part of the world where they had no business being. By the mid-nineteenth century, this was very old news. The same thing had happened on every continent, saving Antarctica.

In this context it is best that I repeat again my governing assumption, that history is a dialectic of bad and worse. The history of European civilization vis-à-vis the world from the fifteenth century to the present day is astounding. The worst aspects of settlement were by no means peculiar to the American West, but some of its better aspects may well have been. For one thing, the settlement was largely done by self-selecting populations who envisaged permanent settlement on land that, as individuals or communally, they would own outright. The penal colonies and pauper colonies and slash-and-burn raids on the wealth of the land which made the history of most colonized places so unbelievably desolate were less significant here. On the other hand, there was a Utopian impulse, the hope to create a model of a good human order, that seems to have arrived on the *Mayflower*, and which flourished through the whole of the nineteenth century. By the standards that apply to events of its kind, the western settlement had a considerable positive content.

I have read fairly extensively over the last few years in nineteenth-century writing about American social and political issues. Whether or not the West would be settled was clearly not in doubt. The question was how, and by whom. It appears to me that the Homestead Act was designed to consolidate the Northern victory in the Civil War by establishing an economy of small-holder farming, of the kind that prevailed in the North, as opposed to plantation farming on the Southern model. English agriculture was very close to the kind practiced in the South, with the exception that the gangs of English farm laborers, though so poor they were usually called "wretches," were not technically slaves or chattels. In attempting to give the western lands over to the people in parcels suitable to making individual families the owners of the means of their subsistence—and the language I am using here is nineteenth century and American—Lincoln contained, more or less, the virtual slavery that followed actual slavery. In the terms of the time, as things go in this world, the policies that opened the West were sophisticated, considered, and benign. No wonder such hope attached to them.

The American frontier was what it was because it expressed a considerable optimism about what people were and what they might become. Writers of the period assumed that human nature was deformed by drudgery, poverty, contempt, and self-contempt. They were obsessed with the fact that most people in most places—including American blacks on plantations and American whites in city slums—lived lives that were bitterly unworthy of them. So it is not surprising that their heroes lived outside society, and neither did nor suffered the grueling injuries that were the stuff of ordinary life. In Whitman the outsider is a visionary. In Thoreau he is a critic. In the vernacular tradition of western myth he is a rescuer and avenger. In every version he expresses discontent with society. So it is not surprising that he is the creation of generations that accomplished more radical reforms of society than had ever been attempted anywhere before.

This brings me around again to an earlier point, that there is no inevitable conflict between individualism as an ideal and a very positive interest in the good of society.

Obviously I have an axe to grind here. My one great objection to the American hero was that he was inevitably male—in decayed forms egregiously male. So I created a female hero, of sorts, also an outsider and a stranger. And while Sylvie obviously has her own history, to the degree that she has not taken the impress of society she expresses the fact that human nature is replete with nameless possibilities, and, by implication, that the world is accessible to new ways of understanding.

Perhaps it was a misfortune for us that so many interesting ideas were associated with access to a habitable wilderness. The real frontier need never close. Everything, for all purposes, still remains to be done.

I think it is a universal sorrow that society, in every form in which it has ever existed, precludes and forecloses much that we find loveliest and most ingratiating in others and in ourselves. Rousseau said, men are born free, yet everywhere they are in chains. Since the time of the Hebrew prophets it has been the role of the outsider to loosen these chains, or lengthen them, if only by bringing the rumor of a life lived otherwise.

That said, I must say too how beautiful human society seems to me, especially in those attenuated forms so characteristic of the West —isolated towns and single houses which sometimes offer only the merest, barest amenities: light, warmth, supper, familiarity. We have colonized a hostile planet, and we must staunch every opening where cold and dark might pour through and destroy the false climates we make, the tiny simulations of forgotten seasons beside the Euphrates, or in Eden. At a certain level housekeeping is a regime of small kindnesses, which, together, make the world salubrious, savory, and warm. I think of the acts of comfort offered and received within a household as precisely sacramental. It is the sad tendency of domesticity—as of piety—to contract, and of grace to decay into rigor, and peace into tedium. Still it should be clear why I find the Homestead Act all in all the most poetical piece of legislation since Deuteronomy, which it resembles.

Over years of time I have done an archeology of my own thinking, mainly to attempt an escape from assumptions that would embarrass me if I understood their origins. In the course of this re-education I have become suspiciously articulate and opinionated about things no doubt best left to the unself-conscious regions of the mind. At the same time, I feel I have found a place in the West for my West, and the legitimation of a lifelong intuition of mine that the spirit of this place is, as spirits go, mysterious, aloof, and rapturously gentle. It is, historically, among other things, the orphan child of a brilliant century.

I think it is fair to say that the West has lost its place in the national imagination, because by some sad evolution, the idea of human nature has become the opposite of what it was when the myth of the West began, and now people who are less shaped and constrained by society are assumed to be disabled and dangerous. This is bad news for the national psyche, a fearful and anti-democratic idea, which threatens to close down change. I think it would be a positively good thing for the West to assert itself in the most interesting terms, so that the whole country must hear, and be reanimated by dreams and passions it has too casually put aside and too readily forgotten.

12. *Housekeeping:*
New West Novel, Old West Film

Sheila Ruzycki O'Brien

While "Old West" and "New West" sometimes refer to chronological occurrences in the western part of this continent, the terms can also be considered theoretical. Old West tales are replete with images of competition and solitude. Fiction writers and filmmakers frequently depict traveling beyond the geographical boundaries of society as a means of leaving that society behind, the American land providing both a playground and a testing ground for male prowess. Readers and viewers can tell the good guys from the bad, and the linear plot ends with a clear win for the good guys. As Patricia Nelson Limerick notes, within the traditional Western "the dominant feature of conquest remained 'adventure.' "[1] New West writers, in contrast, recognize the complexity of western life: their tales are less clear-cut in terms of both character and plot; protagonists are not necessarily white men;[2] and cooperation as well as competition can be a means of survival and success.

Marilynne Robinson's novel *Housekeeping*,[3] set in post-World War II northern Idaho, provides such a New West alternative, but with some Old West flavor. Robinson builds on the foundation of traditional fiction and film Westerns, creating protagonists who are outsiders, yet she makes her central characters female drifters who do not try to dominate other characters or their environment. She also emphasizes the lasting, even heroic, community between these women. In the film *Housekeeping*,[4] director Bill Forsyth offers quite a different perspective from the novel, shaping the story into a version

173

of an Old West narrative and so undercutting Robinson's New West approach. He makes escape seem a simple and pleasurable option, exaggerates the confrontational quality of the community, and de-emphasizes the lasting adult bond between the women travelers.

One of the central Old West myths underlying the public's sense of the West is that of the lone traveler. Frederick Jackson Turner helped mold this myth in his 1893 speech, "The Significance of the Frontier in American History," by claiming that the frontier created a "dominant individualism." Associated with this brand of individualism were "freshness, and confidence, and scorn of older society, impatience of its restraints and its ideas, and indifference to its lessons"— as well as a lack of artistic ability. These qualities all supposedly led to the survival of the fittest. Turner's theory became embedded in popular culture, and his smaller-than-life vision of the American frontiersman sprang into larger-than-life legends on the Hollywood screen.

We are all familiar with such heroes as appear in films like *The Man Who Shot Liberty Valance, Shane, The Searchers,* and *Will Penny.* These men fall in love or enter a loving family circle, and then exit after a victory, still alone (or with sidekicks), but more admired.[6]

Such a view of American heroes is not restricted to film. In "Melodramas of Beset Manhood," Nina Baym has rightly asserted that those who shape the traditional American literary canon have historically possessed a limited sense of what constitutes American themes.[7] One accepted American literary theme concerns the solitary white male on the move, flashing his superior wit, skill, and consciousness as he vanquishes savages or saves the (overly) civilized. Related to this hero is the male who travels with a companion, usually a racial "other," a more foolish person, or an animal, all familiar pairings in film as well as fiction.[8] All these heroes (men such as Natty Bumppo, Huck Finn, and Nick Adams) are basically Old West loners following the semi-mythical trail of Daniel Boone and Davy Crockett. They are men who could handle tools from rifles to fishing poles, and they are famous for their inability to sustain emotional commitments.

Supportive, nonviolent family bonds are sometimes central in the traditionally popular literature and film of the West, and they have become more prominent with the recent publication of many pioneer diaries, Native American stories, and other texts only recently considered as American western literature through the revisions of New West critics and historians. In the traditional Western, families are of-

ten a foil for the hero's solitude; wholesome white families also counterpoint the depiction of Indians as savage and provide the hero with
good rescuing material. Sometimes a hero even marries. After all,
marrying a woman in a traditional Western was not like marrying in
Philadelphia. Audience members know the wife will probably require
continued rescuing, and so the hero can remain a hero. Marriage also
(supposedly) creates a nice, tidy ending, although not quite on a par
with riding off into the sunset leaving dead bad guys and admiring,
longing beauties in the dust, forever frozen by the narrative in attitudes of vanquishment and desire.

Robinson shapes *Housekeeping* into a New West tale in part by
undercutting the value of Western loner status—without dismissing
the viability of outsider status. The two principal characters, the narrator Ruth and her Aunt Sylvie, are inundated by examples of the
"solitary traveler—Old West" pattern within their family, yet these
examples provide little sustenance.[9] Their loner relatives are dead, distant, or otherwise departed, the western myth of the loner having def-
initely undermined this family. Both of Ruth's maternal grandparents
are loners, responsible in terms of material care such as housing and
food—the grandfather even supplies artwork—but emotionally disconnected from each other and from their children;[10] Ruth's father is a
traveling salesman who deserted his family; her mother committed
suicide by taking a solo car trip into the lake. Ruth's Aunt Sylvie, too,
is an independent traveler until she recognizes Ruth's pained loneliness as well as her own and becomes involved in her niece's life. This
commitment, Elizabeth Meese has noted, "stands in strict contrast to
Kerouac's male fantasy of life on the road."[11]

Robinson also reshapes the traditional American Western by
focusing on intense relationships between women, an uncommon approach in both Old and New West narratives except in pioneer diaries. As Adrienne Rich notes, "the essential female tragedy" is the
daughter's loss of a mother or the mother's loss of a daughter, yet
"there is no presently enduring recognition of mother-daughter passion and rapture."[12] Martha Ravits points out that *Housekeeping* does
recognize such loss and passion as well as some healing achieved
through Sylvie's wise foster mothering.[13] However, Ruth's loss of her
sister Lucille to the confines of rigid normalcy remains an unhealed
wound at the end of the text, a continuing sorrow that contributes to
the novel's lack of closure.

One way in which Robinson meshes her New West approach with

Old West traditions is by having two women stand together against the conservative forces of society—the forces joined by Ruth's sister Lucille. As with the loners in classic Westerns, the women's free spirits chafe at the confines of civilization. Ruth and Sylvie must leave well-intentioned but narrow-minded townspeople and family behind, since this group will not permit female adventures. While Ruth and Sylvie's first overnight journey together works as a catalyst for growing awareness and affection, it impels the traditional community to attempt separating Ruth from Sylvie. They assume, as one church-woman states, that "young girls should lead an orderly life,"[14] and this "orderly life" does not include the "unfeminine" activities of hopping trains or spending the night in a boat. Ruth refuses to abandon Sylvie and her own quirky self, and so to avoid a custody hearing, the two leave established society behind. Like many "good-bad" men in traditional Westerns, Ruth and Sylvie live in both legal and self-imposed exile. While morally good, they cannot fit into a restrictive society. Respectability is impossible, and Ruth herself notes that she and her aunt are social outcasts and "drifters."[15]

In addition to expanding women's roles in western fiction, Robinson creates two central characters who overturn a sense of hierarchy common in western literature and film. According to Alicia Ostriker, emotional closeness can be "derived from acknowledged likeness, not from the patriarchal relationships of dominance and submission."[16] Pairs in Old West literature and film tend to be socially and/or intellectually uneven: Natty Bumppo and Chingachgook, Huck and Jim, the traditional Western hero and his sidekick—the Lone Ranger and Tonto, Gene Autry and Frog, Roy Rogers and Gabby Hayes, Tom and Pompey (a black man) in *The Man Who Shot Liberty Valance,* as well as most male/female and adult/child pairs. Ruth and Sylvie's relationship, despite their difference in age and their status as aunt and niece, is one based on similarity. While Ruth and Lucille at first yearn for a dominant parental figure who will punish them for breaking rules, Ruth soon recognizes that she shares Sylvie's quirkiness and doesn't want it repressed.[17] Lucille, on the other hand, clings to a rigid order as a means to hold chaos at bay, and so she moves in with her "normal" home-economics teacher. The fact that the tale is told by Ruth as an adult narrator open to the wanderings and questions of her own mind emphasizes the success of her un-repressive relationship with Sylvie. It also underscores that as a grown woman, Ruth chooses to continue her relationship with her aunt.

The lack of domination between the two central characters echoes their refusal to dominate or even control the environment, an enormous contrast to their Old West counterparts who forced land, animals, and machines (as well as women and minorities) to do their bidding. Even mythic outsiders in the Old West tradition are insiders in the sense that they support the development of the West, either directly or indirectly. Sylvie and Ruth form a new breed of western outsider; they are outsiders who are not loners and who neither implement changes in their environment nor act as catalysts for change. They do not fight nature. In fact, Sylvie's "housekeeping" welcomes leaves, wind, water, and animals into the house.[18] Neither mines nor gardens are dug, no dams are built, no horses broken. The lack of forcefulness of any kind confirms that they do not conform to the Old West tradition.

Like Sylvie's house, Ruth's narrative remains untidy; Ruth will not beat it into shape to provide a false sense of control or to simplify her story. The traditional Western follows a linear pattern, complete with a tidy ending, providing the audience with a bourgeois sense of contentment that Roland Barthes calls "plaisir."[19] By the time she begins her story, Ruth has accepted the untidiness inherent in both her life and her thoughts. Her nonlinear narrative mirrors her mental and geographic rambles and presents a striking contrast to a traditional Western.[20] She wanders away from plot, pursuing questions often left unanswered.[21] The narrative does not thrust itself forward, but takes tangential and circuitous paths. The ending of the text, chronologically close to its beginning, is far from neat and far from "happy."[22] Ruth, though still close to Sylvie, longs for her lost sister Lucille; she is still wandering and continually becoming more of a social outcast.

Bill Forsyth's film version of *Housekeeping* provides an intriguing counter to the structure and emphasis of Robinson's novel. It offers a visually rich symbolic texture but flattens the emotional range of the book as well as its open narrative structure. The shift in medium necessitates some of this flattening, but the direction it takes is worth discussing. While Forsyth maintains an ending centered on Robinson's female travelers (although Robinson has stated that Forsyth briefly considered a concluding marriage between Sylvie and the sheriff),[23] he does instill more of the American traveler's mystique into the film than is evident in the novel. Traveling is glorified without modification. In addition, the us-vs.-them/outsider-vs.-society theme is accentuated. Although Robinson depicts the community of

Fingerbone as threatening to separate Ruth from her aunt, the sheriff and the visiting churchwomen are citizens concerned with Ruth's welfare—not merely the pompous lawman and the tight-lipped, condescending matrons of the film—and Robinson herself verbally underscores the town members' concern rather than their rapacity.[24] Thus, Forsyth's "them" are clear enemies, representations of self-serving bastions of society, such as Twain's Miss Watson and Colonel Sherburn in *The Adventures of Huckleberry Finn* and the ladies' moral society in *Stagecoach* (portrayed by John Ford as worse enemies than Apaches).[25] By establishing their enemy status, Forsyth promotes the simplified black-and-white quality of Old West tales.

As the film clearly pinpoints evil in the restrictions of traditional society, it simply exalts the means of being victorious over such restrictions: transience. Through striking visuals, Forsyth underscores the joy of escape provided by travel. As the flood settles in on Fingerbone shortly after Sylvie's arrival, and rising water destroys even the possibility of normal housekeeping, Sylvie responds by singing and happily dancing a quick step through the water with Ruth. (In the novel, Ruth's memory of the scene is much more serious: "Sylvie took me by the hand and pulled me after her through six grand waltz steps."[26]) Lucille, the family member who tries to cope by maintaining order and decorum, futilely tries to sweep floating objects, including a suitcase, into a closet. However, as Ruth and Sylvie make waves, the suitcase (which has a very minor role in the novel) cannot be repressed; it dances out of the closet, topped with a lamp shade and almost wriggling with pleasure as it foretells a future in which the dancers elude the strictures of respectability.

Another visual glorification of travel occurs at the very end of the film. Forsyth cuts off Ruth's description of her travels with her aunt and her sadness over losing contact with her sister. His final image is simpler and happier: a shot of the railroad tracks glowing in the darkness, looking like a ladder to heaven, enticing the viewer with a sense of limitless possibilities.

Not only does the director elevate the flatly positive travel myths of popular culture, but he also undermines the continuous relationship of the two women by using young Ruth's child voice for the voice-over narration, instead of the adult narrative voice of the novel. "Ruthie" never becomes "Ruth" in the film; the striking opening line of the novel, "My name is Ruth,"[27] is gone, ousted by a teenage voice giving information about "Grampa," a word that replaces Ruth's word choice, "Grandfather." By transforming the narrator Ruth into Ruthie, Forsyth undermines the equality within the women's relationship, creating the inequality common in Old West narratives; he also can justify curtailing not only the nonlinear complexity of Ruth's adult mind but also the final section of the novel focusing on Ruth's adulthood. (When I asked Robinson if she approved of Forsyth's ending, she replied emphatically, "No. Not at all. Absolutely not."[28])

The final sequence in the film limits but also undercuts the importance of the women's continuing relationship—and even makes the fact of their survival somewhat ambiguous. As the tracks glow on the screen, the viewer is left considering the travelers' danger in crossing the railroad bridge. Only those conscious of the framework of Ruth's retrospective narration—or those who have read the book—are assured of a safe crossing. (I have seen this movie in theaters numerous times, and each time the room rustled with "Did they make it?" as the credits rolled.)

Forsyth does present positive and entertaining female characters in his film, and his work accomplishes some of the novel's goals. The protagonist remains female—and Sylvie's network of female transient friends is intact—but Forsyth's *Housekeeping* is more a "me, too," contemporary version of the Old West than is Robinson's novel, since his film curtails some of Robinson's revisions of Old West myths.

In his film Forsyth backs away from what I consider Robinson's central revision, her response to what is so often glorified—or at least depicted as necessary—in the Old West tradition: isolation. Robinson's Ruth and Sylvie live as adult outsiders; they choose to exercise their Old West independence, yet their lives are not glorious. However, their New West desire to maintain, respect, and nurture each other provides them sustenance throughout their travels—and this adult affection that softens the dark side of isolation Forsyth omits. Such a New West value was not even considered by Frederick Jackson Turner in his depiction of the American West as a survival-of-the-fittest world, but to Ruth and Sylvie—and to the rest of us—survival can depend on it.

Notes

1. Patricia Nelson Limerick, *The Legacy of Conquest: The Unbroken Past of the American West* (New York: Norton, 1987), 19.

2. Two historians at the forefront of presenting the diversity of the West are Patricia Nelson Limerick, *The Legacy of Conquest,* and Susan Armitage, "Through Woman's Eyes: A New View of the West," in *The Women's West,* ed. Susan Armitage and Elizabeth Jameson (Norman: University of Oklahoma Press, 1987), 9–18. Critic Jane Tompkins provides a perceptive analysis of the relation between culturally diverse historical perspectives and literary analysis in " 'Indians': Textualism, Morality, and the Problem of History," *Critical Inquiry* 13, no. 1 (Autumn 1986): 101–19.

3. Marilynne Robinson, *Housekeeping* (New York: Farrar, Straus and Giroux, 1981; New York: Bantam, 1982).

4. *Housekeeping* (1987, Columbia), directed by Bill Forsyth.

5. Frederick Jackson Turner, "The Significance of the Frontier," in *The Early Writings of Frederick Jackson Turner* edited by Everett E. Edwards and with an introduction by Fulmer Mood (Madison: University of Wisconsin Press, 1938; Freeport, N.Y.: Books for Libraries Press, 1969), 185–229.

6. *The Man Who Shot Liberty Valance* (1962, Paramount), directed by John Ford; *Shane* (1953, Paramount), directed by George Stevens; *The Searchers* (1956, Warner Brothers), directed by John Ford; *Will Penny* (1968, Paramount), directed by Tom Gries.

7. Nina Baym, "Melodramas of Beset Manhood: How Theories of American Fiction Exclude Women Authors," *American Quarterly* 33 (Summer 1981): 122–39.

8. Leslie A. Fiedler discusses mixed racial pairings in *Love and Death in the American Novel,* rev. ed. (New York: Stein and Day, 1966).

9. For a fuller analysis of how *Housekeeping* incorporates and reshapes canonical and non-canonical depictions of western travelers, see Sheila Ruzycki O'Brien, "*Housekeeping* in the Western Tradition: Remodeling Tales of Western Travelers," in *Women and the Journey,* edited by Susan McCleod (Pullman: Washington State University Press, 1993).

10. I find Ruth's grandfather a major character in *Housekeeping*. Many other critics claim that male characters in the text are only marginal or used as a point of departure. See Elizabeth Meese, *Crossing the Double Cross: The Practice of Feminist Criticism* (Chapel Hill: University of North Carolina Press, 1986), 55–68; Thomas Foster, "History, Critical Theory, and Women's Social Practices: 'Woman's Time' and *Housekeeping,*" *Signs: Journal of Women in Culture and Society* 14, no. 1 (Autumn 1988): 73–99; and Phyllis Lassner, "Escaping the Mirror of Sameness: Marilynne Robinson's *Housekeeping,*" in *Motherpuzzles: Daughters and Mothers in Contemporary American Literature,* ed. Mickey Perlman (New York: Greenwood Press, 1989), 49–58.

11. Meese, *Crossing*, 64. A similar point is made by Dana Heller in *The Feminization of Quest-Romance* (Austin: University of Texas Press, 1990), 93–104.

12. Adrienne Rich, *Of Woman Born: Motherhood as Experience and Institution* (New York: Norton, 1976), 237.

13. Martha Ravits, "Extending the American Range: Marilynne Robinson's *Housekeeping*," *American Literature* 61 (Dec. 1989): 644–66. Roberta Rubenstein also focuses on the mother-daughter bond between Sylvie and Ruth as a means of coping with loss in *Boundaries of the Self: Gender, Culture, Fiction* (Urbana: University of Illinois Press, 1987), 211–30.

14. Robinson, *Housekeeping*, 185.

15. Ibid., 213.

16. Alicia Ostriker, *Stealing the Language: The Emergence of Women's Poetry in America* (Boston: Beacon Press, 1986), 327.

17. For a related discussion, see Lassner.

18. Sylvie's free-form housekeeping and her harmonious relationship to the environment have been frequent issues of concern among Robinson critics. See, for example, Foster, Kirby, and Lassner, as well as Anne-Marie Mallon, "Sojourning Women: Homelessness and Transcendence in *Housekeeping*," *Critique* 30, no. 2 (Winter 1989): 95–105.

19. Roland Barthes, *Image-Music-Text* (London: Fontana Press, 1977), 9.

20. Limerick discusses the imposition of a rigid, linear chronology on western history in her introduction to *The Legacy of Conquest*.

21. For a related discussion of *Housekeeping*'s narrative structure, see Meese.

22. For a detailed feminist analysis of narrative endings, see Rachel Blau DuPlessis, *Writing beyond the Ending: Narrative Strategies of Twentieth-Century Women Writers* (Bloomington: Indiana University Press, 1985).

23. Marilynne Robinson, *Housekeeping* Symposium at Sandpoint, Idaho, June 1988.

24. Ibid.

25. *Stagecoach* (1939, United Artists), directed by John Ford.

26. Robinson, *Housekeeping*, 64.

27. Ibid., 3.

28. This discussion occurred during Robinson's visit to my "American Women Travelers" class at the University of Idaho in October 1989.

Bibliography

Armitage, Susan. "Through Woman's Eyes: A New View of the West." In *The Women's West*, edited by Susan Armitage and Elizabeth Jameson, 9–18. Norman: University of Oklahoma Press, 1987.

Barthes, Roland. *Image-Music-Text*. London: Fontana Press, 1977.

Baym, Nina. "Melodramas of Beset Manhood: How Theories of American Fiction Exclude Women Authors." *American Quarterly* 33 (Summer 1981): 122–39.

DuPlessis, Rachel Blau. *Writing beyond the Ending: Narrative Strategies of Twentieth-Century Women Writers*. Bloomington: Indiana University Press, 1985.

Fiedler, Leslie A. *Love and Death in the American Novel*. Rev. ed. New York: Stein and Day, 1966.

Ford, John (director). *The Man Who Shot Liberty Valance*. Paramount, 1962.

———. *The Searchers*. Warner Brothers, 1956.

———. *Stagecoach*. United Artists, 1939.

Forsyth, Bill (director). *Housekeeping*. Columbia, 1987.

Foster, Thomas. "History, Critical Theory, and Women's Social Practices: 'Woman's Time' and *Housekeeping*." *Signs: Journal of Women in Culture and Society* 14, no. 1 (Autumn 1988): 73–99.

Gries, Tom (director). *Will Penny*. Paramount, 1968.

Heller, Dana A., *The Feminization of Quest-Romance*. Austin: University of Texas Press, 1990.

Kirby, Joan. "Is There Life after Art: The Metaphysics of Marilynne Robinson's *Housekeeping*." *Tulsa Studies of Women in Literature* 5, no. 1 (Spring 1986): 91–109.

Lassner, Phyllis. "Escaping the Mirror of Sameness: Marilynne Robinson's *Housekeeping*." In *Motherpuzzles: Daughters and Mothers in Contemporary American Literature,* edited by Mickey Perlman, 49–58. New York: Greenwood Press, 1989.

Limerick, Patricia Nelson. *The Legacy of Conquest: The Unbroken Past of the American West*. New York: Norton, 1987.

Mallon, Ann-Marie. "Sojourning Women: Homelessness and Transcendence in *Housekeeping*." *Critique* 30, no. 2 (Winter 1989): 95–105.

Meese, Elizabeth. *Crossing the Double Cross: The Practice of Feminist Criticism*. Chapel Hill: University of North Carolina Press, 1986.

O'Brien, Sheila Ruzycki, "*Housekeeping* in the Western Tradition: Remodeling Tales of Western Travelers." In *Women and the Journey,* edited by Susan McCleod. Pullman: Washington State University Press, 1993.

Ostriker, Alicia. *Stealing the Language: The Emergence of Women's Poetry in America*. Boston: Beacon Press, 1986.

Ravits, Martha. "Extending the American Range: Marilynne Robinson's *Housekeeping*." *American Literature* 61 (Dec. 1989): 644–66.

Rich, Adrienne. *Of Woman Born: Motherhood as Experience and Institution*. New York: Norton, 1976.

Robinson, Marilynne. *Housekeeping*. New York: Farrar, Straus and Giroux, 1981; New York: Bantam, 1982.

Rubenstein, Roberta. *Boundaries of the Self: Gender, Culture, Fiction*. Urbana: University of Illinois Press, 1987.

Stevens, George (director). *Shane*. Paramount, 1953.

Tompkins, Jane. " 'Indians': Textualism, Morality, and the Problems of History." *Critical Inquiry* 13, no. 1 (Autumn 1986): 101–19.

Turner, Frederick Jackson. "The Significance of the Frontier." In *The Early Writings of Frederick Jackson Turner,* edited by Everett E. Edwards and with an introduction by Fulmer Mood, 185–229. Madison: University of Wisconsin Press, 1938. Repr. Freeport, N.Y.: Books for Libraries Press, 1969.

13. Reading the Myth of the West

Helen Lojek

Frank South's 1981 *Rattlesnake in a Cooler* and Mark Medoff's 1984 *The Majestic Kid* are rarities on the contemporary American stage, plays that deal with the "myth" and the "reality" of the American West. The works face directly what have become central problems for many western writers: what to make of the myth and its relation to reality, and whether literature and life demand choosing one over the other. South's play rejects myth so determinedly that his myth-accepting protagonist seems doomed from the start. Medoff's play works out a more complex response that, without fully affirming the myth, allows his protagonist to look to it for guidelines and make a healthy transition to a new age. In large part, the very different fates of these protagonists are a product of the very different ways in which they, and their creators, "read" popular western myth. Not *what* the myth is, but the *function* assigned to myth, determines the ultimate shape of the reconciliation of myth and reality in these plays.

Realistic suspicions that snowmobiles and hydroelectric dams and the tourist trade have more to do with life in the West than do Lone Rangers and Cisco Kids have long been forced to yield before the simplistic popular-culture image of the West as a country of cattle drives and gleaming six-shooters and unstainable white hats—an image that retains as apparently unshakable a grip on the American imagination as does that which links the South with Miss Scarlett and Ashley. There are, of course, other (often related) mythic Wests: the frontier that was Deerslayer's dominion; the vast plains where a homesteader could pit himself against nature to carve out a Little House on the Prairie; the mountains where luck and determination could yield the

184

fabulous Treasure of the Sierra Madre. But the cowboy legend, as Robert Athearn has pointed out, "is the most enduring of western folklore."[1] Mention the West and listeners most likely imagine cowboys in chaps who tip outsized hats to women and use lightning draws and deadeye marksmanship in the service of justice. Athearn, borrowing a term Joseph Hergesheimer first used in the *Saturday Evening Post* in 1922, calls this "the perpetual west," where "nothing would ever change" and "Americans could place their hopes for the future."[2] As Archibald MacLeish put it, the West is a country of the mind and therefore eternal.[3]

As Athearn's and MacLeish's terminology suggests, of course, both past and present western realities are absorbed by this myth of the perpetual West. That perpetual West—nurtured by generations of dime novels, silver screen images, country western ballads, and television series—often persists most vigorously in the imaginations of easterners who have never crossed the Mississippi River, much less the one hundredth meridian, and may therefore retain a notion that the West remains another chance, an escape hatch from the problems besetting the overpopulated urban East, a frontier of opportunity unclosed despite Turner's best efforts.

Both of these plays deal with such easterners. The protagonists—South's from Kentucky, Medoff's from Chicago by way of New York—are professionals who have, as children, absorbed images of the West from the songs and movies of popular culture. And it is the myth of the perpetual West to which they adhere: neither protagonist pauses to reflect that a myth based on a brief nineteenth-century phenomenon is unlikely to match the twentieth-century reality. Instead, both move west hoping to find the mythic world of country western music and cowboy films. Neither, of course, finds that world, and therein lie both tales.

South and Medoff begin their plays by emphasizing the vehicles of popular culture through which their characters have absorbed the myth. At the start of *Rattlesnake,* audience and protagonist listen to five country western songs, lasting almost ten minutes. And Medoff suggests that as the audience enters *The Majestic Kid* "an old cowboy movie should be showing."[4] Audiences for both plays, then, begin by reacting directly to the powerful, simple images of popular-culture myth. And so, in a sense, the audiences begin where the protagonists begin—with their minds set by images gleaned from popular culture. The ends of the plays remind us of these pop culture influences by returning to the opening references. South ends with one final country western song; Medoff parodies the stock conclusion of Westerns in which the hero of the film rides off into the sunset.

South's _Rattlesnake_ is a one-character play, but the unnamed protagonist, who is waiting to be hanged for murdering a patrolman, replays scenes from his past, so we hear the words of others, even if we do not see them on stage. As a preschooler in Lexington, Kentucky, "while Mom baked oatmeal bread and Daddy finished Dentistry school,"[5] he absorbs a steady diet of country western music, which he and his mother use as an escape from life in a Kentucky apartment. One day the radio announcer makes an offer: "If you'd like to hear those heifers on the open range, if you'd like to see that sunset over those mountains, or feel those reins in your hands, you either go out west, or buy this album. 'Tex Ritter, Singin' For You' " (2). His mother buys the album. And gradually an image of the Great Southwest, where he "was due," develops in his mind: "There's something stark and solid about the west. It's cleanliness. There's something washed out, removed. There is something in day to day living elsewhere that doesn't exist in Colorado, Utah, or New Mexico. Whatever it is that's missing, it's [sic] absence makes things better for me" (2).

What is missing in this mythic West is, pretty clearly, family, responsibility, order, regularity—but it takes him a while to realize this. First he grows up (after a fashion), goes to medical school, and begins family practice. One day in the supermarket a woman accidentally hits him while reaching for a copy of _Family Circle,_ and he ends up marrying her. They settle in Boonsborough, its very name an echo of the western tradition for which he yearns, and it is not long before he is oppressed by the family circle he has begun to create: his wife criticizes his fondness for "sentimental ballads," and he suddenly balks at having children and begins to neglect his family practice. The circle is too confining: "[M]y road was all planned out and smoothed for me, had been for as long as I could remember, all I had to do was keep walking, stay married, have kids, get wealthy, start to twitch, and get palsy as the walls closed in" (2). Instead, he opts to leave his wife and practice and light out for the territory, the West, where less is more.

The doctor aspires to become the familiar figure of the free, rootless westerner, wandering unfettered by women. His attraction to the mythic West is part of a general tendency described by Ray Billington.

In the "West that they created in their imagination . . . each individual could carve out his own destiny. . . . All who glorified the pioneering past shared . . . an urge to escape the pressures of modern society."[6]

The country western songs with which the play begins suggest that the principal modern incarnations of the unfettered westerner admired by the doctor are truckers and rodeo cowboys. The doctor, who gives no hint he has ever been within smelling distance of a horse, aims to be a rodeo cowboy.

Sure enough, he finds work on a ranch in Greeley, Colorado, the first place he gets off the bus. True, it's a dude ranch. True, his job is not to ride and wrangle, but to glue tips back on pool cues and clean the swimming pool. Equally true, he is pleased with his appearance— with how "authentic" he looks in his faded, torn-up jeans, beat-up boots, and cowboy hat.

From this point on, it seems as though the doctor has been reading Richard Slotkin's *Regeneration through Violence*. Wishing to begin anew, to get off the "greased track" he has been on since the womb, to re-form his life, he (apparently unconsciously) links regeneration with violence so tightly that he cannot separate the two. Sent out to shoot skunks in the dump, he imagines the skunk who appears at the burrow hole as a "poor provider" who has been thrust from his "home" by others willing to sacrifice him for the greater good. Frenziedly, the doctor blasts away, and then turns his gun on "a flock of magpies all heading for church." Having exterminated these reminders of Kentucky family life, he offers to spare the "witnesses"—three rabbits—if they run. They do not run, so he kills them, too, and concludes this parody of a Western with a rousing "Ride'm cowboy" (7).

At the suggestion of Jim, the wrangler and rodeo cowboy who has gotten the doctor his job, he leaves Greeley and goes with Jim to Cheyenne for Frontier Days. Westerners from Buffalo Bill Cody to the current residents of Jackson Hole have worked hard to exploit the myth of the West, marketing versions of it to eastern tourists and to themselves. Frontier Days is a classic example of that tendency to "wild up" the contemporary West, and the doctor loves it. It is another example of the extent to which the myth, based on the past, can subsume present realities. As one of the play's opening songs puts it,

A hundred years ago he was a hero
Born when he was needed by someone

His way of life had reason and meanin'
And the world had a place for restless men (D)

Unlike the songwriter, however, the doctor fails to realize that the world has changed. Loner heroes no longer have a clear "place," and Frontier Days celebrations are not reality but play.

The doctor admires Jim for the barely submerged violence in his nature. Jim pounds the steering wheel as he drives, rescues the doctor from a bar fight, and pitches a sugar jar through a restaurant window when the eggs don't suit him. It is the last incident that leads to real trouble. When a New Mexico highway patrolman tries to arrest Jim for the sugar jar episode, the doctor "rescues" his pal by hitting the patrolman on the head with a tire iron and killing him. For the doctor the myth is attractive not only because it allows escape from conventional Kentucky life, but also because it converts complex realities into simple patterns of right and wrong, patterns that reveal an appropriate course of action. Western myth dictates absolute loyalty to his partner, and so he "defends" Jim by killing the patrolman.

Jim, however, is not pleased by this demonstration of the doctor's commitment to the primal frontier bonding between partners, recognizing in it an oversimplified view of the world, a view that is essentially childlike, appealing only to a "kid."

> [T]hat dead weight back in New Mexico is your first big ol notch in your fucking gun isn't it? Who the fuck are you anyway? Some fucking clerk on vacation? . . . you're just a trigger happy kid, no matter how old you say you are. No but you were going to save my life, how were you to know that he was just a cop who was going to bruise me up some screw me for about a hundred dollars and send us on our way? (11)

Jim, who lives in the real West (also sometimes known as the New West), understands that a cowboy's image is, in fact, an image and need not entail ultimate, irreversible acts of violence against authority. He knows "there's still no more elbow room than before," and makes adjustments. But the doctor, fleeing domesticity, seeking manly independence, cannot separate his need for a new life—a regeneration—from violence. Remembering the killing, he observes, "At least once I moved under my own steam and felt the pressure of one life pushing against another. I guess I just always wanted to feel definite, unforgiving, and male. Or maybe I just always wanted to be a killer" (2). Realist Jim objects to movies such as *The Misfits,* Arthur Miller's archetypal easterner's view of the West. That film features Clark Gable's definitive, romantic refusal to work for wages because he is "some kind of last of the cowboys." Jim regards such sentiments as "shit" (11). The romanticist doctor, on the other hand, is fond of describing things as "just like in the movies," and finds Jim's reaction to the tire iron killing bewildering. The pop-culture descriptions of cowboy-dom have failed the doctor. He is not sure what Jim regards as appropriate, and he concludes that "they should issue cowboy guide books, like driver's manuals" (12).

After the murder, Jim and the doctor are picked up by three drunken cowboys who enlist Jim in a kind of league against the doctor. Parodying the traditional western tormenting of the tenderfoot, they "jocularly" threaten the eastern doctor with a rattlesnake curled up on the dashboard, and with another stored in a cooler in the trunk. The doctor, no doubt unconsciously recognizing here an opportunity to demonstrate that the West has made a Man of him, responds with a second outburst of violence, flinging the cooler in the faces of his tormentors, before they subdue him and turn him in for murder. He accepts his fate with equanimity, never challenging Jim's false report of how the murder happened, pleased that they have left him his hat, the definitive symbol of the figure into which he has tried to make himself.

By the end, of course, the doctor is the rattlesnake in the cooler—a coiled, confined creature, perpetually threatening violence and with no further human connections. And he has become that because of the way in which he read the myth of the West. Seduced by images of manly independence and rootless lack of confinement, he goes west to pursue those images. Though the myth does not match the reality of the West he finds, he never adjusts his aim. He has wanted a guidebook to being a cowboy, and he treats the myth as that guidebook, believing that if he mimics its image of the cowboy he will become the thing itself. His attitude is reminiscent of that of Faulkner's Sutpen, who believes he can become a southern gentleman by following a "recipe." For the doctor, the myth is not a myth at all, but an alternative to the life he has and despises in Kentucky. Seeking escape from the family circle, he selects the cowboy guidebook provided by Tex Ritter songs and attempts to follow it. Conceiving (or, I am arguing, misconceiving) myth as a guidebook to an alternative reality, the doctor opens the way to confusing violence with manliness, and clothes with the man. He never really notices that reality fails to match the myth, and continues to behave in ways he imagines can be set to a Tex Ritter tune.

A healthier notion of the nature and function of myth might have saved him from the rope he dangles from at the end of this play—as a healthier understanding of myth does indeed save Medoff's central character in *The Majestic Kid*.

Medoff's play is longer and more complex than South's, the humor is lighter, the conclusion is not bleak but hopeful, the pattern is not ironic but comic. But the central situation is parallel indeed. Aaron Weiss has come to New Mexico with his childhood friend and fellow attorney, AJ. Their idealistic efforts to improve the administration of justice in the Bronx have not yielded much success, and they have come west to help the Apaches regain some of their tribal lands. As children AJ and Aaron had played cowboys, and the shaping influence of the myth of the West is apparent. AJ describes their case as a "last stand," and Aaron acknowledges that

> I came . . . "out west," because I imagined I could still somehow become who I've wanted to be since I was nine years old, could climb out of the Saturday matinee of my childhood and become at twenty-nine who I was then: The Majestic Kid. Who knew it was possible to help people without hurting other people; a hero who bloodlessly snuffed out injustice wherever it lurked; who could commit his very life, against whatever obstacles, to fulfilling precious ideals. And who inevitably, in the end, preserved and returned to its rightful owner the land. (8)

The elements of the western myth that inspire Aaron, of course, are considerably more benevolent and less violent than those that inspire the doctor in *Rattlesnake*—are, in fact, often both positive and valuable. But the broad outlines of the cowboy myth are the same.

Aaron, too, absorbed this myth from popular culture—from the Laredo Kid, the silver screen cowboy who made nine-year-old Aaron think of himself as the Majestic Kid. A rootless, womanless hero who sings love songs to his horse, has a draw like quicksilver, and never deserts a "saddle partner," Laredo comes to New Mexico with Aaron. He is a figure of memory and imagination, but one who actually appears onstage, slightly paunchier than he was once, still singing his outdated cowboy songs, bewildered at the world (and the women) of the eighties, but there nonetheless as guide for Aaron.

In New Mexico Aaron also encounters violence, especially in the person of Judge William S. Hart Finley, whose reactions to Aaron range from a threat to "whip your undies down and tie your ding-dong in a knot" (5), to physical attack, to threatened death by gunshot. In fact, Aaron more than once must be rescued from the unspeakable judge by Lisa, the "gal" who according to Laredo's code is there to be rescued. And Aaron, like South's doctor, finds a world more complicated than the one promised by the pop-culture myth. In New Mexico good and evil are very difficult to separate. The judge with the silver screen name is cruel, crooked, exploitative, and violent—but he can also quote Benjamin Franklin and John Dryden, and he genuinely loves Lisa (even if he is fond of quoting from property rights law to justify his attempts to control her). The Apaches, whom Aaron believes must be mystically united to their land, want to regain it primarily to build a resort hotel. They wear polyester, serve Sara Lee cheesecake, and prefer watching Bob Hope and Sammy Davis to doing tribal dances. Aaron's notion of the code of the West ("Do unto others as you would have others do unto you") collides directly with the judge's code of the West ("You piss in my trough, I poison your well")—which Laredo renders as "You wee-wee in my trough, I poison yore well" (35).

Both South and Medoff specifically associate the myth of the West with youth. Jim calls South's doctor a "kid, no matter how old you say you are." And Aaron refers to himself as an "aging boy." The difference, of course, lies in who recognizes this link between myth and youth. Unlike South's doctor, Medoff's lawyer recognizes that the myths of his childhood do not match the reality of his adulthood. His initial reaction to the disparity is to drop out of the contest altogether, to quit trying to save the world and go to computer school. It seems clear that the Laredo Kid, who stands baffled in the background, searching vainly for the script that controls the action, will offer no real help. A lovable, comic buffoon, bewildered by this New West, Laredo continues to say "dukey" for "shit," "caboose" for "ass," and "redskins" for "Indians"; the meanings of words like "toxic waste" and "fornicate" elude him completely; and he (like Aaron) thinks *Fanny Hill* is a tale of pioneer adventure.

Aaron, however, does not fall into the trap of attempting to force reality to match the silver screen myth. From the start he realizes that Laredo *is* a myth. When Laredo teaches Aaron to fight, for example, what he teaches him is a series of movie "thocks" that involve no actual physical contact and so prevent any serious injury. And Aaron practices his quick draw not with a six-shooter but with his forefinger. Further, Aaron has absolutely no desire to duplicate Laredo's rootless wandering. What Aaron wants is precisely that family circle that neither Laredo nor South's doctor could handle—and he wants it with Lisa, a modern woman of the West who sings "Home on the Range" with new meaning, cooks, ropes, and has a mystical, spiritual sympathy with the land and the people of New Mexico.

The one significant variation between the myth as the doctor absorbs it from Tex Ritter and the myth as Aaron absorbs it from Laredo is the attitude toward the land. Laredo loves the land, and the feel for western geography that Aaron has absorbed from him is reinforced by Lisa. In fact, it is reverence for the land that links past and present in Aaron's perpetual West: "we came west, hand carrying our remaining faith in the future of the species, to work for the Apaches who were trying to reacquire ancestral lands" (18). No one in *Rattlesnake* demonstrates such awareness of the land. This spiritual, "almost religious" response to the land is one quality that John R. Milton cites when distinguishing between the western (an inferior, formulaic exploitation of the West) and the Western (a higher literary product, capable of dealing with character and "several kinds of reality").[7] The existence of love of the land in Laredo's mythology indicates both the range of elements possible in popular-culture images of the West and Aaron's instinct for adhering to life-affirming rather than to violent elements of the myth.

Aaron's relationship with Lisa provides two other clear examples of the way in which—instead of attempting to shape his life to the myth—he preserves only those portions of the myth that match his own priorities. For decades now, commentators have noted that the myth of the Old West, in which "space and isolation become basic themes . . . is especially damaging to writing about ordinary women's lives, since community rather than individualism was basic to them."[8] Blanche Gelfant points out that "just as the West held the promise of innocence, so also it promised manhood. It defined the terms for manhood by its ritual, which, in the American novel, might be modified in its details, but never in its exclusion of women. The young hero going West was to leave all women behind." Females are not only an encumbrance, but a reminder of the feminine side of men's natures, a side they can no longer endure as they grow up.[9]

Aaron's ability to deal with this myth of the West, which he has absorbed from movie after movie, depends in large part on his ability to analyze it in terms very close to those used by such recent commentators. In describing the Laredo Kid's "other identity"—the protective identity Laredo assumes when he is not wearing a mask and saving gals—Aaron notes, "You always played a mild-mannered drifter who was ineffectual and damned with a sensitivity we now associate with femininity. You just didn't address the fact that was your female side."

"That was just *pretend*," protests Laredo. "That wasn't me. Me was the guy who put on the black duds and mask and rode a white horse to the gal's rescue" (49–50). Aaron is not convinced.

> I lurched into adolescence steeped in the male-male and the male-horse relationship. . . . And shallow dipstick that I was, I failed to comprehend the obdurate indifference all you guys displayed toward women . . . they scared the crap out of you. All you "kids." The Durango Kid, Ringo Kid. Cisco, Sundance, Billy *the* Kid. The Laredo and Majestic Kids. Little boys scared to death of having to meet a woman face to face and deal with her not as a *gal*, but as a woman, and protected from her by a hundred and nine scripts with the same plot. (62)

"I'm not a man. I'm just an aging boy adapting badly to a world run amok," Aaron realizes (57). Realizing this, however, he moves to change.

Lisa has pointed out the limits of the myth perpetuated by Westerns:

> The movie makes the woman capable as the dickens . . . but too dumb to recognize that the mild-mannered drifter is really the hero in the mask and black duds. . . . That way they won't have to get married. . . . what would be a tad more useful today would be: They get married and have children, and you have a series of movies about a family facing the challenges of ranch life together. (28)

And gradually Aaron is brought to realize he wants neither to rescue Lisa nor to be rescued *by* her, but to develop a shared relationship. From this shared relationship, he hopes, will develop a family, and from that "a sense of community, of something larger than any of us" (40–41). Thus he specifically rejects two major elements of the myth, womanlessness and individualism, opting instead for family and community.

Battered against the limits of what he has learned from Laredo, bewildered by the failure of the myth to match the reality, Aaron loses his temper and yells his most serious charge against his old mentor: "Stop talking to me about cowboy movies! This is my real life!" (53). Laredo and his values, however, are not defeated.

> *What I stand fer ain't important no more—that whut yore saying? Cuz yore gonna be thirty years old, preservation a the land, right'n wrong, doin unto others what you'd have them do unto you ain't important no more? THAT WHUT YORE SAYIN TO LAREDO?* . . . No. Course it ain't. Cain't be. Was, there wouldn't be no hope fer no one nowhere in this public. (53)

In the end Aaron decides that Laredo is just as correct about basic values as he is incorrect about language and women. When Aaron makes his final—nonviolent—stand, he makes it because of his commitment to the basic values of Laredo's world. "I'm just not interested in living in a world where people behave like this" (67), he says firmly, and goes from there.

Thus Aaron never really abandons the Laredo Kid. He can hang onto the mentor of his youth because he recognizes Laredo's mythic, fictional character. For Aaron, Laredo is not a guide to achieving manhood, but a myth that posits an ideal shape for the world. The separation of myth and reality is emphasized by Laredo's constant reading of scripts, and by his advocacy of movie "thocks" and quick-finger draws rather than actual violence. This myth is not a reflection of reality (past or present), then, but a wish that reality were as simple as white hats and black hats. Because he recognizes Laredo as myth, rather than guidebook, Aaron can learn from him and adapt what is valuable in the myth to guide his life in the New West.

Early in the play, Aaron confesses to Laredo that he has "grown so far away from the example you set." "Grown away from faith in justice and redemption, from love of the land?" replies Laredo. "Ut—yore teasin' your Laredo, you l'il dickens, you" (9). And, of course, eventually Aaron discovers that Laredo is correct. Aaron may have grown away from love of horses and independence and toward love of Lisa and the family circle. He may have been forced to abandon his conviction that the hero always rescues the gal and that good and evil are easily distinguishable. But he has not lost his commitment to justice and redemption and love of the land. Those values may be difficult to pursue; the world may be so complicated that he cannot even be sure particular actions will yield the desired goals; but Aaron still believes in the bedrock of Laredo's commitment to shaping a better world. It is that basic commitment that finally gives Aaron the confidence to "wing it" in a world ungoverned by scriptwriters.

Aaron learns from a great many factors in this play. He learns from Lisa, and from the judge, and from the experience of New Mexico itself, and from his own instincts. What he learns from the forces of the New West, however, though it will modify the lessons of the silver screen myth, will not totally destroy that myth. Finally, it is because Aaron recognizes that it is a myth that he can preserve what he continues to value about the shape it attempts to impose on the world, letting the rest go. At the end of the play, as Laredo heads off into the sunset, Aaron—repeating an old game of theirs—beats Laredo to the draw for the first time, getting his shooting finger in the air before Laredo gets his six-shooter out of the holster. It is Aaron's final coming of age, one that would have been far more difficult had he not learned much of value from Laredo.

What Aaron recognizes and South's doctor does not is that myths do not reflect reality. As Richard Slotkin explains it, "Myths are stories, drawn from history . . . and through periodic retellings those narratives become traditionalized . . . increasingly conventionalized and abstracted."[10] Myths project "models of good or heroic behavior that reinforce the values of ideology."[11] Rather than realism, then, the goal of myth is didacticism—the embodiment of values and modeling of ideal behavior. An attempt to "read" myths realistically is doomed to failure, since they lack the ambiguity of real life. An attempt to follow their pattern precisely leads only to disaster, since the pattern lacks the flexibility necessary for modification in response to changing circumstances. His vision shaped by the myth, South's doctor cannot see the real West and does not understand why the guidebook will not work. He accepts without question the ideology embodied in the western myth's metaphors, using an abstract vision of the past to guide his present concrete behavior. Aaron, on the other hand, with Lisa's help, analyzes the myth and its ideology, occasionally arguing with both. To use the currently popular term, Aaron "rehistoricizes" the myth and is thus able to abandon those portions that do not fit him or the New West, and pursue the values he continues to respect.

Further, he understands that—the world being more complicated than the myth—there is no guarantee he will succeed in achieving his goals, even if he adopts more flexible methods than Laredo's. Without commitment to good over evil, and to the land, however, life seems worth little to Aaron, and so the myth has served its purpose and provided a clearer sense of direction than he would otherwise have had. Like Robert Athearn, he recognizes that "though the legend can bring out many of our weaknesses, it more often speaks to the best in us and reminds us that we can be better than we are."[12]

Medoff has defined the function of myth—which he sees as one means for providing continuity, linking past, present, and future—in terms that closely parallel Athearn's.

> I want [my children] to have what I had—the luxury of bearing a mythology out of the past into the present which they can respect, a tradition of heroism to which they can aspire, from which they can take hope in the present and conjure a future worth living.... What Laredo taught Aaron has to be discarded, but adapted for a new age, a new manhood.[13]

Aaron's success in making the transition to a new age and manhood is not without ironies. If Leslie Fiedler is correct that "the Western story in archetypal form is...a fiction dealing with the confrontation in the wilderness of a transplanted WASP and a radically alien other, an Indian,"[14] then Aaron's Jewishness separates him from an archetype that he otherwise matches quite nicely. But if we remember that an important characteristic of this mythic western hero is his ability "to solve...problems in an innovative manner, while never surrendering an uncritical faith in a better tomorrow,"[15] then there are ways in which Aaron adheres *more*, not *less*, closely to the myth than does South's doctor, who is so locked within the patterns projected by popular culture that he cannot free himself to innovate.

Primarily, however, Aaron succeeds (not as a hero, but as a person) because he is a better reader of myth. He can deal with the conflict of myth and reality because he recognizes that the purpose of myth is not to reflect reality but to model behavior. He balances emotional attraction to the myth with intelligent analysis of it and so—like all good readers everywhere—he comes to fuller understanding and appreciation of both the fiction and the reality.

Notes

1. Robert G. Athearn, *The Mythic West in Twentieth-Century America* (Lawrence: University Press of Kansas, 1986), 23.

2. Ibid., 63.

3. Quoted in John R. Milton, *The Novel of the American West* (Lincoln: University of Nebraska Press, 1980), 41.

4. Mark Medoff, *The Majestic Kid* (New York: Dramatists Play Service, 1986), 3. Subsequent references to this text are given in parentheses.

5. Frank South, *Rattlesnake in a Cooler*. Typescript from Bret Adams (agent): New York, 1981, 2. Subsequent references to this text are given in parentheses.

6. Ray Allen Billington, *Land of Savagery, Land of Promise: The European Image of the American Frontier in the Nineteenth Century* (New York: W. W. Norton, 1981), 314.

7. Milton, *The Novel of the American West*, xiii.

8. June Underwood, "The Civilizers: Women's Organizations and Western American Literature," in *Women and Western American Literature*, ed. Helen Winter Stauffer and Susan J. Rosowski (Troy, N.Y.: Whitston, 1982), 9.

9. Blanche H. Gelfant, "Reconsideration," *New Republic*, May 10, 1975, 22.

10. Richard Slotkin, *The Fatal Environment: The Myth of the Frontier in the Age of Industrialization, 1800–1890* (New York: Atheneum, 1985), 16.

11. Ibid., 19.

12. Athearn, *The Mythic West*, 274.

13. Mark Medoff, "Adiós, Old West," lecture at Boise State University, Boise, Idaho, Feb. 25, 1988.

14. Leslie A. Fiedler, *The Return of the Vanishing American* (New York: Stein and Day, 1968), 24.

15. Athearn, *The Mythic West*, 50.

Bibliography

Athearn, Robert G. *The Mythic West in Twentieth-Century America*. Lawrence: University Press of Kansas, 1986.

Billington, Ray Allen. *Land of Savagery, Land of Promise: The European Image of the American Frontier in the Nineteenth Century*. New York: W. W. Norton, 1981.

Fiedler, Leslie A. *The Return of the Vanishing American*. New York: Stein and Day, 1968.

Gelfant, Blanche H. "Reconsideration." *New Republic*. May 10, 1975: 20–26.

Medoff, Mark. "Adiós, Old West." Lecture at Boise State University, Boise, Idaho, Feb. 25, 1988.

———. *The Majestic Kid*. New York: Dramatists Play Service, 1986.

Milton, John R. *The Novel of the American West*. Lincoln: University of Nebraska Press, 1980.

Slotkin, Richard. *The Fatal Environment: The Myth of the Frontier in the Age of Industrialization, 1800–1890*. New York: Atheneum, 1985.

South, Frank. *Rattlesnake in a Cooler*. Typescript from Bret Adams (agent): New York, 1981. South's play is not in print. The typescript differs at some points from the Robert Altman production (ABC Video Enterprises, 1982). When variations exist, I have relied on the typescript.

Underwood, June. "The Civilizers: Women's Organizations and Western American Literature." In *Women and Western American Literature*, edited by Helen Winter Stauffer and Susan J. Rosowski, 3–16. Troy, N.Y.: Whitston, 1982.

14. Stone-Eyed Griffons: Mythology in Contemporary Montana Fiction

Nathaniel Lewis

There is a motto: Montana Is What America Was. This sort of expression is common enough, found on T-shirts and bumper stickers in many western states. The intended meaning is clear: Montana is the last frontier of...the western landscape, the pioneer spirit, individual liberties, and, too often, the last home of vigilante justice, where "a man can be a man," and so on. In its way, the phrase is a striking one, even an exciting one, yet the problems inherent in such thinking are enormous. For one thing, as soon as this commercialized jingoism occurs, we can be sure that Montana is no longer in that pristine condition. More disturbing, though, are the subtle uneasiness and anxiety dormant in such a statement: it seems as much aimed at convincing native Montanans of their own situation as it is directed at nonwestern tourists. The speaker of the motto looks backward, not forward, and stands eye level with an idealized perception of a western past. That ideal is blatantly historicized and nostalgic, woefully idealistic (as if those historical imaginings ever existed), and intellectually dishonest. It seeks to honor a "culture that...never quite existed," in a phrase from Mary Clearman Blew. The concern is as much with a national perception of a mythic past as with a limited perception of a mythic present.

This evaluation is perhaps rather obvious, for the idea of a western art as well as the hopes for Rocky Mountain tourism have traditionally been centered on "the myth of The Western: gunslingers and settlers and savages, invading armies and law-bringing," as William

Kittredge writes in his masterful collection of essays, *Owning It All*.[2] Western artists have been looking backward and responding to their own history, even while being suspicious of that history. Again, William Kittredge: "The myth has been an insidious trap for those who would write about the American West, a box for the imagination. For a long time it was as if there was only one legitimate story to tell about the West, and that was the mythological story."[3] Kittredge knows what he is talking about, being both artist and critic, and one of the central figures in the blossoming group of Montana writers.[4] These men and women are part of an emerging set of western writers who have begun to challenge the mythological delusions with a vengeance, filled with resentment toward the weight of public perceptions and expectations. In his essay "Doors to Our House," Kittredge considers the need for a western writing that is "antimythological,"[5] that runs "clear of mythic and legendary cobwebs," that sees "straight to the actual."[6] The exhortation is both bold and practical, and the meaning self-evident.

As a call for a "realistic" representation of modern western landscape and society, the idea appears worthy of high appreciation and enactment but, as Kittredge himself immediately reflects, "sometimes you have to wonder about that. As a friend of mine says, 'I ask for truth, and what do I get? Candor.' "[7] Kittredge suggests that candor can be "part of the impulse to see straight to the . . . heart of things," but it can also be meaningless violence and despair, "only hearts torn apart while we watch."[8] In other words candor can be helpful in overturning the old sentimental myths, but it does not necessarily lead to any insight into the elusive contemporary "actual." In response to Kittredge, author David Long incisively asks, "what *is* the actual in our time? Wilderness or clearcut? Amber waves of grain or Minuteman silos?"[9] Indeed, images of missile silos, ugly land development, and mined-out mountainsides are every bit as "mythological" as cowboys and Indians, equally vulnerable to various readings and interpretations. The question of what is "actual" or "true" in the New West cannot be answered by writing; language is metaphorical and not designed to *be* or even represent that "actual," but always to create new fictions. The West, like any region, will always be the product of myth. ("Life imitates Art," declared Oscar Wilde.) What western art needs then is not an "antimythological" writing, but the creation of a *new* mythology, or a set of new mythologies. And I believe that ultimately this is Kittredge's point: western writers need to reinvent and rewrite the West through imaginative fiction. "In the American West we are struggling to revise our dominant mythology," Kittredge states, "and to find a new story to inhabit."[10]

The Montana writers are progressing toward that new, revised story, that new mythology. David Long remarks that "in the place of those received and unreliable myths about the West, artists are offering up personal mythologies."[11] I do not take that "personal" to imply a writing (or other art form) limited to personal understanding or personal significance, but rather a new set of common and vital mythologies expressed through an individual's vision: personal experience raised to cultural mythology. The creation of myth might be thought of as the struggle to make language a renewed and active force, to produce images that are thought to contain that "actual." In speaking of the creation of myth, I have in mind the process by which individual writers—and as I am suggesting, a cluster of contemporary Montana writers—press the particular and concrete toward the general and abstract, while always hanging on to the particular. When a number of geographically related writers perform in this way, the result is a sort of regional mythology: that is, a mythology arising from general cultural conditions and attitudes and beliefs.[12]

These authors are consequently both myth destroyers and myth creators. They twist and distort the outdated, "unreliable" myths until they shed their old associations; the writers use a style both strong and direct, with the uncanny effect of staring down a reader, of daring anyone to watch the carnage. But they also arrive at new and startling images: through the most visceral and sentient language, operating in a spectacularly visual landscape with concrete, rugged, often violent prose, these men and women are creating symbols—symbolic actions—that help form our emerging perception of today's West. In the end, this form of symbolization is dramatic, challenging, communicative. David Long accurately sees in the contemporary Montana art a point where "autobiography and metaphor merge," where specific individual accounts are lifted into the realm of collective myth.[13] Kittredge, who is always sensitive to how his own autobiographical narrative "keeps becoming fiction,"[14] writes that "stories are valuable precisely to the degree that they are for the moment useful in our ongoing task of finding coherency in the world."[15] These writers have pushed their language to the point that experience becomes raised to symbolic action, images raised to new and explosive signification, the concrete bridged into the abstract. The result is that their stories, images, language, literature—all become myth, a new western myth.

The phrase "symbolic action," used above, will remind most readers of the critical vocabulary of Kenneth Burke, and indeed Burke's essay, "The Philosophy of Literary Form," suggests a pattern of poetic action and symbolization that illuminates the achievement of these Montana writers. Although this essay uses only his model—this is not a paper on Burke or his ideas—an early line from his essay stands out as a response to that motto, Montana Is What America Was. Burke writes, "critical and imaginative works are answers to questions posed by the situation in which they arose. They are not merely answers, they are *strategic* answers, *stylized* answers."[16] We might say that these writers are doing just that: responding with strategic answers to their historical situation, taking apart old myths, and thus simultaneously posing new questions for the future.

Burke posits that a rhetorical strategy, a piece of writing, in fact "any verbal act," is a "symbolic action."[17] He continues by identifying three levels of symbolic action: (1) the bodily or physical level, which includes sensory and natural imagery; (2) the "personal, intimate, familiar, familistic level," which often seems to suggest relationships and social structures; and (3) the abstract level.[18]

Burke's first level of symbolic action is that of the physical, that of "kinaesthetic," muscular imagery. His examples are instructive: "gripping, repelling, eating, [and] excreting."[19] Perhaps the most immediately striking characteristic of the Montana writers is the physical, naturalistic, carnal nature of their work. The vast, often hostile landscape of the Northern Rockies serves as an appropriately intimidating physical setting, although these writers evoke a similar power of place from many western regions, including California, the American Southwest, and Mexico. The main focus, however, falls on the all-too-human characters of each story: interaction with the land, sexual relations, and graphic violence are all central forms of action, and rarely independent of one another. The authors choose a language that echoes this rough, physical level: clean, rugged, unadorned, and usually unmetaphorical; the Montana writers shoot with precise aim, straight and accurate. The difficulty for the narrators and characters lies in determining what the proper rules are concerning the physical, for the traditional structures of interpretation have failed. Patricia Henley, for example, in her collection *Friday*

Night at Silver Star, examines the ambiguous and confusing sexual and social rules that exist for her characters. As one character says in response to a painful but therapeutic massage, "don't stop. If it hurts, it's good."[20]

At the heart of much Montana writing is a violence of one sort or another, though frequently it is merely threatening or inchoate. Even when only an allusion, though, the violence is consistently brutal, ugly, and described in nauseatingly precise detail. Worst of all, it seems to be random and without meaning; unlike the violence of the Old West, romantically remembered as a pioneering ("civilizing") necessity, the modern violence fails to bring productive order or understanding to the characters' world. Often the violence is reflected in the harsh landscape, but just as often it is associated with sexual imagery, until the lines of delineation between the violent and the sexual become indistinct. This is epitomized in Jim Harrison's long story "Revenge," a tale of unsettling physical retribution that takes place in Mexico.[21] A betrayed husband breaks in on his adulterous wife and her lover as they lie in bed; Cochran, the unfortunate discovered man, is forced to watch while his lover's lips are sliced with a razor, "the pimp's ancient revenge for a wayward girl." Then the woman's eyes are pried open and she is compelled to view her lover, Cochran, being kicked in the groin. We soon learn that the woman is later forced into a heroin stupor and brought to a public brothel where she is repeatedly raped, while the man is left in the open to die, "his testicles inflated from [the] groining."[22]

Notable here is not only the mingling of violent and sexual imagery, but the fact that both of the lovers, as well as the reader, are compelled to watch the brutality, which is dispassionately described. Harrison even warns us to be prepared, although he suggests that we, too, are obliged to watch. As he wickedly phrases it, "let us perch on the log mantel, an impassive stone-eyed griffon, for it is best to have stone eyes for what we are going to see."[23] There is a challenge implicit in these words, a sort of staring contest in which the reader must gaze, too closely and too long, onto the scene of the savagery.

A good deal of the physical foundation of the Montana writings results in this sort of intimidation of both character and reader, a warning that things may get ugly, and that each individual is always isolated in the watching. The landscape, which at one literary time might have been sublime and transcendent, now either dwarfs and frightens, or depresses with its hard and ragged look. Sexual intimacy more often leads to emptiness and sadness than to satisfaction or communication, to lonely lust rather than love. Violence is disruptive, random, sudden, alienating. Over and over, a character—and, by being forced into close visual proximity, the reader—is left alone to make sense of all the activity. Each story abandons its reader, who must interpret the world, sort through the images, grope with past and present situations: the reader is left alone to attempt an understanding of the text of the new, confusing, unfamiliar set of mythologies.

The Montana writers challenge the reader in a decidedly personal manner, thus elevating each work to the second level of symbolic action, the familistic, personal level. The authors thrive on this level, both by establishing an intimacy with the reader, and by returning over and over to the power of the western family. Yet although the sense of family and community strongly influences each story, the happy, tightly knit clan of the American imagination does not live here. One finds, rather, an unpleasant duality in the family's emotional effect. On the one hand, there is an inescapable "connectedness" about the family structure: each person is bound to the acts and sorrows of the others. On the other hand, to echo one of William Kittredge's titles, "we are not in this together." In other words, there seems to be no escape from the pain and anxiety of the family network, but neither does there seem to exist any permanent support or compensating human communication.

This idea is played out to different effects with different emphases by these writers, but one image is representative. In David Quammen's story "Walking Out," a young boy sets forth on an uncomfortable hunting trip with his father. Both become badly, gruesomely, wounded—bears and guns—but it is left to the boy to carry his delirious father out of the wilderness. After a wrenching journey through the snow and storm, he arrives at a cabin, only to be told that his father, whom he has been struggling to deliver, has been dead for at least a day. Although his assertion is questionable, the boy responds, "I know that."[24] The picture of a desperate, wounded boy lugging his dead father for miles, perhaps knowing the man is already dead, conveys the plight of each individual weighed down by a lifeless yet inescapable family. By extension, the image also suggests that each individual carries a heavy and useless past, one that cannot be thrown off yet has ceased to engender any life. If Quammen is alluding to Virgil's Aeneas carrying his ailing father Anchises from burning Troy, then he's making an ironic comparison—the classical idea of a valuable and necessary past contrasts markedly with the implied modern notion of an unusable one.

Similarly, both of the mid-1970s, Montana classics—Norman Maclean's *A River Runs through It* and Ivan Doig's *This House of Sky*—revolve around the theme of family and the suffering seemingly inherent in the family structure. Yet these books incorporate an internal sense of transcendence that overcomes the anguish of painful memory. We feel exhilaration at the authors' literary abilities—though perhaps Maclean's novella is equally unnerving in its evocative power and emotion. To many later writers, however, the impact of the family is more openly enervating and frightening, and the love is often hollow or disastrous; one might say that these stories are haunted by family.

In fact, almost all the Montana writers at one point or another describe familial troubles in intimate detail. Of course the theme is hardly unique to Montana writing (one immediately thinks of much southern literature, for example), but the dichotomy between individual isolation and debilitating kindred attachment seems significantly pervasive in these stories. James Crumley's detective Milo and his deceased father spring to mind, as do Lucien Taylor's unique household in Thomas McGuane's novel *Something to Be Desired,* the struggling group in James Welch's *Winter in the Blood,* the Ludlow clan in Harrison's "Legends of the Fall," the crazed family in William Kittredge's "The Soap Bear," and so on. To that group of sad kindred relations Rick Bass has recently added a memorable short story titled "Choteau," named in part for the Montana town known for its prison. The story ostensibly has nothing to do with blood ties, but rather with hunting and the wild, fantastic character of Galena Jim Ontz. Although most of the story is told in an amusing, exaggerated, almost dreamlike voice, the entire tone is changed by the revelation that Galena Jim "has a son, Buck, nineteen years old, who is in the state prison in Choteau, a lifer, maximum security, for killing a man. Buck is his son from a long-ago marriage, his only son. . . . Jim doesn't talk about it much. Usually he just talks around the edges, like: 'Wonder what Ol' Buck's doing tonight?' or something like that."[25] The words radically change the emotional direction of the tale, as well as offer a clue to the significance of the title. What had been a type of adventure narrative becomes instead the story of a man's loss and confusion.

Usually, as in "Choteau," a single troubled family member symbolizes the destructive influence of family, an "other" character whose spirit invades the story. Sometimes, though, this relationship is reversed, and it is the narrator who causes the family pain, knowingly or not. A mentally unstable, unreliable narrator from Mary Clearman Blew gives this chilling description of his family and the "authoritarian figures of [his] childhood": "all children stand in the shadows of giants. My particular giants, my parents, were ordinary farm people. I am the younger of two brothers. My brother, Miles, still farms the old ground. He and I remain on good, if remote, terms. My father is dead, my mother senile."[26] In this short passage, the progression from conventional family history to unhappy personal disclosure surprises the reader: it begins on comfortable, common ground ("all children," "ordinary farm people"), hints at an unpleasant side ("good, if remote"), and finishes with the simple but disconcerting facts about the narrator's parents.

These Montana stories convey a grim feeling of familial emotion, and are effective because they are told in a deeply personal, intimate manner. While this emotional violence is akin to the physical violence, here the effect is much more subtle and delicate—and much more unsettling. We as readers may not want to know quite so much about an obviously doomed marriage or slowly dying father, may even resent an author for the clear, awful vision of human families torn apart. In Jim Harrison's "Legends of the Fall," for example, the emotional violence visited upon the Ludlow family is far greater than the physical violence to any individual character. The patriarch Ludlow, after sending his three sons to war, feels grave doubts and presentiments and, in what must be a last, desperate form of Montana prayer, realizes that "he would have gladly given his ranch to have even one son back."[27] As is so often the case, the reader must watch too closely as decaying family structures create pain and misery, the account being told in an uncomfortably personal voice.

Richard Ford's stories in *Rock Springs* succeed in exactly this way, in part because they are among the most consciously "told" of these writings. There is a sustained suggestion that he, or rather each narrator, is telling something very private that needs to be revealed; the reader, willingly or not, subsequently becomes part of the story, a present and necessary audience. The tone is familiar, informal, intimate, as if we are looking too deeply into the narrator's eyes while he speaks. Nearly every story in *Rock Springs* opens with a first-person narrative voice letting us into its private circle. "This is not a happy story. I warn you," begins "Great Falls," and the shadow cast by these words hangs over the entire story.[28] The threat is similar to that made by the narrator of another literary Ford, Ford Madox Ford, who cautions that *his* tale (*The Good Soldier*) "is the saddest story I have ever heard." The effect of Richard Ford's balanced sentence—"I warn you"—is stunning and ominous. The narrator demands that each reader be present for the kill, be close to the disintegrating family. Another Ford story opens with this long expository sentence: "All of this that I am about to tell happened when I was only fifteen years old, in 1959, the year my parents were divorced, the year when my father killed a man and went to prison for it, the year I left home and school, told a lie about my age to fool the Army, and then did not come back."[29] In effect the story has just been told, and there is no turning back for the reader who can only continue listening for the sad details, perhaps with the slim hope that the title, "Optimists," is not merely sarcastic or bitter.

Ford's rhetoric draws the reader into each tale, makes the reader feel at once present and alone. There is no doubt after a while that these stories are as much about the reader, as much about anyone who chances upon them, as they are about a specific character. It is the reader who is forced into consciously interpreting the text. This is made clear in the closing paragraph of Ford's title story, "Rock Springs." The narrator, Earl, is running from the law with his girlfriend Edna and his daughter, reaching the end of an exhausting day in which his life is giving every indication of falling apart. After being told by Edna that she is leaving him and realizing that only harder times lie ahead, he walks out to the motel parking lot intending to steal a car. Looking into the back of a Pontiac, he ends the story this way:

> I had a funny sensation at that moment and turned and looked up at the windows along the back of the motel. All were dark except two. Mine and another one. And I wondered, because it seemed funny, what would you think a man was doing if you saw him in the middle of the night looking in the windows of cars in the parking lot of the Ramada Inn? Would you think he was trying to get his head cleared? Would you think he was trying to get ready for a day when trouble would come down on

him? Would you think his girlfriend was leaving him? Would you think he had a daughter? Would you think he was anybody like you?[30]

Ford's strategy is a spinning breakdown of character delineation. He turns on the reader, forcing that reader into the story by avoiding a straightforward ending, and instead firing a series of personal questions. In essence, the reader is placed behind that other light in the motel room next to Earl's own, watching the action and then being forced into making judgment on that action. The development is deft and impressive: subtly Ford himself, or perhaps a new, critical voice, has entered the scene, for it is not Earl, the story's narrator, who is asking these intrusive questions. The "I" of Earl is now replaced by the "he," standing for both Earl and that rhetorically imagined, anonymous man in the parking lot. It is as if in midparagraph the story ended with Earl peering through cars; and, as in a frightening, nightmare college textbook, personal and dangerous study questions have been added after the text. The reader stands beside the cold narrative voice considering what to make of the scene, how to interpret the signs, how to read the mythology. Finally, in a cruel twist, the reader is forced back into the story by being asked whether Earl is anybody like him or her. The answer is ambiguous, for few would at first empathize with the amoral, bad-luck car thief Earl; yet the question pulls out the rug, and each reader is left alone and confused.

The effect of this non-ending is a leap from the motel room and parking lot into the realm of literary reflection, a move beyond the fictionally specific place and time into a metaphysical dimension. This is the third level of symbolic action, the abstract level, a level that emerges from the first two levels. Perhaps this level marks the separation of mere candor from the truth, to return to William Kittredge's terms. That is, while candor can be mired in "our nostalgia for the old days,"[31] these writers have dislocated the present from the past. They offer no simple truth, of course, but by demolishing the comfortable and false old myths, and by creating unfamiliar new ones, they force each reader to stand alone and wide-eyed, gazing on the pain of physical existence and confronting a new, frightening world.

Each writer in his or her way conducts a struggle with the kind of language and literature that seems doomed to perpetually recreate a false past. Montana Is What America Was. An individual who accepts this thinking is involved in an artificial re-creation of that past

and in misreading the present. On a literary level, this misprision results in a pathetic and harmful delusion, what Paul de Man in his own
critical context termed the self-mystification of the self in crisis. These
writers are fighting off that need to escape into self-mystification: first
by the shock of random physical violence, then by painful family and
personal exposition, and finally by a brutal literary re-creation. And,
again, the reader is forced into facing the same interpretive difficulties: contemporary Montana fiction is hardly escapist literature.

Ultimately, the state of Montana acts as the stage, the physical setting for the works, and this is a central theme: the concrete, physical
world is never completely shed. But the glare of the modern human
crisis is not limited to Montana: the abstract world is not limited to
any road map. While the landscape is western, and the new regional
mythology is western, the Montana writers finally reach toward a national consciousness. At the abstract level, their concerns with language and self-mystification make demands on us all, wherever we
live. Through careful if sometimes agonizing readings of the Montana
texts, we come to both a new understanding of today's West and also
a revised vision of today's America. By writing these mythologies not
only for their own state and the evolving West but for the entire country, contemporary Montana authors are ahead of their time, creating
the literature that will someday be called the new mythology of the
Modern. In this sense, Montana Is What America Will Become.

Notes

1. Mary Clearman Blew, *Lambing Out and Other Stories* (Columbia: University of Missouri Press, 1977), 20.

2. William Kittredge, *Owning It All* (St. Paul, Minn.: Graywolf Press, 1987),
170.

3. Ibid., 171.

4. The list of fiction writers includes Rick Bass, Mary Clearman Blew, James
Crumley, Rick DeMarinis, Ivan Doig, Richard Ford, Patricia Henley, David
Long, Norman Maclean, Thomas McGuane, David Quammen, James Welch,
and many more. The phrase "Montana writers" is a felicitously liberal one and
encompasses writers born in Montana, writers who have lived in Montana, and
even writers who have only used the state as a stage for their work. A few helpful
introductions to Montana's recent literary history are William Kittredge's essay
collection *Owning It All*, and specifically "Doors to Our House"; Kittredge and

Annick Smith's Montana anthology *The Last Best Place;* and Christy Porter's review essay, "Bright Lights, No City," in the *Los Angeles Times,* Mar. 19, 1989, pt. VI.

5. Kittredge, *Owning It All,* 171.

6. Ibid., 177.

7. Ibid.

8. Ibid., 178.

9. David Long, "Straight to the Actual," in *Montana Spaces,* ed. William Kittredge (New York: Nick Lyons Books, 1988), 173.

10. Kittredge, *Owning It All,* 64.

11. Long, "Straight to the Actual," 174.

12. The Montana writers are keenly aware of how fiction works to create a regional mythology, of course, and this self-awareness can lead to some very amusing reflections. As Thomas McGuane wryly comments: "It always made me very suspicious that *no one* from Yoknapatawpha ever went to Miami. Faulkner certainly left no stone unturned for himself; but the denizens of his books he locks up in this morbid Cloud-Cuckoo-Land where everybody has mule trouble while the author rides up and down Sunset Strip in a convertible." But McGuane doesn't entirely let himself off the hook, either, admitting with an implicit wink that "I like to gesture at the cloverleaf ramps and exclaim, 'The earth is good, Pablo.' And like a lot of other ropers, I like to get a leetle loaded and rope horned cattle" (*An Outside Chance* [New York: Penguin, 1982], 221).

13. Long, "Straight to the Actual," 174.

14. Kittredge, *Owning It All,* 18.

15. Ibid., 19.

16. Kenneth Burke, *The Philosophy of Literary Form* (1941; reprint, Berkeley: University of California Press, 1973), 1.

17. Ibid., 8.

18. Ibid., 36–37.

19. Ibid., 36.

20. Patricia Henley, *Friday Night at Silver Star* (St. Paul, Minn.: Graywolf Press, 1986), 63.

21. Although Jim Harrison does not live in Montana, he may be loosely considered a Montana writer by association, being a regular visitor to the state, friends with several Montana writers, and the author of a celebrated Montana story, "Legends of the Fall." "Revenge" is one of three stories (along with "The Man Who Gave up His Name" and "Legends of the Fall") included in the collection titled *Legends of the Fall* (New York: Delacorte, 1979). Strictly speaking, "Revenge" is not a Montana story, but because it is firmly linked to the Montanan "Legends of the Fall," and because the story so clearly represents a major motif in Montana writing, I have decided to include it for discussion. For a lively article on Harrison and his friends, Thomas McGuane, Guy de la Valdène, and Russell Chatham, see Jim Fergus, "The Sporting Club," *Outside Magazine,* Mar. 1989, 40.

22. Harrison, *Legends*, 34, 4.

23. Ibid., 33.

24. David Quammen, "Walking Out," in *Blood Line* (St. Paul, Minn.: Graywolf Press, 1988), 41.

25. Rick Bass, "Choteau," in *The Watch* (New York: Norton, 1989), 43.

26. Mary Clearman Blew, "Forby and the Mayan Maidens," in *The Last Best Place*, ed. William Kittredge and Annick Smith (Helena: Montana Historical Society Press, 1988), 886.

27. Harrison, *Legends*, 213.

28. Richard Ford, *Rock Springs* (New York: Atlantic Monthly Press, 1987), 29.

29. Ibid., 171.

30. Ibid., 26–27.

31. Kittredge, *Owning It All*, 178.

Bibliography

Bass, Rick. "Choteau." In *The Watch*, 34–47. New York: Norton, 1989.

Blew, Mary Clearman. "Forby and the Mayan Maidens." In *The Last Best Place*, edited by William Kittredge and Annick Smith, 886–98. Helena: Montana Historical Society Press, 1988.

———. *Lambing Out and Other Stories*. Columbia: University of Missouri Press, 1977.

Burke, Kenneth. *The Philosophy of Literary Form*. 1941. Reprint. Berkeley: University of California Press, 1973.

Doig, Ivan. *This House of Sky*. New York: Harcourt Brace Jovanovich, 1978.

Fergus, Jim. "The Sporting Club." *Outside Magazine*, Mar. 1989, 40.

Ford, Richard. *Rock Springs*. New York: Atlantic Monthly Press, 1987.

Harrison, Jim. *Legends of the Fall*. New York: Delacorte, 1979.

Henley, Patricia. *Friday Night at Silver Star*. St. Paul, Minn.: Graywolf Press, 1986.

Kittredge, William. *Owning It All*. St. Paul, Minn: Graywolf Press, 1987.

———. "The Soap Bear." In *We Are Not in This Together*, 37–67. Port Townsend, Washington: Graywolf Press, 1984.

———, ed. *Montana Spaces*. New York: Nick Lyons Books, 1988.

Kittredge, William, and Annick Smith, eds. *The Last Best Place*. Helena: Montana Historical Society Press, 1988.

Long, David. "Straight to the Actual." In *Montana Spaces*, edited by William Kittredge, 169–78. New York: Nick Lyons Books, 1988.

Maclean, Norman. *A River Runs through It*. Chicago: University of Chicago Press, 1976.

McGuane, Thomas. *An Outside Chance: Essays on Sport*. New York: Penguin, 1982.

———. *Something to Be Desired.* New York: Random House, 1984.

Porter, Christy. "Bright Lights, No City." *Los Angeles Times,* Mar. 19, 1989, pt. vi.

Quammen, David. "Walking Out." In *Blood Line,* 1–41. St. Paul, Minn.: Graywolf Press, 1988.

Welch, James. *Winter in the Blood.* New York: Harper and Row, 1974.

15. Investment in Place: Thomas McGuane in Montana

Nancy S. Cook

Although Thomas McGuane never has been considered primarily a regional writer, in recent years most of his work has used Montana as its setting. While many writers who are natives of the region struggle to overcome the label "regionalist," McGuane has embraced the region as a resident and has used it as a setting for his fiction. Whether because he writes about the present or because he had achieved some national recognition before taking on the region, McGuane's work has eluded pejorative classification as "western."

Perhaps a contemporary setting allows certain regional books to escape that derogatory term, "western." Gerald Haslam claims, "When western books are set in the present, critics seldom call them western: the national myth allows the West only a past."[1] Though the contemporary setting may have allowed critics to take McGuane's work seriously, they might accurately claim that it *is* western, in the pejorative sense, for it depends upon a mythic notion of a western past. More important, the Old West, as mythic construct, becomes the locus of value for the characters and authorial personae in McGuane's work. Throughout the past decade he has written of the present-day West, but with a profound uneasiness about being at home in it.

McGuane's brand of regionalism doesn't celebrate the modern West, with its rapid growth and urban oases. After noting the "antipathy" Montanans have for "dudes" and "pilgrims," he adds: "Nevertheless, Montana is my home, my adopted home; and anyone who has moved here from somewhere else has had to endure a bit of patronizing. Over the years, though, many local pontiffs have turned in the old homestead for a snappy burger franchise where seldom is heard a discouraging word. *Hold the mayo! Side of fries!* and like that."² McGuane sees himself as the "true" Montanan, eschewing profit, keeping archaic traditions alive, acting as a preservationist. Any attempt by fellow citizens to earn a buck the modern way becomes the object of scorn, for it mars the pastoral scene.³

McGuane's discomfort, I will suggest, derives from nostalgia for a masculine ideal commonly identified as part of the western mythos, as well as from a problematic sense of place. The masculine ideal, says the Western, is place specific. In the West there are places where men can be MEN, or at least there ought to be such places. But for the male western writer, adherence to these beliefs can present problems. In a world where physical prowess and action are valued over verbal acuity and symbolic manipulation, the writer may become his own worst enemy, for the act of writing betrays the virtues he expounds. McGuane tries to resolve this dilemma by delineating an enabling place for his New Westerners. I see these efforts as utopian, for although they are rendered by means of realist conventions, they deny the actual. McGuane depicts a diminished, ruined modern West as a foil to illuminate the potential of the mythic one. Next to an ideal Old West, the New West is doomed to failure, for it never can compare favorably.

McGuane uses Montana as the setting for *Nobody's Angel* (1981), *Something to Be Desired* (1984), several essays in *An Outside Chance* (1980), and more than half of the stories in *To Skin a Cat* (1986). A native of Michigan, he has taken to Montana with the zeal of a convert. He bought a ranch, he learned to rope competitively, he raises, works, and shows his own champion cutting horses, he hunts, he fishes, and he writes about all of these things.

An Outside Chance, a collection of essays on sport, reveals the stake McGuane has in his Montana residency. In "Roping from A to B," he comments on his development from outsider to insider. He takes the reader through his initiation into the world of horses, then into roping, then into competition roping. Along the way, he appropriates western language as well, tracing the etymology of certain roping terms from Spanish through their corruption by westerners and into current usage. For instance, McGuane knows that the 'McCarthy' as it is known in Montana, is really a corruption of the Spanish word *mecate,* a rope "which the Spanish hackamore horsemen wound and tied into reins and lead rope"; and 'dally' is a corruption of *dar la vuelta,* which means "to take a turn, a wrap around the saddle horn with the lariat to stop the creature in question."[4] After defining dally, he adds: "The transposition of *dar la vuelta* into dally is in the great Western tradition of corrupting language into the grunting of the midland yokel who levels the same Mortimer Snerd suspicion upon all human products, but starts with language."[5] McGuane's etymology lesson acts as a kind of reclamation project, restoring to his sport the linguistic richness that the cowhand, or here, "midland yokel," has destroyed.

Words, like people and the land, hold a history and he has learned to manipulate that history as easily as he can gallop across his acreage. For McGuane, the ability to "dally" represents an act of historical preservation, with the rodeo as a kind of folk museum. In this scholarly role, he goes beyond mastery of the event itself to master the discourse of roping. Readers may recognize McGuane's expertise as a roper because he has mastered the language of roping and can render its particularities with precision.

The act of roping becomes McGuane's initiation rite, his way of belonging to a place defined in archaic terms. For him Montana is off-road and open land. As an immigrant, he says, "*I* felt sourceless for sure, born in the Midwest of New England Irish parents, my own son born on the West Coast."[6] Roping becomes a way of grafting himself to a place, a way of acquiring a home, becoming an insider. For him, Montana seems less a place than a set of initiation rites in the Hemingway tradition.

McGuane bears the physical marks of a roper: roughened, even mangled hands. He writes that "there came a day when I couldn't find the saddle horn and broke my thumb in a few places, tearing the end off it." During his subsequent trip to the emergency room, the nurse, also an insider, takes one look, then asks, "Miss your dally?"[7] She signifies that she, too, recognizes both the codifying system and McGuane's position in it. While his dedication to the sport may be impressive, his readers may wonder if there is a greater significance. As if in response, he muses: "Is roping the proper concern of mankind? Let's dust this one off. Roping teaches us about horses, cattle, and eternity. Sherwood Anderson wrote about horses. Not about airplane saboteurs, serial orgasm, or 'L.A. space.' "[8] Roping, then, ties him to a place and to a history. More important, it ties him to a myth, one of a utopian, *eternal* West. Writing about it ties him to a literary history, too, though he selects Anderson as a precursor from among more obvious choices such as Hemingway and Faulkner. Here McGuane situates himself not so much with the Sherwood Anderson of *Winesburg, Ohio,* but with him as author of *Horses and Men,* a lesser-known work about horse racing, that is, within the context of *subject* rather than place. In fact McGuane generally seeks to distinguish himself from authors who are identified with a particular place, or who have been lauded for their portrayal of a place. He clarifies:

> The vulgarity we call the "sense of place" is a fairly nelly sub-instance of schizophrenia, saving up facts, preferably inherited, about locale. It's like when Southerners talk about losing the war; you want to puke. It always made me very suspicious that *no one* from Yoknapatawpha ever went to Miami. Faulkner certainly left no stone unturned for himself; but the denizens of his books he locks up in this morbid Cloud-Cuckoo-Land where everybody has mule trouble while the author rides up and down Sunset Strip in a convertible.[9]

McGuane seems to proclaim his modernity, defining himself in opposition to Faulkner. Yet his work relies on a mythic past as much as Faulkner's does, though not as self-consciously. After having gone to considerable lengths to show Montanans and his readers that he has acquired his facts about locale the hard way, McGuane's resentment of those who simply inherit local color comes as no surprise. But his criticism of Faulkner seems particularly misplaced when we remember Faulkner's books and life: he raised mules and he also was a horseman. Moreover, like Faulkner, McGuane is no stranger to Hollywood. Throughout his career he has worked both as a screenwriter and as a director. For McGuane, the ability of the writer to represent a place, *his* place, is related to his ability to participate in traditional, even archetypal activities tied to that place.[10] In other words, a writer must live authentically. Eschewing Faulkner, McGuane positions himself as a true, though unadmitted, son of "Papa" Hemingway. The writer must live the life in order to write it, and history, even family history, just isn't good enough.[11] It seems as if he must participate in the rituals of manhood rather than in rituals of community. While roping is the putative subject of "Roping from A to B," in it McGuane ponders his role as a writer, as well as his relation to other writers, whether realists, regionalists, or sportswriters.

Throughout, the relation between actor and writer remains entwined. Later in the essay, McGuane affirms his need to feel authentic, as a resident of Montana, over and above his identity as a writer:

> I looked at my hand, crooked thumb, rope burns, enlarged knuckles, and I felt good because I was afraid, as a writer, I would always have these Ivory Snow hands; and, in fact, some cur said I had *writer's hands,* which really got to me, as I am someone who wants to be a rugged guy in the West and not some horrid nancy with pink palms. At the same time, you don't want to be the one roper they call "Flipper." This is just a message to other arty types out there in the Rocky Mountains: roping is a good fast way to acquire local-color hands.[12]

If we read any irony here, we must remember that McGuane claims that he *does* have mangled hands. His irony rests in the notion that roping is a "good fast way to acquire local color," for he writes his essay not to tell the reader how to rope, but to show the unknowledgeable the complexities and dangers of roping. He has passed muster, so in some sense he now represents manhood Montana style. At this point we might recall that mastery also requires language and the writer's tools, for it was McGuane's knowledge of the history of the language of roping that gave him the advantage over the "midland yokels" who corrupted the vaqueros' terms mecate and dar la vuelta. Yet even within the sarcastic statement that he has found a "good fast way to acquire local color," one can sense McGuane's contradictory attitude toward history. If one can acquire authenticity as a westerner the fast way, what's wrong with fast food, or acquiring a western urban style the fast way? McGuane's hands may signify his acquisition of a set of codes that represent the West to some, but they can never signify a western heritage.

Perhaps McGuane's stylistic appropriation of the discourse of the West *poses* an ironic distance, as for example, when he distinguishes himself from other ropers, those "midland yokels" who corrupted the Spanish roping terminology. But the pose is disingenuous. He cannot sustain an ironic stance for he is unable to remain restrained, controlled, or detached: he cannot accept the incongruities within his adopted region or within his own fictional landscape. Rather than irony, what readers get in McGuane's writing is an ironic tone, which allows him to gloss over the contradictions inherent in his writing. In place of irony, McGuane creates paradox. Peter Schwenger describes the problem as it relates to Norman Mailer, but it fits McGuane, too: "His devotion to manhood runs a certain risk of contamination through the act of writing, even when Mailer is writing about manhood. Like any consciously 'manly' writer, his situation is paradoxical: he asserts his manhood in a way that the 'real' man considers unmanly."[13] Although McGuane attempts to negotiate this problem by coaxing the reader to believe that his roping skills make him a better writer, a better rancher, and a better man, in fact, roping simply makes him a better roper. And as is true for Mailer, the very means by which he performs his aggressive one-upmanship, by means of language, becomes suspect according to his own criteria. Therefore the linguistic advantage McGuane may gain over the "midland yokels" can never satisfy. Though his mangled hands may impress the locals at the rodeo, they can never impress the reader except through the vocation that their deformity denies.

McGuane's obsession with authenticity evokes Hemingway's response to a review by Max Eastman, where Eastman labeled Hemingway's writing as belonging to "a literary style, you might say, of wearing false hair on the chest." Meeting Eastman in the offices of Scribner's, Hemingway ripped open his own shirt, revealing a hairy chest, then uncovered Eastman's hairless one, slapped him in the face with the offending review, then tackled him.[14] As proof of his accomplishments as a roper and his authenticity, McGuane's mangled hands stand in for Hemingway's hairy chest.

McGuane's attitude becomes further complicated when we note that the essays in *An Outside Chance* originally appeared in *The Atlantic Monthly, Motor News, Outside, Quest,* and *Sports Illustrated.* None of these publications targets the horseman or the sports specialist, nor do any of them have a particularly large circulation in the Rocky Mountain region.[15] If McGuane writes neither for his neighbors, the fellow inhabitants of his region, nor for fellow horsemen, then he must be writing for the "horrid nancy with pink palms." He offers the uninitiated and the rootless a lesson in dues paying. In the West one can create a new identity for oneself, but must pay for one's new/old roots. Presumably Faulkner never paid his dues because he rested on the roots of his family tree and cruised the "Sunset Strip in a convertible."

While it may be horrid to be cursed with "writer's hands," in part it is through McGuane's writer's skills that he can demonstrate that he has paid his dues, as I have argued earlier. He has the ability to ferret out the authentic speech that often remains hidden to his neighbors. His use of indigenous colloquial language demonstrates his credentials. McGuane chides John Updike for his needless Francophilia at the expense of American language, citing Updike's transformation of the Kennedy Memorial's eternal flame into the *"flamme éternelle."*[16] As he has demonstrated to his readers, McGuane not only knows how to dally, but also the origin of the word dally. He knows both the technical language of his sport and the language of the men who practice it.

Thus we can expect from McGuane's fiction representations that are grounded in a sense of place. He will write about places he knows, activities he can do, in hopes that his view *won't* be construed as that from a convertible cruising Hollywood. But a sense of place for the New Westerner involves a complex series of negotiations between often competing definitions. For McGuane place is defined through initiation rituals, including the rituals of a specialized local language. He employs a set of realist conventions about the actual, so that what seems to be modern is in fact archaic. While castigating the would-be urban westerner who runs a McDonald's instead of a ranch, McGuane, as a writer, actively sells his view of the region. Furthermore, McGuane's authentic West is also a mythic one. He inhabits a West that also belonged to "Papa" Hemingway and to Owen Wister. In many ways it is the Wild West of the late nineteenth century, of cowboys, ranchers, hunters and trappers, and outlaws. Although McGuane is quite careful with clichés, his use of setting and space often belies his ostensibly ironic stance. In fact, these inconsistencies produce a radical, if unaware, self-contradiction rather than irony: that is, paradox.

McGuane's position within Montana culture, at least as he writes about it, is anachronistic. He has chosen to defend an idealized notion of a nineteenth-century American West, and to pursue sports and recreation, hobbies, and businesses that will afford him status according to mythic standards. His is not necessarily the ideal held by the average Montanan, native or not, but rather a peculiarly literary and filmic ideal. McGuane has created himself as the archetypal westerner.

Yet even as he creates his voice as mythic westerner, he naturalizes that creation, which effaces it under a gloss of contemporary quotidian life. His daily life and chores, however, are essentially different from those of most Montanans. In "The Heart of the Game," McGuane writes about his ranch chores:

My chores of late had consisted primarily of working on screen-plays so that the bank didn't take the ranch. These days the primary ranch skill is making the payment; it comes before irrigation, feeding out, and calving. Some rancher friends find this so discouraging they get up and roll a number or have a slash of tanglefoot before they even think of the glories of the West. This is the New Rugged.[17]

Here McGuane claims that writing is just a way to pay the bills. The strategy here, at least as old as Castiglione, is to efface the effort of writing, to treat the real nature of his work in an offhand manner. Although he mentions screenwriting, presumably "The Heart of the Game," too, is a way of making the payment, so the reader subsidizes those activities that are truly important for him to do, and if we pay, he will tell us about them. He is our surrogate. Like his protagonist, Chet Pomeroy, in *Panama* (1978), McGuane stands in as a "carica-ture" of his reader's own desires.[18] But McGuane does not stand in for his "rancher friends," for unlike them he relies on writing, not ranch-ing, to make the payment. Rather he stands in for the "horrid nancy with pink palms," the reader who works all week to support a pas-time. There is nothing new about "the New Rugged" for the Montana rancher without another income. "Making the payment" is a basic skill for the average rancher, and always has been. For the average rancher that skill cannot be separated from other ranch activities, for they are inextricably linked. But McGuane occupies a locally anoma-lous position because he can make his "nut" externally, at what he does. For him, ranching is not a means of life support, but of life en-hancement. His approach to "the primary ranch skill" may be like those of rancher friends, but those friends would be the Ted Turners, Calvin Kleins, or Peter Fondas, that is, the tycoons, actors, painters, or other writers of the region.

All this might be better fitting for biography were it not manifest in his fiction. In "Roping from A to B," McGuane has removed at least one fictive layer. Yet his Montana fiction demonstrates the same ethos at work, revealing a paradoxical and troubled relation to west-ern space.

In the Montana short stories of *To Skin a Cat*, McGuane's charac-ters enact a nineteenth-century mythic ideal in a modern Montana.[19] As exaggerations of the McGuane persona, they choose behavior that is outlawed, outside social or legal norms, in response to modern social pressure. McGuane's sympathy and affection for them seem really to be a fondness for their outlaw ethic. Like him, they accept a code or myth of the West. He works to make an outlaw position seem an understandable reaction to the frustrations of modern life: town life, divorce, separation from meaningful or useful work. He presents characters who are, or who long to be, anachronistic, who need a simpler, nineteenth-century pastoral environment whether they know it or not.

The narrator of "Flight" tells of a visit from a particular hunting buddy during grouse season in Montana. Dan Ashaway, the visiting hunter from Philadelphia, is terminally ill. Dan and the narrator go hunting with Dan's two superbly trained hunting dogs in country they have hunted together before. The land resonates with events from their earlier trip as well as with evidence of earlier hunters: "antelope blinds the Indians had built," "eagle traps," "old cartridge cases . . . 45–70s; maybe a fight, maybe an old rancher hunting antelope with a cavalry rifle" (159). On the trip Dan tells the narrator that his illness is terminal, but in mythic western fashion they say nothing more about it. As the dogs go off in search of game, Dan simply says, "This is it," then tells the narrator the particularities of caring for the two pointers. This exchange not only reveals an intimate knowledge of hunting dogs (in much the same way that McGuane's discussion of the term dally reveals an intimate knowledge of roping), but also it conveys the intimacy of the men's relation to each other. With a "Wish me luck," Dan walks over a rim and shoots himself with his shotgun (160). Without even a confirming glance, the narrator whistles for the dogs, heads for his truck, and the story ends.

Readers can accept the narrator's behavior only if they understand the literary codes that inform it. They must accept a world of few words, where meaning inheres in the silences. They must accept the notion of a heavily encoded specialized language. And they must accept that when men have guns, death is likely to occur. Readers must believe that a special bonding occurs between the two men through the transfer of the prized hunting dogs. They must believe, along with Ernest Hemingway, that suicide by shotgun when faced with illness is a noble act. All these codes must operate if the story is to be successful in its short five-and-a-half pages. McGuane fashions meaning in minimal space by setting his readers into a fictive world that contains many familiar signifiers. Once they recognize the signs, then Dan Ashaway's disappearance, like an old buffalo leaving the herd, makes sense.

Although set in contemporary Montana, which frequently is distinguished from the past, McGuane's world remains archaic rather than modern. His fiction often represents a world with a limited, if not dismal, future, so his characters cling to bits of frontier ethic to maintain dignity or integrity within a diminished environment. These characters become interesting and plausible only to the extent that the reader understands the underlying codes. McGuane's notion of this ethic seems to be derived from both literary and filmic sources, and in many instances it seems to be an eastern point of view. In *The Mythic West in Twentieth-Century America*, Robert Athearn lists some of the qualities of an eastern point of view. The easterner tends to lament the despoiling of the "Old West."[20] Business pursuits outside of ranching are viewed as a kind of commercial pollution. Easterners "believe the West's most valuable commodities are wild, magnificent scenery, excitement, adventure, a bit of rusticity, and an occasional whiff of imagined danger. In other words, the chance to escape, briefly to be sure, the dailiness of their lives."[21] These "eastern" desires operate as unstated motivation for many of McGuane's characters. Often those characters who aren't motivated by these desires become the object of scorn.

The mythic West offers many useful signifiers. First, it is inhabited by men with guns. It can be a world of absolutes, where compromise is unnecessary, even undesirable. McGuane capitalizes on our notions of the western hero. Robert Warshow describes the western hero as a gentleman, a man of leisure. He is melancholy, a man for whom "life is unavoidably serious."[22] He is a man who always defends "the purity of his own image—in fact his honor."[23] And he is a man who is the source of moral ambiguity, for "he is a killer of men."[24] McGuane places his characters within this signifying system, whence they proceed to search for a safe place.

Second, the mythic West is a place in which women occupy a marginal position at best. "Like a Leaf" is the story of a widower who has moved off the ranch and into town. In attempting to hang onto his sanity and put his life back together since his wife's death, he has been seeing a doctor, presumably for psychiatric care. The story, in first-person narration, follows his progress with the doctor and with the unmarried woman who lives across the street. The woman remains unnamed throughout, referred to as "the person" or simply as "she." The narrative structure allows the possibility that at least some of the events are a dream or fantasy—the narrator says at one point, "Doc and I agree on one thing: it's all in your head"—but the story represents the actions as real (42). Whether part of the narrative's reality or part of the narrator's fantasy, the signifying codes remain the same.

From the opening line of "Like a Leaf," McGuane manipulates a series of underlying assumptions. The narrator begins: "I'm underneath my small house in Deadrock" (39). Deadrock is a fictional small town resembling McGuane's adopted hometown of Livingston, Montana.[25] The story begins not in possibility, in the wide open spaces where the narrator might have as many spatial options as he has narrative ones, but rather in the claustrophobic crawl space beneath a small house in town. This is domestic space with a vengeance. The narrator lets us know that the possibilities are indeed quite limited when he tells us that although this house is what is known as a "starter" home, for him, "this one is it" (39).

Where ample space might once have been desirable, now it represents his loss. Without the mooring of a lasting marriage, or more important, without his vocation as a rancher, any expanse has become uncomfortable for him as he informs, "I bought a youth bed to reduce the size of the unoccupied area" (41). Diminution itself offers no relief either, for among his other problems, the narrator shakes. His shaking seems a mockery of the mythic valorization of motion over stasis, though the narrator retains some belief in the idea that both space and unrestricted motion represent freedom, for often he uses spatial metaphors. When he describes his wife's death, he says, "She just nodded her pretty face and headed out. I sat there like a stupe" (40). A little later he mentions his depression and how "when you're like that you need someone or something to take you away" (41).

Although the narrator sometimes claims that the diminution of his life has its good points, his own terms of comparison question his assertions. We learn that he is underneath the house "distributing bottle caps of arsenic for the rats that come up from the river and dispute the cats over trifles. I represent civilization in a small but real way." A few paragraphs later he tells us: "I was one of this area's better cattlemen, and town life doesn't come easy. Where I once had coyotes and bears, I now have rats." McGuane's narrator is a man trapped by domesticity twice over. No longer having a ranch to run, he lives in a "starter home" in town, and having become used to married life, he feels its absence. McGuane's ethos dictates that a rancher without a ranch is a lunatic and that any amount of space that is less than unlimited becomes claustrophobic.

Most of the comparisons between life in town and life on the ranch reinforce feelings that ranch life, though not perfect, is better. When the narrator emerges from underneath the house and returns inside, he notices flies. He recalls: "We never had flies like this on the ranch. We had songbirds, apple blossoms, and no flies" (40). The narrator often connects ranch life with his deceased wife, with her views about various aspects of town life offered as counterweight to his town experiences. After the narrator reveals his compulsion for window-shopping, he adds: "My wife couldn't understand this. Nature was a shrine to her" (42). Of "the person," who is having an affair with his neighbor (he calls this neighbor "Impact Man"), the narrator remarks: "With her bounce, her cigarettes, and her iffy hours, she makes just the kind of woman my wife had no use for" (46).

As in other McGuane fiction, use value is connected with the land, and here, by extension, with the dead wife. When he window-shops, the narrator regards things his wife "would never buy, not risqué things but things that wouldn't stand up" (45). By extension their love has a kind of use value, for it is the kind that stands up, even through death. Unlike "Impact Man's" affair with "the person," the narrator's relationship to his wife had meaning. He says, "We didn't impact, we loved each other" (40). At the story's end the narrator addresses his dead wife once again, affirming her values: "Tomorrow we'll shop for something nice, something you can count on to stand up" (55).

The narrator's relation to "the person," whether actual or imagined, carries pronounced elements of aggression. In McGuane's contemporary West, the western hero may fight other men, himself, or women. In "Like a Leaf," the narrator sees himself as the woman's adversary more than her seducer, for the thrill of pursuit is the thrill of the hunt. When he thinks about the possibility of a "fling" with "the person," he sees that "all this has a sporting side, like hunting coyotes." As a Montana cattle rancher, his hunting coyotes would be without use value, another thing his dead wife probably would scorn (42).[26] After watching "the person," whose "wantonness overpowers" him, the narrator throws his dinner at a passing dog, finding he has "a taste in my mouth like the one you get in those frantic close-ins hunting coyotes" (44–45). Later when he describes her movement, he notes that she "swings her shoulder bag like a cheerful weapon" (46). She has eyes that "dance with cruel merriment," and wears cologne that savages his nerves (49, 51). But the story turns as the narrator shifts from the hunter to the hunted. After he attempts to back out of his by-now dangerous seduction, she becomes the aggressor. As he says, "Please no, Please no," she "clambers roughly atop," has her way with him, and looks at him "with her raging victorious eyes." As he tells it, "In short, I've been raped" (51).

Feminized, he bursts into tears, then not wanting to go to a public place, he takes her to visit his friend Al, a prison guard. Soon Al finds himself in a compromised situation analogous to the narrator's. While "the person" is in the prison yard visiting the prisoners, they both wait for her, "like a pair of sea captain's wives in their widow's walks." She signals them and they "wave back . . . flapping away like a couple of widows" (54). Al and the narrator realize what they must do to right the situation, and relieved, they laugh until the tears come again. In the best Gary Cooper sense, they understand that "a man's gotta do what a man's gotta do," and Al gives the narrator his gun. The narrator then takes "the person" to a contemplative spot on the river, where the river moves,

> but not enough to erase the stars from its surface, or the trout sailing like birds over its deep pebbly bottom. The little homewrecker kneels at the end of the sandbar and washes herself over and over. When I am certain she feels absolutely clean, I let her have it. I roll her into the pool, where she becomes a ghost of the river trailing beautiful smoky cotton from a hole in her silly head. (55)

With the calm observance of the hunter, the narrator details the scene before dispatching his prey as he might a coyote. His shaking seems to have stopped, for he hits his mark. Having eliminated "the little homewrecker," he stands alongside other western heroes such as Shane, who, as outsiders, come into a community and eliminate the disruptive element. They can't belong for they are killers, but they perform a necessary task. In death (and much like the dead wife), the woman becomes aestheticized and merges with the scene, her death naturalized by it. The narrator's reward for dispatching the predatory woman is a moment of harmony with and appreciation for the naturalized scene. The woman's reward for her acts of predation is death.

Though the narrator has represented "the person" and his

deceased wife in oppositional terms, they have more in common than initially might be apparent. They both occupy positions that are outside the ethos presented. The wife's words echo in the narrator's head, making the adjustment to ranch life on his own impossible and making town life tawdry and unsubstantial. His dependence upon her has incapacitated him. Yet, in part, through the memory of her words the narrator is able to reject community, "the social whirl," and do what he must (55). So she becomes useful to the extent that her memory can be opposed to "the person," but her usefulness both to the narrator and to the story depends upon her absence. Moreover, both women represent talk more than they do action. The narrator recalls his wife's words and opinions more than her movements or deeds. And though "the person's" crime may result from her predatory sexuality, she dies for what she *says*. After having compromised Al sexually, and having arranged an encounter with the prisoners, she threatens, "Be cool now, Al, . . . or I talk" (54). Al and the narrator then decide she must be killed. In the world of "Like a Leaf," women, whether home builders or homewreckers, can make men dangerously dependent. Consequently, to maintain the myth of masculine domination, one way or another women must be exiled in the end. The exile of women from McGuane's Montana might go unnoticed by many of his readers, who seem mostly sympathetic to his cause. Initially, his assumed audience consisted primarily of men, for this story originally appeared in *Playboy*.

While the narrator of "Like a Leaf" has done his job, he is homeless at the story's end—left by the river, neither in town nor back at the ranch. McGuane's characters seek but never find their own safe place, even though McGuane imagines the possibility for his characters as well as for himself. But to do so under the terms he has articulated, he has had to deny his craft, his literary precursors, the community around him, and the present. In fact, paradoxically McGuane's work might betray, in Leslie Fiedler's terms, "a lust for un-reason, a nostalgia for a time when insanity could be heroically lived out in a landscape indistinguishable from nightmare."[27] Like the narrator of "Like a Leaf," McGuane creates his own literary crawl space, which limits not only his own efforts but denies an alternative sense of place either to actual Montanans or to his readers. In effect, though retaining its stylistic elements, he eschews realism in favor of a brand of romance, where the ethical standards are mythic, where men should be MEN, and where townies and women disturb the peace.[28]

Though working within the confines of realism, McGuane refuses to confront the uneasy relation between contradictory views of the contemporary American West. Instead he resorts to a mythic, nineteenth-century view of the American West to resolve conflicts in his work that cannot be so easily resolved in contemporary society, even in Montana. In so doing, McGuane denies Montana a viable present, recreating it as a shabby wax museum, where dusty stuffed coyotes, disheveled Custers, and rusty six-shooters recall for tourists the ideal of an adventurous past. As a result, for McGuane's readers contemporary Montana, with its burger franchises and starter homes, is doomed to disappoint.

Notes

1. Gerald W. Haslam, ed., *Western Writing* (Albuquerque: University of New Mexico Press, 1974), 4.

2. Thomas McGuane, *An Outside Chance: Essays on Sport* (New York: Farrar, Straus and Giroux, 1980), 213.

3. I use pastoral in two ways here. First, I mean that which is rural, even bucolic. Second, I use it in the Empsonian sense, that is, as a place where one can escape to work out conflict and where the complex becomes simplified.

4. McGuane, *Outside Chance*, 210–11. McGuane defines both dar la vuelta and mecate adequately, but not completely. Fay Ward, for example, not only indicates an intermediate step in the Americanization of dar la vuelta to dally-welta, but also gives a definition as it applies to roping and a more literal translation, meaning "to give her a turn." Ward provides a more specific definition for mecate, referring to it as a hair rope made from either the mane or tail hair of horses. But Ward has a different agenda, for his book functions as a handbook that shows how to use the information given, as the book's title suggests. Fay E. Ward, *The Working Cowboy's Manual* (New York: Bonanza Books, 1983), 157–59.

5. McGuane, *Outside Chance*, 210.

6. Ibid., 215.

7. Ibid., 212.

8. Ibid., 216.

9. Ibid., 221.

10. Gender-specific pronouns are used here because they reflect McGuane's gendered notions about place.

11. McGuane particularly rejects Faulkner, who had such a strong tie to his region through family history. In an interview with Larry McCaffery and Sinda Gregory, McGuane talks of his Irish immigrant family as perpetual outsiders: in

Ireland, in Massachusetts, in Michigan, and McGuane himself in Montana. Larry McCaffery and Sinda Gregory, *Alive and Writing: Interviews with American Authors of the 1980s* (Urbana: University of Illinois Press, 1987), 203.

12. McGuane, *Outside Chance*, 222.

13. Peter Schwenger, *Phallic Critiques: Masculinity and Twentieth-Century Literature* (London: Routledge and Kegan Paul, 1984), 20.

14. Ibid., 37.

15. This assertion is based on my 1986 survey of circulation data for approximately fifty magazines, which was conducted for an unrelated project.

16. McGuane, *Outside Chance*, 221.

17. Ibid., 229.

18. Jerome Klinkowitz, *The New American Novel of Manners: The Fiction of Richard Yates, Dan Wakefield, and Thomas McGuane* (Athens: University of Georgia Press, 1986), 136.

19. Thomas McGuane, *To Skin a Cat* (New York: Vintage Books, 1986). Subsequent page references included in the text are to this edition.

20. Robert G. Athearn, *The Mythic West in Twentieth-Century America* (Lawrence: University Press of Kansas, 1986), 1.

21. Ibid., 131.

22. Robert Warshow, "Movie Chronicle: The Westerner" (1954), in *The Immediate Experience: Movies, Comics, Theater and Other Aspects of Popular Culture* (Garden City, N.Y.: Doubleday, 1962), 137.

23. Ibid., 140.

24. Ibid., 142.

25. McGuane has moved farther out of town and closer to Big Timber, Montana, but he still spends time in Livingston (so I'm told).

26. While Montana sheep ranchers have cause to hunt coyotes, for often they kill sheep, as a rule coyotes don't represent a threat to cattle ranchers.

27. Leslie A. Fiedler, *The Return of the Vanishing American* (1968; reprint, New York: Stein and Day, 1976), 164.

28. I use romance in terms of an American tradition, following descriptions by Henry James and Richard Chase, among others.

Bibliography

Athearn, Robert G. *The Mythic West in Twentieth-Century America.* Lawrence: University Press of Kansas, 1986.

Fiedler, Leslie A. *The Return of the Vanishing American.* 1968. Reprint. New York: Stein and Day, 1976.

Haslam, Gerald W., ed. *Western Writing.* Albuquerque: University of New Mexico Press, 1974.

Klinkowitz, Jerome. *The New American Novel of Manners: The Fiction of Richard Yates, Dan Wakefield, and Thomas McGuane*. Athens: University of Georgia Press, 1986.

McCaffery, Larry, and Sinda Gregory. *Alive and Writing: Interviews with American Authors of the 1980s*. Urbana: University of Illinois Press, 1987.

McGuane, Thomas. *An Outside Chance: Essays on Sport*. New York: Farrar, Straus and Giroux, 1980.

———. *To Skin a Cat*. New York: Vintage Books, 1986.

Schwenger, Peter. *Phallic Critiques: Masculinity and Twentieth-Century Literature*. London: Routledge and Kegan Paul, 1984.

Ward, Fay E. *The Working Cowboy's Manual*. New York: Bonanza Books, 1983.

Warshow, Robert. "Movie Chronicle: The Westerner" (1954). In *The Immediate Experience: Movies, Comics, Theater and Other Aspects of Popular Culture*, 135–54. Garden City, N.Y.: Doubleday, 1962.

16. "Bring Forth the King's Remembrancer!": Folklore as History in the Work of Ivan Doig

Elizabeth Simpson

In the old days, in blizzardy weather, we used to tie a string of lariats from house to barn so as to make it from shelter to responsibility and back again. With personal, family, and cultural chores to do, I think we had better rig up such a line between past and present.
—Wallace Stegner

As a child growing up in one of the subregions of the West, Oregon's Hood River Valley, I was aware of profound discontinuities in the history of my home place, shifts in economics and demographics that separated the present from the past. My friend and neighbor, Paul Keir, told me tales of his own boyhood in the valley, recounted memories of Indians exercising their ponies on the sandbars of the Columbia River. On the wall of his study hung a photograph of Indians dipnetting salmon at Celilo Falls. On horseback rides, he would take me to Indian encampments where a little digging would unearth handcarved wooden stirrups and cooking spoons.

My mother, who had come to live in the valley in the 1940s, told me about signs appearing in local store windows during the Second World War, No Dogs or Japs Allowed, and about how the minister of the Episcopal church lost three-quarters of his congregation by railing

230

against the wartime internment of the Japanese and the confiscation of their orchards and homes.

By the time I heard these stories, the Indians of the valley were represented only by Indian Charley, who rode in local parades. Celilo Falls had long disappeared behind the John Day Dam, and the tidy orchards planted and nurtured by the Japanese had become anonymous sections of the large holdings of wealthy whites. Now when I go back for a visit, I see the homes of childhood friends converted to bed-and-breakfasts, and old cafés reborn as "ethnic" restaurants that serve the wind surfers who have discovered the Columbia River.

The discontinuities in the history of my home place are not unique, nor do I recount them here from nostalgia. Rather, they illustrate a problem for western writers and historians, a problem deftly articulated by Wallace Stegner in "History, Myth and the Western Writer," first published in 1967, and deftly answered, ten years later, in the work of Ivan Doig.

In his essay Stegner argues that historical discontinuity is the central fact of western experience. He notes that the nineteenth-century settlement of the West often amounted to little more than a raid on its resources: one place after another was stripped of its minerals, its timber, its water, its grass, and then abandoned. Furthermore, the get-rich-and-get-out mentality created a large migrant population that precluded the development of stable communities in the West. Stegner notes: "Despite their colorful history, there has hardly been a *continuous* community life in an Aspen or a Telluride; and when oil-fields are superimposed on orchards in California, something disruptive has happened in the life of both people and towns."[1] Stegner argues that the absence of stable communities prevented the development of traditions that could serve as foundations of personal and regional identity as they had in New England, the Midwest, and the South. In turn, the lack of historical continuity, tradition, and regional identity fragmented western literature.

Stegner divides western writing into two categories, each of which manifests the writer's sense of historical discontinuity. The first category, the formula Western, focuses on a brief (and heavily mythicized) period of history and ignores the present altogether. The formula Western not only reinforces the absence of community-based continuity, but actually raises this absence to the status of a genre motif. The cowboy hero usually lives in relative isolation and makes his own rules: he may come to the aid of a beleaguered town or a helpless schoolmarm (often breaking social mores or laws to do so), but he rides off again into the sunset, happily unencumbered by social restrictions or family life. In the formula Western, community is regarded not as a source of strength, but as a refuge for the weak.

The second category Stegner calls "western literature with a small *w*," in which he includes the work of Walter Van Tilburg Clark, Willa Cather, and A. B. Guthrie. He points out that these authors lived in the West and therefore wrote from a strong sense of place, rather than from the western myth. But they were frequently overwhelmed by what had happened in that place, the urbanization and industrialization that defiled a fragile landscape. Their attitude toward the past, therefore, was nostalgic, even elegiac, and their attitude toward the present one of disgust. Their work, according to Stegner, does not provide westerners with a sense of regional identity, nor a feeling that their lives are linked meaningfully with the past. He argues that westerners lack a sense of "a personal and *possessed* past" that should arise from a sense of historical continuity.[2]

Stegner's essay has all the power of a paradigm, all the authority of his own experience as a writer, historian, literary scholar, and resident of the West. However, in the years since the publication of "History, Myth and the Western Writer," there has been an explosion of writing in and about the West, some of the most vital and innovative writing in America. Many of these writers have moved away from the two categories of western writing Stegner describes. Rather than focusing on history writ large, the political and economic events that have disrupted life in the West, they focus on history writ small, the folk traditions within which westerners can locate themselves.

Foremost among these writers is Ivan Doig, westerner by birth and by choice. Doig writes from a strong sense of place, and one of his main thematic concerns is to "place" westerners in their world. But unlike Stegner, Doig defines "place" not only in terms of location but also in terms of folklore. In his work a person's "place" often refers to membership in folk groups whose traditions and stories create continuity between the present and the past, and thereby provide a sense of personal and regional identity.

Interestingly, Stegner considered folklore as a possible source of continuity and rejected it, noting that it was usually "an improvisation on an occupational theme—logging, riverboating, railroading, cowboying," and that even though western folkore was lasting, it, like the formula Western, did not reflect the reality of daily life.[3]

Stegner's dismissal of folklore is not surprising, considering that he was working from a concept of folklore that defined it as a study of cultural remnants or curiosities, bits of Indian legend or Grandmother's quilts, interesting as artifacts but essentially irrelevant to the present. However, during the time Stegner was writing, professional folklorists were expanding the possibilities of folkloric study, defining it not only as a study of artifact but also as an examination of living processes and traditions. According to folklorist Jan Brunvand, "Folklore comprises the unrecorded traditions of a people. The study of folklore records and analyzes these traditions because they reveal the common life of the mind below the level of 'high' or formal culture, which is recorded by civilizations as the learned heritage of their times."[4]

Brunvand's definition marks an important shift from Stegner's paradigm in its emphasis on folklore as *commonality* rather than curiosity, and its distinction between formal and informal history. The "common life of the mind" is manifested in oral, customary, and material traditions that are shared among members of folk groups and informally passed from generation to generation.

Doig's awareness of folklore has enabled him to articulate, as Stegner did, the interdependence of tradition and community. Where he differs from Stegner is in his recognition that community is not necessarily dependent on location. It is clear from Stegner's essay that he defines "community" in terms of place—towns like Aspen and Telluride, whose integrity has been threatened by major events. Doig is also aware of uneven urban development in the West, and he documents it in his memoir *This House of Sky*. He describes a Montana dotted with abandoned homesteads, each named for the first family that tried, and failed, to make a life there. Towns are divided between ramshackle buildings that meet the needs of the present and huge empty carcasses of grander edifices, such as resort hotels and auditoriums, that recall dreams of a past that did not survive into the present.

Equally ephemeral are the populations of Montana. In his novels *English Creek* and *Dancing at the Rascal Fair*, Doig records the vicissitudes of political and ecological history that brought settlers to the West and sent them away again: the Homestead Act, the depression, Montana winters, droughts and forest fires, the influenza epidemic of 1919. Under these circumstances, the instability of towns and populations is not surprising.

But Doig is also aware that "community" is created not only by location but also by culture, and that the relationship between community and tradition is dual: communities create tradition, but tradition
also creates communities. All of us are members of many culture-
based communities: ethnic, familial, religious, occupational, frater-
nal, avocational, recreational. Our work habits, our knowledge of
crafts, our aesthetics and foodways and dress codes, our sense of con-
vention and propriety are shaped by the folk groups we belong to,
and these groups are only partially determined by where we live and
who our neighbors are.

One brief example from *This House of Sky* will illustrate what I
mean. This is a scene where Ivan, his father, Charlie Doig, and the
rancher McGrath are tallying sheep:

> McGrath has kept the count steady with his chopping hand.
> When Dad does the count, he stands half-sideways to the river
> of sheep, his right hand low off his hip and barely flicking as
> each sheep passes. I have seen buyers, the men in gabardine suits
> and creamy Stetsons, with other habits—pointing just two fin-
> gers, or pushing the flat palm of a hand toward the sheep—as
> they count. The one trick everyone has is somehow to pump the
> end of an arm at each whizzing sheep, make the motion joggle a
> signal to the brain.[5]

In this passage and others like it, Doig redefines "community" to
mean a group of people whose common ground is knowledge and tradition, rather than place. The rancher McGrath, Charlie Doig, and
the buyers in gabardine suits are, regardless of where they live, members of the same community. They all know the same things: the difficulties of finding good herders; how to dock lambs and castrate them;
how to "jacket" a motherless lamb so that another ewe will take him;
when to shear and when to sell; when to throw the flock on new
grass; how to train a dog that will "run on wool." Skills like these are
informally acquired, passed from person to person, and connect the
people who share them. The rancher carries these traditions with him
as a snail carries its house on its back. And he will therefore have
more in common with other sheep ranchers, herders, and buyers in
other parts of the country than he will with the banker in his own
hometown.

Even though much of the working population in Montana is migrant, its members are not homeless, nor are they strangers to one

another. In *English Creek*, for example, the same men come together year after year for seasonal jobs such as haying or lambing or fire-fighting, and form effective crews because they know one another well and know how to work together. The temporary communities they create are oddly cosmopolitan: the men swap stories, talk about other towns and ranches they have seen, learn from one another's experiences. Their communities are work-related, rather than place-related, but are nonetheless stable and meaningful.

Folk life creates bonds that stretch across time as well as space: people follow the traditions of their predecessors but reshape those traditions according to changing needs. The traditions of folklife are both stable and innovative: they have their roots in the past but remain viable because they change with changing circumstances.

For example, the first two novels of the Montana trilogy, *English Creek* and *Dancing at the Rascal Fair*, follow the fortunes of the McCaskill family through three generations from the homesteading period in the 1800s through the beginning of the Second World War. Doig examines the continuities and changes in the cultural life of the region in scenes that focus on its folk life: dances, rodeos, picnics, ranch life. In *Rascal Fair*, which takes place in the late-nineteenth and early twentieth centuries, homesteaders dance Scottish dances to songs they brought with them from Scotland, such as "Tam Lin" and "Sir Patrick McWhirr." Two generations later, descendants of these immigrants dance square dances to western songs like "The Dude and Belle." The tradition of community dances has remained stable; the dances themselves have changed over time. Similarly, the turn-of-the-century rodeos in *Rascal Fair* are impromptu affairs held in somebody's corral. The rodeos in *English Creek*, two generations later, are more elaborate but still feature events that recall the past. The clothing worn by the riders and ropers, the skills they demonstrate, the patter of the announcer, the rules of the contests between men and animals would be meaningless if they did not deliberately recreate earlier rodeos and celebrate the traditional work of the cowboy.

The past is important in Doig's work: he is a historian as well as a writer, and major historical events inform the plots of his novels and shape the lives of his characters. In *Rascal Fair*, immigrants move west in response to the Homestead Act and spend their lives meeting the act's demands and struggling against its shortcomings. They experience the development of the railroads that expand their markets, and the establishment of the national forests and the grazing acts that restrict their access to grasslands. They suffer the devastation of wars and diseases.

These events are history writ large and compose the formal histories that order and interpret the past. In them we perceive the fragmentation Stegner talks about. But even though our lives are shaped by these events, we are usually unaware of their lasting significance—they are best understood in retrospect. Our sense of a "personal and *possessed* past" is created by history writ small—family history, local history, the kind that usually does not make its way into textbooks. Knowledge about our past and present worlds is essential to the formation of personal and regional identity. In *This House of Sky*, Doig defines memory as "a set of sagas we live by, much the way of the Norse wildmen in their bear shirts. That such rememberings take place in a single cave of brain rather than half a hundred minds warrened wildly into one another makes them sagas no less."[6] In this passage, Doig makes the point that the memories that tell us who we are take the form of *saga*, or story, and accordingly the narrative structures of his books consist of complex interweavings of stories told by Doig himself (*This House of Sky, Winter Brothers*), by a self-conscious narrator (*English Creek, Dancing at the Rascal Fair, Ride with Me, Mariah Montana*), and by various raconteurs in all of his books. The point is not only that Doig's books are full of good stories but also that these stories function as the figurative "line between the past and the present" that Stegner called for. Telling stories is a means of realizing, in both senses of that word, an individual's life and of placing that life in a historical continuum.

In *This House of Sky*, for example, Doig recounts the stories of his father, Charlie, and his grandmother, Bessie Ringer. Charlie's stories take the form of personal narratives: reminiscences about his family and about the pastoral idyll that he and Ivan's mother, Berneta, lived out in their mountain summers before her death. He tells occupational stories that succinctly and often humorously characterize skinflinty ranchers or half-crazy sheepherders, or recall mishaps on the job. He tells tales of adventure that center on his own brushes with death. Through his stories Charlie re-creates himself, his family, and life in the valley, and he thereby teaches his son how to live in that place. Bessie's stories recall Ivan's babyhood and early childhood, times before language could have shaped experience for the boy himself. At the end of *This House of Sky*, Doig acknowledges his debt to his father, saying, "It was you, in your burring troubadour's way of

passing to me all you knew of the valley and the Basin, who en-
chanted into me such a love of language and story that it has become
my lifework."[7]

Doig locates regional, as well as personal, identity in memory
and story. In a passage from a book of stories read aloud by the
schoolchildren in *Rascal Fair,* Doig illustrates the importance of oral
tradition:

> *"One more sun," sighed the king at evening, "and now another
> darkness. This has to stop. The days fly past us as if they were
> racing pigeons. We may as well be pebbles, for all the notice life
> takes of us or we of it. No one holds in mind the blind harper
> when he is gone. No one commemorates the girl who grains the
> geese. None of the deeds of our people leave the least tiny mark
> upon time. . . . Oblivion has been the rule too long. What this
> kingdom needs in the time to come is some, umm, some blivion.
> There, that's it, we need to become a more blivious people.
> Enough of this forgettery. But how to do it, it will take some
> doing. What's to be done? Tell me that, whoever can."*
>
> *"If you will recall, sire, this morning you named a remem-
> brancer."*
>
> *"Eh? I did? I mean, I did. And what a good idea it was, too.
> For a change things are going to be fixed into mind around here.
> Send me this remembering fellow."*
>
> *"Bring forth the king's remembrancer!"*[8]

The king does not appoint a court recorder, but a storyteller, who
will "fix things into mind." He does not comment on the need to recall wars and plagues, but "the blind harper" and "the girl who
grains the geese." The king knows that without the ordering power of
story, events and people remain isolated and meaningless, and a kingdom that has no sense of its own past and people can have no meaningful present or future.

Each of Doig's books is graced by a remembrancer, such as Toussaint Rennie, who appears in both *English Creek* and *Dancing at the
Rascal Fair.* Toussaint recounts events he has experienced and
thereby personalizes the impersonal past. Part Indian, part white,
very old but still vital in the 1930s, Toussaint belongs to two cultures
and two centuries. By his own account, he witnessed most of the history of western Montana: the decimation of the Native American
tribes and the buffalo herds, the great cattle drives, the construction

of the Valier irrigation project, the establishment of homesteads, the growth of the town of Gros Ventre. Toussaint holds the valley in his memory. When he refers to an incident in the life of Jick, the young narrator of *English Creek,* Jick marvels:

> If I was a Toussaint topic, just what did that constitute? The mix of apprehension and surmise was all through me. Plus a flavor of something which seemed surprisingly like pride. Better or worse, part of me now was in Toussaint's knowledge, his running history of the Two. In there with Phony Nose Gorman and the last buffalo hunt and the first sheep and the winter of '86 and Lieutenant Black Jack Pershing and the herded Crees and— and what did that mean? Being a part of history, at the age of fourteen years and ten months: why had that responsibility picked me out?[9]

The stories that Toussaint tells remain alive in Varick McCaskill and his sons, Alec and Jick. They feel the resonance of history when they look over hay fields in the valley and picture the buffalo and the cattle herds that once grazed there. Historical significance for them is not nostalgia for the past, but an understanding of how they fit into the life of the valley that preceded them and that will continue after they are gone.

Oral history is the provenance of the folk: it is literally "his story" and "her story," and its significance lies in the personalizing of events and in the details of daily life that are so often neglected in formal histories.

In *Winter Brothers,* Doig comments on the limitations of formal history and implies the need to supplement it with oral history. *Winter Brothers* explores the journals of James Swan, a pioneer of the Northwest coast. Swan recorded much of the tribal histories of the Makah and Haida Indians, and Doig notes that these histories become abbreviated through time as historians use them for different purposes. For example, Stingess, a Haida woman, spent an evening telling Swan about the practice of tattooing. Swan recorded only part of the information in his diaries, and Doig included even less in his book. Once oral history became formal history, something was lost. Of this process of abbreviation, Doig notes:

> How elliptical, literally, the past becomes. Stingess culls from what may have been an evening-long narrative an answer for

Swan. Who chooses as much of it as he thinks worth cramming into his diary pages. At my hundred years' remove, I select lines from his and frame them in trios of editing dots. From her Haida tradition to Swan's white tribe to my even paler version. The logical end of the process signaled by my ellipses, I suppose, might be for the lore of Haida tattooing to compress down to something like a single magical speck of print, perhaps the period after the news that Stingess had got tired of all the chit-chat and hobbled home. But I've heard it offered that a period is simply the shorthand for the dots of an ellipsis. That a story never does end, only can pause. So that would not complete it either, the elliptical transit from Stingess to Swan to me to whomever abbreviates the past next.[10]

History writ large is inescapable. Our lives are, as both Doig and Stegner emphasize, determined by major events. But a personal, a possessed past, that links people one to another and makes the present meaningful, is essential to the creation of personal and regional identity. Writers who explore that relationship are well on their way toward developing a regional literary canon.

The West described by Stegner is echoed in my own home place, where changes in economy and demographics have created major discontinuities in the valley's history. The Indians and their way of life, the small Japanese farms, are gone for good, and the little town that once served the needs of surrounding farmers and ranchers now caters to wind surfers. But the West described by Ivan Doig is also reflected in the valley. The past continues into the present in the stories that Paul Keir and my mother told, and through their words I can watch the Indians run their ponies on the sandbar, witness the intolerance that swept the Japanese from their homes. And I pass those memories, and my own, on to those who come after me. The lariat from the past to the present is, as Stegner knew it must be, woven of our words.[11]

Notes

1. Wallace Stegner, "History, Myth and the Western Writer" (1967), in *The Sound of Mountain Water* (New York: Doubleday, 1969), 191.

2. Ibid., 199.

3. Ibid., 191.

4. Jan Harold Brunvand, *The Study of American Folklore: An Introduction* (New York: W. W. Norton, 1968), 1.

5. Ivan Doig, *This House of Sky: Landscapes of a Western Mind* (New York: Harcourt Brace Jovanovich, 1978), 166.

6. Ibid., 10.

7. Ibid., 273.

8. Ivan Doig, *Dancing at the Rascal Fair* (New York: Atheneum, 1987), 131–32.

9. Ivan Doig, *English Creek* (1984; reprint, New York: Penguin Books, 1985), 152–53.

10. Ivan Doig, *Winter Brothers* (New York: Harcourt Brace Jovanovich, 1980), 202.

11. Those interested in more detailed commentary on folklore and history in the work of Ivan Doig may consult Elizabeth Simpson's *Earthlight, Wordfire: The Work of Ivan Doig* (Moscow: University of Idaho Press, 1992).

Bibliography

Brunvand, Jan Harold. *The Study of American Folklore: An Introduction.* New York: W. W. Norton, 1968.

Doig, Ivan. *Dancing at the Rascal Fair.* New York: Atheneum, 1987.

———. *English Creek.* New York: Atheneum, 1984; New York: Penguin Books, 1985.

———. *This House of Sky: Landscapes of a Western Mind.* New York: Harcourt Brace Jovanovich, 1978.

———. *Winter Brothers.* New York: Harcourt Brace Jovanovich, 1980.

Simpson, Elizabeth. *Earthlight, Wordfire: The Work of Ivan Doig.* Moscow: University of Idaho Press, 1992.

Stegner, Wallace. "History, Myth and the Western Writer." *American West* 4 (May 1967): 61–62, 76–79. Reprint in *The Sound of Mountain Water,* 186–201. New York: Doubleday, 1969; Lincoln: University of Nebraska Press, 1980.

17. Spiraling around the Hinge: Working Solutions in *Always Coming Home*

Mary Catherine Harper

In her 1983 article, "A Non-Euclidean View of California as a Cold Place to Be," Ursula K. Le Guin describes how she is sometimes asked what kind of books she will continue to write, "books about the terrible injustice and misery of our world" or "escapist and consolatory fantasies." The choice of "misery" books, according to Le Guin, would limit her to writing about worlds with free, yet unhappy, people in them, while deciding on "escapist" writing would result in happy but enslaved populations. Her choice then is a blanket "no."[1] At first glance, the answer is inappropriate. Le Guin appears to sidestep the issue. But she does offer an explanation: "Back round once more. Usà puyew usu wapiw!"[2] This statement translates from Cree to mean "He goes backward, looks forward."[3]

This translation is as cryptic as Cree is to us. It is only when read in conjunction with Le Guin's *Always Coming Home,* her work in progress in 1983, that the full implications of her use of "He goes backward, looks forward" can be realized. *Always Coming Home* contains a personal vision of life where one may refuse to participate in either/or thinking, where one may refuse the cultural dualisms that Americans find themselves trapped in today. This cross-genre "novel" significantly places what we see as opposites—backward and forward—in dialogue with each other. It is a dialogue between

American "binarism" and the thought or possibility of an other-than-binary life.

Of course, *Always Coming Home*'s examination of binarism is situated in the same place that Le Guin has identified in "A Non-Euclidean View of California as a Cold Place to Be" as *the* both/and place: California. In "A Non-Euclidean View" Le Guin employs California as a trope of both binary and other-than-binary thought, but in her fiction text she creates a literal both/and California setting. To be precise, through the agency of fantasy, *Always Coming Home*'s action takes place in a future utopic Napa Valley and simultaneously in the Napa Valley we know today. In this double place, then, it is possible to be in both the present (or past, depending on one's perspective) and future, to be both backward and forward, hot and cold, and ultimately in both a binarist and other-than-binarist mode. In the dual setting Le Guin works out alternatives to the polarization of high and low, of better and worse, and especially of progressive and primitive.

Always Coming Home is not the first work in which Le Guin has tackled philosophical dualism. She has previously built dualism into the cultural fabric of her fictional societies. In works such as *The Dispossessed* and *The Left Hand of Darkness* she uses the concept of opposing forces to create her thematics of division and unity. Dena C. Bain explicates Le Guin's use of the yin-yang principle of the Taoist quietist philosophy in "The 'Tao Te Ching' as Background to the Novels of Ursula K. Le Guin." Bain states that the basic myths underlying several of Le Guin's works are "the concepts of wholeness, of presence, of reconciling forces which appear totally opposed, but which, in the moment of complete reduction and return to the Uncarved Block, are invariably revealed to be necessary complements."[4]

In *The Dispossessed* the principle of opposites as complementary parts of a whole is represented by the two worlds, Anarres and Urras. Anarres, the desert moon of Urras, is populated by the descendants of dissidents who migrated from the planet. *The Left Hand of Darkness* also presents the conflict between two groups of people and two ideologies on one planet, Gethen. The inhabitants of Gethen are obsessed with the idea of opposition and unity for good reason. Not only must they contend with divisive political and social factions but they must also reconcile the very notion of divided wholes to their naturally hermaphroditic selves. As in *The Dispossessed, The Left*

Hand of Darkness illustrates that final opposition is never possible, for opposites depend on each other for definition. Each is formless without the other.

Always Coming Home employs the same yin-yang principle as the previous novels and, like *The Left Hand of Darkness* and *The Dispossessed,* presents two sets of people with differing ideologies. These are the process-oriented Kesh and the dualistic Dayao. Unlike the previous works, *Always Coming Home* is concerned with the subtle uses and abuses of the Taoist principle of unity in opposition. Unlike the previous novels, *Always Coming Home* defines the yin-yang principle, not in terms of opposition or duality, and not in terms of an overriding unity of two forms, but in terms of the meandering processes by which the principle actually functions. Those processes are symbolized by the statement, "He goes backward, looks forward."

Before going into the process-oriented focus of the text, it is important to clarify why *Always Coming Home* shifts the focus from the "unity in opposition" principle to a process orientation. In the novel an oppositional approach to culture formation is presented as an unhealthy tendency toward the valuation of only one-half of a two-part system. The dualistic Dayao are trapped in an us/them or self/other mentality to which the unity-in-opposition principle is especially susceptible. According to *Always Coming Home,* the self/other mentality distorts the unity principle by setting up hierarchies based on "good" and "bad" and by elevating a part of the system so high that it is seen as "self-unified" and, therefore, the proper measure of any phenomenon's value. Stone Telling, the half-Dayao wise woman in *Always Coming Home,* describes the Dayao dualism when her father, Terter Abhao, takes her from her Kesh village into his Dayao city:

> One is not the universe; he made it, and gives it orders. Things are not part of him nor is he part of them, so you must not praise things, but only One. The One, however, reflects himself in the Condor; so the Condor is to be praised and obeyed. And the True Condors and One-Warriors, who are all called Sons of the Condor or Sons of the Son, are reflections of the reflection of One, and therefore also to be praised and obeyed. The tyon are very dim and faint reflections far removed from One, but even so they have enough of his power to be called human beings. No other people are human. The hontik, that is women

and foreigners and animals, have nothing to do with One at all; they are purutik [*sic*], unclean, dirt people. They were made by One to obey and serve the Sons.[5]

The hierarchically structured Dayao society pampers its aristocratic males and exploits its women and slave classes, thus taking the notions of better and worse or high and low to an extreme. Thus, the high valuation of "One," his "Son," and "Son's Sons" leaves no room for any kind of unification with the "others": women, foreigners, and animals.

The Dayao leaders are obsessed with controlling others, even those outside their political boundaries. They are described as "civilised, aggressive, and destructive" (402). The most important political item on the Dayao agenda is to conquer neighboring peoples and rule their lands in a feudal fashion. As is usual for conquerors, the Dayao tend to privilege their life-style over that of the subjugated and see the technology that accompanies their city life as progressive, and the agrarian life-style of their neighbors as atavistic.

By the end of the Dayao section of the novel, however, the Dayao "way" has self-destructed. A series of computer-stored messages explains that while the Dayao are superior to the Kesh in terms of industrial technology and could easily destroy the Kesh with small weapons such as guns and grenades, they insist on putting all their resources into huge, cumbersome war machines that are powered by fossil fuels. Ironically, they live in a future world that has almost lost its "worldwide technological web" as well as its fossil fuel resources. Despite the futility of large industrial-based projects, they expend their time, resources, and the patience of their slave labor on war measures inappropriate to their time and place (403–4). The final outcome of the Dayao obsession with progress, civilization, and control of all surrounding lands is a slave revolt that disrupts the Dayao culture. J. R. Wytenbroek explains the significance of the outcome:

Their society is a machine that, set going, cannot stop. Those who start the machine become part of the machine, until, finally, they become the machine and no longer control it.... However, the war machine here is breaking down, collapsing under its own weight of greed and power. The society begins to destroy itself from within because of the potency of its own disease, which is overwhelming it.[6]

The Kesh explanation of the Dayao decline is voiced by Stone Telling: "A hundred years or more ago they obeyed one of their Condors who had a vision and said that One had commanded them to build a city and dwell in it. When they did that they locked their energy into the wheel, and so began to lose their souls" (208). The Dayao self-destructed because of their inflexibility, their inability to break the mold of either/or thinking. The Kesh warn against Dayao-like dualized behavior in pithy aphorisms like "*better* and *worse* are eggsucking words, they leave only the shell" (332).

Besides exposing the limitations of a dualistic approach to one's culture, *Always Coming Home* offers an alternative approach, one that has the power to affirm a variety of solutions to the problem of structuring reality. In terms of approaching the task of restructuring reality *Always Coming Home* is unusual. It does not slide easily into the formulaic solutions we have come to expect in the science fiction and fantasy genres that Le Guin uses as her foundation. But that is no surprise, for while Le Guin has always used the basic science fiction and fantasy tenet of complementation between civilization/culture/technology and nature/primitivism, that is, the belief that the institutions and activities of civilization are dependent on what is identified as an opposite natural state, she does not allow that tenet to simplistically drive the structures of her stories. Instead, she critically examines the restrictions of employing dualized sets of contrasting or oppositional elements that fill up each other's lacking features. At the same time, she stretches toward complex relationships. As Charlotte Spivack states in *Ursula K. Le Guin,* the fiction of Le Guin "offers a thrilling personal vision of a universe, a whirling, expanding infinitely peopled universe, with harmony in its vast movement and unity in its complex diversity."[7] That personal vision and the intricate narrative, character, and image structures that it powers set Le Guin's work both inside and outside the science fiction and fantasy arenas.

That vision is also the source of present critics' inability to classify her work satisfactorily. Harold Bloom has recently defined her genre as romance and has placed the whole of the multiple forms of science fiction under that category.[8] An earlier critic, George Edgar Slusser, is more tentative about genre. He uneasily and provisionally defines Le Guin's work as science fiction in *The Farthest Shores of Ursula K. Le Guin* and then posits the idea that Le Guin's novels are complex forms that "shift in focus away from the celebration of balance and toward the problematics of balance."[9] Le Guin's theme of balance as problematic is yet to be fully explained.

James W. Bittner is even less sure of the Le Guin territory and declares that the development of Le Guin's work is still unknowable and that each new work interacts with and alters the structure of her previous works.[10] What Bittner (and to some extent Slusser) is picking up on is the figuration of process as structure in Le Guin's works, a fluid figuration that crosses and often confuses genre boundaries. Critics in the future will have to contend with Le Guin's flexibility of form if we are to understand the structure of Le Guin's nontraditional social vision of the processes of affiliation building, the creation of flexible relationships that support both individual and communal needs.

In *Always Coming Home* it is the Kesh people who represent this process-oriented alternative, this going backward, looking forward way. Le Guin herself explains that the imaginary Kesh people of *Always Coming Home* do not recognize the dichotomies of their predecessors, who just happen to be us. As they organize their psycho/socio/political structures, they do not use a hierarchy. Instead, they organize around "central and less central."[11]

The idea of centrality is important to Kesh life, but not necessarily in the way one might think. What is central is not so much a place or thing as a way of going. For the Kesh, centrality is the action of a continual return. As Charles Crow puts it in "Homecoming in the California Visionary Romance," "Kesh civilization represents a return—a coming home—to enduring human values."[12] Here we see that even the title, *Always Coming Home,* suggests that Kesh civilization is a never-ending act of returning to a communal center.

The concept of centrality is further suggested in *Always Coming Home* by a recurring image, namely the "heyiya-if," the "hinge." The hinge is that which is centered, yet changing, becoming, moving sideways, around itself and within itself, a symbol of "keeping many different things in mind and observing their relations and proportions" to one another (331). This "continual act of returning" has a particular visual shape in *Always Coming Home.* It is drawn as an empty hinge in the center of a doubly spiraled form.

Yes, it is the yin-yang symbol, but the shape of the symbol is modified. For one thing, the form is not closed off by a circle's circumference. The form is left open. The symbol is further modified in that the uniformity of the black-and-white sign is dispensed with. Instead,

Figure 1

(ACH, 338)

(ACH, 158)

(ACH, 327)

(ACH, 300)

(ACH, 513)

each black-and-white drawing differs from all others in some way. Also, the clear differentiation into halves is thwarted because the initial curved line of the traditional yin-yang symbol often turns into a complex spiral at each end. Finally, the center of the stylized design, the hinge, is usually empty. This heyiya-if, then, is somewhat contrary to the traditional, fully connected yin-yang symbol. As such, it suggests open-endedness, flexibility in the relationship between its halves, and gradual change rather than unity in opposition.

In its various forms the hinge appears at regular intervals throughout *Always Coming Home*, which is cunningly devised as an anthropological text, complete with drawings of Kesh town structures, local flora and fauna, and maps of an area that can be identified as the future Napa Valley of California. The hinged form is present in the stylized drawings of birds, animals, and Kesh town charts. Hinge drawings appear in the songs, chants, biographical sketches, and sociological and ecological descriptions that the fictional anthropologist,

Pandora, has collected. The drawings of a hinge in the center of a spiraling form reiterate the importance of centering in the dynamic Kesh way.

On another level, the hinge image is developed as a complex symbol that embodies the actual dynamic, the actual connectionist Kesh style of life that is always mindful of the process of living around the hinge. The use of the hinge as a manifestation of its own dynamic is apparent in several places in the text. For example, the Kesh's particular niche in *Always Coming Home*'s historical framework is that of a hinge between past and future. Historically, the Kesh don't actually exist; they are an imagined group. But they are connected to the past because they are patterned after several groups of Native Americans who inhabited the Pacific Coast.[13] At the same time, the Kesh are also associated with the future, because in *Always Coming Home* they are placed in our distant future. The past and future thus converge in the Kesh. They are described in *Always Coming Home* as a people who "might be going to have lived a long, long time from now in Northern California" (ix). In other words, the Kesh live simultaneously in our probable past and our possible future. The present isn't left out, either, for it is the immediacy of the present that *Always Coming Home* highlights. As stated at the beginning of the text, "All we ever have is here, now" (ix). Therefore, past and future spiral and converge at the hinge that is the embodiment of the immediate now.

The historical placement of the Kesh is not the only thing affected by the hinge's function as a structuring principle. Pandora, the anthropologist character of *Always Coming Home* who is gathering ethnographic information on the Kesh, discovers the consequences of the heyiya-if as the Kesh's guiding image. She reports her initial difficulty in locating the site of Sinshan, the Kesh town she plans to study. She first looks for a wall, a gate, and sacred buildings in what she suspects is the central part of the town. This type of search is in keeping with traditional archaeological methods. But Pandora suddenly realizes that her assumption of a gate and wall is silly. That is what a northern European or Mediterranean town would contain. She explains her revelation: "there was never a wall; what on earth did they need a wall for? What I had taken for the gate was the bridge across the meeting of the creeks. And the sacred buildings and the dancing place not in the center of town, for the center is the Hinge, but over in their own arm of the double spiral" (3). In short, only after Pandora applies the concept of life around a hinge is she able to reconstruct Sinshan.

She correctly hypothesizes that there is no meeting building in the center of Sinshan. The center is empty because the Kesh see their town structure as moving around the hinge instead of going toward it. Also, because they see themselves as meandering in side steps and in reversal patterns, the town is set up in a double spiral around the center. The left and right arms of the spiral extend from the hinge and run around it. One arm of the spiral consists of the careful placement of the heyimas, the communal activity buildings. The other arm is fashioned into the living quarters of the Kesh. The place for ceremonies rests in the arm of the communal spiral. The ideas of never reaching the center and of always coming home through the forward-backward process of affiliation building are therefore structured into Kesh towns. The town dwellers literally live their lives moving around the center. Their town experience is both a real and symbolic expression of a hinged way of life.

The image of the hinge and the consequent turning around it not only characterize the immediate Kesh town experience but also the science of the Kesh. For example, the Kesh see cosmic order in terms of spinning around. In one of their poems is a description of the earth as a larger version of a Kesh town:

> Ballround, earth-town.
> Each street meets
> itself at length.
> Old are the roads,
> long are the ways,
> wide are the waters. (420)

In another poem we see a similar description:

> Earth goes turning,
>   earth goes turning spinning,
>   spinning the day-course
>   between shining and darkness.
> What lies between south and north
> is the axis of turning;
> what lies from west to east
> is the way of turning. (420)

It is the movement and the connectedness that are important in these poems. The axis of the earth is not described except in terms of its relationship to the turning, and the focus is on the dynamic that results from gyrating around the core image. It is the spinning around the central image, then, and not the image itself, which is meaningful.

This emphasis on the dynamics of a relationship can also be seen in the spiritual life of the Kesh. In the longest of *Always Coming Home*'s autobiographical tales, the central wise woman, Stone Telling, describes a four-day vision quest. She states: "The hinge of my walk had been the golden hill; the coyote had sung to me; and so long as my hand and the rock touched each other I knew that I had not gone wrong, even if I had come to nothing" (23). Stone Telling sees her spirit in terms of the inscrutable contact between herself and the rock hinge.

The mysterious hinge-to-human dynamic is manifested in the Kesh's ceremonial life, also. One ceremony especially illustrates the obliquity of the dynamic. This is the wine festival, celebrated during the autumnal equinox. During this festival, the Kesh participate in what is called the "Reversal," a ritualistic reversal of their personalities. For example, in one Reversal a normally shy and inhibited man straps on a huge ceremonial penis and runs around poking it at women (28). The Reversal or Dionysiac free-for-all is probably the ultimate expression of "He goes backward, looks forward." The purpose of the Reversal is to acknowledge the necessities of that other side of human nature, the chaotic side, and to remind the Kesh that everyday human personality is never separate from it.

The hinge concept, "heyiya," affects the intellectual reality of the Kesh as well. For example, in the "Serpentine Codex," one of the Kesh's written texts, is a reference to how the categorizing of reality is accomplished by "a fundamental grammatical maneuver of the language" that places great value on the disruption of what might be considered traditional scientific, social, and political truths. For example, though four is an even number, it is also considered an odd number and is used often in conjunction with the numbers five and nine. These three numbers are considered semisacred as a reminder of the arbitrariness of truth and as a formal acknowledgment of the interdependence of all numbers in the system of mathematics. Likewise, egalitarianism, specifically the practice of valuing all persons equally without regard to gender, is the social and political mode (46–50). The idea is that traditional categories of an oppositional nature and the accompanying binarist terminology, such as "male and female" or "odd and even," do not exist. Furthermore, any possibility of creating opposition-based classes and explanations is thwarted by a language expressing both/and or multiple relationships.

Even more important than the valuation of flexible relationships over duality is the subtle understanding that any preoccupation with specific organizational patterns, such as the number of work/sacred houses or the exact differentiation between fact and fiction, earth and sky, and mortal and immortal, is inappropriate and "childish" (46). In fact, the Kesh even see the making of a god or gods out of hinge principles as too specific a task and, therefore, silly. In keeping with their open-ended dynamic way, they see the concept of the hinge only as a "working metaphor" (52). By the time a member of a Kesh community reaches maturity she or he is expected to understand the subtle fluidity of the social, political, and language structures.

The autobiographical sections narrated by Stone Telling, a woman who is half Kesh and half Dayao, serve as illustration of the transformation of the child-self's confused or rigid way of thinking into what Stone Telling later calls a "gyred" way, a way that perceives the multiple affiliations possible for the individual, the group, and the natural environment (388–90). At the beginning of Stone Telling's autobiography she is a child, ignorant of Kesh thought and sometimes stubborn in her ignorance. After visiting relatives in another village, Stone Telling, or North Owl as she is called then, discovers the Kesh phenomenon of seeing the world backward. When she gets to her village the hills, the houses, and even the inside of her home are perceptually reversed. Stone Telling likes the "strangeness" though she doesn't know yet what to make of her backward world and wants things to return as they were (18–19).

Later, when she goes on a vision quest, Stone Telling comes into contact with her personal hinge, the walk on the golden hill. At the time she is unable to comprehend what the vision means: "I knew something had come to me that I did not understand" (23). But she is open to the inscrutable knowledge. "So long as my hand and the rock touched each other I knew that I had not gone wrong, even if I had come to nothing" (23). The willing acceptance of subtle connections with her environment is the first step in Stone Telling's understanding of the fluid processes of creating affiliations.

As Stone Telling's story unfolds, she learns through some adolescent rebellion on her part and an excursion into her father's Dayao city that the Dayao's rigid life-style is repressive and the Kesh's dy-namic way of living is healthy. In the Dayao city she is forced to marry a man in whom she has no interest, is treated with no respect, and is faced with accepting the Dayao notions of "enemy" and "law" and "no way for disagreements to come together into agreement" (370–74). Thus, when Stone Telling returns to her village it is with an insider's understanding that the Dayao's way disconnects one from the life-sustaining environment. She calls that "living outside the world" (390).

Stone Telling gladly returns to a life where community and individ-ual relationships take precedence over law enforcement and where problems are solved by consent. That is the manner in which Stone Telling and a lover named Alder decide to take each other in mar-riage. Each of them is unsure about making a commitment at first. They talk about it, think about it, live together for a while, live apart for a while. The decision is a slow process, after much talk about the need for both intimacy and freedom (397–400). By the time Stone Telling fully affiliates herself with Alder, the pattern of her matura-tion process is clear. So is the pattern of Kesh adult life. It is a never-ending, fluid process of creating harmonious relationships between one and another, between individual and community, and between person and nature, all in a spiraling network of relationships.

In stories such as "Stone Telling" the Kesh life dynamic is expli-cated. But *Always Coming Home* not only explicates the Kesh life dy-namic, it manifests it. Pandora's "anthropological" text is like Kesh life. It revolves, reverses, and digresses here and there as it slowly uncoils her information on the Kesh. The short texts comprising the work are of diverse discourse modes that make *Always Coming Home* dynamic in the same way as Kesh life. The anthropological text begins with a song, then moves on to Pandora's note on how she dis-covered the town, Sinshan. This is followed by the first part of Stone Telling's autobiographical account, or what the reader might call a novel narrated in first person, one that orients the reader into the Kesh way. The novel is interrupted by "The Serpentine Codex," which charts social organization and further explains Kesh reality.

Next a metanarrator, or critic, describes Pandora's fear of over-intellectualizing her account of the Kesh. Elizabeth Cummins suggests that the insertion of such a critic is a self-reflexive structural device used to work through the implications of blurring the traditional di-chotomized boundaries between fiction and fact, even between text and critic.[14] The self-reflexive restructuring of these boundaries not only adds to the explanation of the Kesh way but also invites the reader to experience the fiction of *Always Coming Home* as fact, and the fact of self-reflexive critical inquiry as a fictional mode. Even the reader gets to experience Kesh-like relationships.

The excursion into self-reflexivity is then reversed. The next section is made of several unself-conscious stories that might be classed as parables. Then there are a set of poems, a note on Kesh funerary procedures, a group of romantic tales, more poems, and a set of histories, complete with maps. All of this is in the first one hundred fifty pages of the text, slightly more than one-fourth of *Always Coming Home*.

The discourse modes are patterned and balanced in such a way that it is difficult to say, "This text is mostly poetry, or the driving force of the text is narrative, or the text gains coherence by virtue of Pandora's interjections." Each adds to the richness of the overall text and takes part in the theme of Kesh life as a never-ending dialectic. But if one must find a consistent pattern through the text, if one needs to identify the arms around the "hinge" of *Always Coming Home*, then it is probably safe to point to the copious autobiographical accounts as the unifying forms of the text. As Pandora points out, an autobiography, or "telling" of one's life story, is a most sacred thing: it is heyiya. She tells us that "biography and autobiography were written down and given to the heyimas or the lodge as an offering, a gift of life. Commonplace as most of them were, they were a 'hinge' or intersection of private, personal, cyclical being-time, and so were a joining of temporal and eternal, a sacred act" (279). These narratives are the life that keeps moving here and there, backward and forward, in whatever way is necessary for the good of the individual and the community. They function as entry points into the idea of the heyiya and its image.[15]

At the same time we must be skeptical of declaring any form within the huge organic matrix of *Always Coming Home* to be *the* hinge around which all other forms twist. We must reverse our tendency to unify, for to insist on unity is to undermine a theme of the text, a theme based not only on the intricate reversals and snaking path of the text, but also on the very real, very serious philosophy of the Native Americans who are the model for *Always Coming Home*. Theodora Kroeber, respected for her writing on Native Americans of California and known as the counseling mother of Ursula Le Guin, explains that "the Indians [the 'First Californians'] were part of a natural order between whose people and other animal and plant life there was a well-nigh perfect symbiosis."[16] The self/other mentality tended not to figure into their affiliation-oriented relationship with the natural environment. So, to be wise to the healthy way of both the text and Native American peoples like the Coast Miwok and Wappo, the search for the text's unifying principle must be seen, ultimately, as one of those unnecessary categorizing activities in which the Dayao engage. The Kesh would say such overstructuralization calls for a reversal, a switchback, and a focus on developing affiliations once again.

The Kesh would say that the relational idea "He goes backward, looks forward" is unity enough. It is this very attitude that brings *Always Coming Home* to life. Because the text goes backward into the past for its philosophy of living close to the land and then projects itself into the future, the past and future are able to converge. The past way is realized and the future benefits. This is only possible because the idea of event and time boundaries, of dichotomies between past and future, are maneuvered into a minor place in the larger dynamic matrix of past, future, and the hinge, that all-encompassing metaphor that is encountered in the text's fleeting present.

The emphasis on such interrelationships switches us back to the beginning of this reading, to the problem that Le Guin posed in her Yale article, that of the limited two-way choice that American ideology forces on Le Guin as well as on America itself. For Le Guin, "He goes backward, looks forward" is a compelling solution for the contemporary society that has inherited the choking structures of self vs. other, industry vs. ecology, and progression vs. primitivism. As American thought shuns the philosophy of past Native Americans and runs pell-mell toward what Le Guin calls a "one-way future consisting only of growth,"[17] she suggests that "sidetrips and reversals are precisely what minds stuck in forward gear most need."[18]

Thus, when Le Guin is asked what reality she will write, the misery of our unhealthy society or an escape from it, and she says, "no," her answer is appropriate. It is a reversal of the expected answer. It follows the way of the hinge by opening up possibilities for self-reflective discourse and problem solving. Le Guin's answer, like the hinge of *Always Coming Home*, suggests an endless set of working solutions that are negotiable anytime they begin to function poorly. The solutions must address both immediate and future needs, emphasize the interconnectedness of life forms, and manifest their multiplicity in an on-going dialectic whose rules of exchange are never fully defined and codified. One of the Kesh poems clarifies the process through which an appropriate solution moves:

> The solution
> dissolves itself
> leaving the problem behind,
> a skeleton,
> the mystery before,
> around, above, below, within. (418)

Always Coming Home is such a set of solutions. It is a multiplex novel of interrelated genres, characters, critics, events, and ideas that embodies the principle, "He goes backward, looks forward."

Notes

1. Ursula K. Le Guin, "A Non-Euclidean View of California as a Cold Place to Be," *Yale Review* 72 (1983): 179.

2. Ibid.

3. Ibid., 165.

4. Dena C. Bain, "The 'Tao Te Ching' as Background to the Novels of Ursula K. Le Guin," in *Modern Critical Views: Ursula K. Le Guin,* ed. Harold Bloom (New York: Chelsea House, 1986), 223–24.

5. Ursula K. Le Guin, *Always Coming Home* (1985; reprint, New York: Bantam, 1987), 12–13. All future page references to *Always Coming Home* will be made parenthetically in the text.

6. J. R. Wytenbroek, "*Always Coming Home:* Pacificism and Anarchy in Le Guin's Latest Utopia," *Extrapolation* 28 (Winter 1987): 334. Wytenbroek gives a full explication of the Dayao's misuse of hierarchical thinking and the resultant ineffectuality of their stratified power structure.

7. Charlotte Spivack, *Ursula K. Le Guin,* Twayne's United States Authors Series, no. 453 (Boston: Twayne, 1984), 161.

8. Harold Bloom, ed., *Ursula K. Le Guin's* The Left Hand of Darkness, Modern Critical Interpretations (New York: Chelsea House, 1987), 1–2.

9. George Edgar Slusser, *The Farthest Shores of Ursula K. Le Guin,* Milford Series: Popular Writers of Today, vol. 3 (San Bernardino, Calif.: Borgo Press, 1976), 3–4.

10. James W. Bittner, *Approaches to the Fiction of Ursula K. Le Guin,* Studies in Speculative Fiction, no. 4 (Ann Arbor, Mich.: UMI Research Press, 1984), ix.

11. Ursula K. Le Guin, "Text, Silence, Performance," in *Dancing at the Edge of the World: Thoughts on Words, Women, Places* (New York: Grove Press, 1989), 179–87.

12. Charles L. Crow, "Homecoming in the California Visionary Romance," *Western American Literature* 24 (May 1989): 15.

13. Theodora Kroeber and Robert F. Heizer, *Almost Ancestors: The First Californians*, ed. F. Davis Hales (San Francisco: Sierra Club, 1968). Kroeber gives us a clear, brief history of the Yurok-Karok-Hupa Indians of northern California and the Yokut, Pomo, Wappo, and Miwok Indians of north central and central California in this book. The book also includes photos of the last of these peoples. For a more complete understanding of Le Guin's perspectives on the lifestyles of California Indians also see A. L. Kroeber, *Handbook of California Indians* (New York: Dover, 1976).

14. Elizabeth Cummins, *Understanding Ursula K. Le Guin* (Columbia: University of South Carolina Press, 1990), 182.

15. Le Guin, "Where Do You Get Your Ideas From?" in *Dancing at the Edge*, 192–200. This essay explicates Le Guin's understanding of the three-way relationship of narrative, image, and idea.

16. Kroeber and Heizer, *Almost Ancestors*, 24.

17. Le Guin, "Non-Euclidean View," 166.

18. Ibid., 176–77.

Bibliography

Bain, Dena C. "The 'Tao Te Ching' as Background to the Novels of Ursula K. Le Guin." In *Modern Critical Views: Ursula K. Le Guin*, edited by Harold Bloom, 211–24. New York: Chelsea House, 1986.

Bittner, James W. *Approaches to the Fiction of Ursula K. Le Guin*. Studies in Speculative Fiction, no. 4. Ann Arbor, Mich.: UMI Research Press, 1984.

Bloom, Harold, ed. *Ursula K. Le Guin's* The Left Hand of Darkness. Modern Critical Interpretations. New York: Chelsea House, 1987.

Crow, Charles L. "Homecoming in the California Visionary Romance." *Western American Literature* 24 (May 1989): 3–19.

Cummins, Elizabeth. *Understanding Ursula K. Le Guin*. Columbia: University of South Carolina Press, 1990.

Kroeber, A. L. *Handbook of California Indians*. New York: Dover, 1976.

Kroeber, Theodora, and Robert F. Heizer. *Almost Ancestors: The First Californians*. Edited by F. Davis Hales. San Francisco: Sierra Club, 1968.

Le Guin, Ursula K. *Always Coming Home*. New York: Harper and Row, 1985; New York: Bantam, 1987.

———. *Dancing at the Edge of the World: Thoughts on Words, Women, Places*. New York: Grove Press, 1989.

──────. *The Dispossessed: An Ambiguous Utopia.* New York: Harper, 1974; London: Gollancz, 1974.

──────. *The Left Hand of Darkness.* New York: Ace, 1969; London: Macdonald, 1969.

──────. "A Non-Euclidean View of California as a Cold Place to Be." *Yale Review* 72 (1983): 161–80.

Slusser, George Edgar. *The Farthest Shores of Ursula K. Le Guin.* Milford Series: Popular Writers of Today, vol. 3. San Bernardino, Calif.: Borgo Press, 1976.

Spivack, Charlotte. *Ursula K. Le Guin.* Twayne's United States Authors Series, no. 453. Boston: Twayne, 1984.

Wytenbroek, J. R. "*Always Coming Home:* Pacifism and Anarchy in Le Guin's Latest Utopia." *Extrapolation* 28 (Winter 1987): 330–39.

Part 4

Other Voices:
Ethnic Diversity, Old West and New

18. The Choice to Write: Mourning Dove's Search for Survival

Alanna Kathleen Brown

In a letter dated February 29, 1916, to her mentor and friend, L. V. McWhorter, Mourning Dove begins:

> I am writing you today in regards to changing that dedication of "Cogeawea." I think your seggestion strikes about right. You fix it in form and I know it will be all O.K. But I feel like I don't want mention about my Suewappee blood. I think my photo shows the traces of my Indian very strongly and I can see no dispute in that connection. And while on the other hand if I let you mention of my blood, I know all honors will be cast to the white part of me. Savey? I know you will understand. I am plenty dark enough to pass as full blood, to people that does not know the truth. But think it over. I'd rather be Injun[.] I hates to be looked upon Suewappee when I am a writing a novel, of the cowpunchers, with their pals. [4–5;393][1]

The choice to write can hold many dilemmas for a woman. In Mourning Dove's case, one of her critical decisions involved the issue of race. Her choice was a courageous one: "I'd rather be Injun." Its significance is not clear if we do not understand the times and the history out of which that choice emerged.

On July 4, 1876, most Americans were celebrating one hundred years of political existence in special festivities throughout the nation. Only eleven years earlier, the North and the South had been torn by a devastating civil war. This was the period of recovery, of the healing of wounds, of quick industrial and economic development in the East, and the opening of frontier after frontier in the West. The last quarter of the nineteenth century into the first decade of the twentieth century would see massive immigration, particularly from Europeans eager for land and for opportunities closed to them in their home countries. Americans were caught up in a vision called Manifest Destiny.

But Manifest Destiny had a dark side. Fate appeared to require federal policies to maintain it, propaganda to sustain it, and a military to enforce it. There had always been a problem with Columbus's "discovery" of America. Native peoples, complex cultures, were already here. That awkward truth reasserted itself on July 5, 1876, when leaders in Washington, D.C., learned of General Custer's annihilating defeat at the battle of the Little Big Horn River on June 25. The battleground, close to what today is called Billings, Montana, was only a geographical stone's throw away from Yellowstone National Park, the first such wilderness preserve, established by Congress in 1872. The Nez Perce, under the leadership of Chief Joseph, would pass through that park on their attempted flight into Canada in 1877. I doubt that anyone in that band of people thought that he or she trespassed on federal land. What the Nez Perce fled was the radically diminished life of the reservations, and the humiliating encounters with people whose behaviors and attitudes were so strikingly different from their own.

Chief Joseph's people did not make it to Canada, and the Sioux and Cheyenne warriors did not stop the U.S. Cavalry. With the 1890 massacre at Wounded Knee on the Pine Ridge Reservation in South Dakota, the U.S. conquest of indigenous peoples begun centuries before was at an end. The General Allotment, or Dawes, Act of 1887 became the capstone legislation marking that achievement. This act initiated a period of coercive assimilation intended to destroy Indian cultures and to force native peoples into the Euramerican mainstream. In essence, the Indians were to just disappear. It was into this world of hothouse assimilation pressures that Mourning Dove was born.

The details of her early life are sketchy and contradictory. Various documents place her birth date between April 1882 and April 1888.[2] The issue of sexual exploitation also haunts her past. In a November 10, 1925, letter, she states:

I am of Irish decent. I think. That is my grandfather's name was Haynes or Haines. but my father never took his name but went by his step father's name who really raised him. and to save dad's feelings please do not mention any names. it would dig up the past. because in the early days, many white men never married their Indian wives legally, and only cast them aside for white women when thire kind came. and ofcourse my dad was the unfortune one. so let the past rest for his sake.

My grandmother thought no doubt she was corectly married by her Indian tribal cermonies. [9;389]

That violation of another's trust, and of Indian people's marriage customs in general, is also a centerpiece of the corrupt relationship between Densmore and Cogewea in Mourning Dove's novel. But a more poignant story may lie behind the family story already recounted. The allotment records of 1905–6 suggest that it was Mourning Dove's biological father who was named Haines, and who would have abandoned Lucy Stuikin, her mother, and the little baby girl, very early in that child's life. Whether the events happened to Mourning Dove or to her father, Joseph Quintasket, Indians clearly were exploitable, discardable human beings when exposed to Euramerican needs and ambitions. That sexual abuse also prefigured the psychological and spiritual abuse which would follow.

In 1883 a Court of Indian Offenses had been established that made it a crime for Native Americans to speak their own languages, to practice traditional religious rituals, to wear traditional dress, even to wear their hair at the male warrior length. While it was impossible to totally enforce such requirements, the constant harassment by officials, the need for certain ceremonies to go underground, or to be performed in truncated ways, such as powwow dances at the Euramerican Independence Day celebrations, severely weakened the power and significance of tradition for the younger generation during Mourning Dove's lifetime.[3]

Another potent arm of civilization was the creation of federal schools and the expansion of religiously affiliated schools to educate Indian children. These were most often boarding schools where girls and boys were isolated from their parents, and even isolated from other children of their tribe in rooming arrangements. They were forced to speak English all of the time, and to accommodate themselves to "American" dress, diet, and daily discipline. Traditional Indian beliefs were openly ridiculed, and nothing in the curricula encouraged pride in their Indian heritage. To become a dusky mirror image of a Euramerican prototype was the all in all.

Mourning Dove experienced such an education, and this bizarre period of intense repression serves as the backdrop to her spiritual autobiography, *Cogewea, the Half-Blood: A Depiction of the Great Montana Cattle Range,* first drafted by 1914 and eventually published with extensive editing and cowriting in 1927. What led her to write that Western Romance? Or later to dedicate so much of her energy to collecting and writing up Okanogan legends? What moved her late in her life to create a manuscript on the assimilation pressures impacting her people? Her childhood and young adulthood did not bode well for such ambitions.

Mourning Dove grew up on Kelly Hill, near the Kettle River, just outside of Boyds, Washington, on the Colville Reservation. She was of Colvile,[4] Arrow Lakes, and probably Irish descent. Her English name was Christine Quintasket; her Indian name was Humishuma, or Mourning Dove. According to school records, she first attended the Goodwin Mission School of the Sacred Heart Convent at Ward, Washington, in 1895. That school was only about ten miles downriver from Kelly Hill. As with many other Indian children, the new environment was so foreign that Christine got sick and had to go home. She returned to the mission school in 1898–99. Unfortunately that was the year in which federal funds were cut for Indian education in church-related schools. Protestant Americans had become anxious about what appeared to be tax-supported Catholic proselytism, and educational support was redirected to the religious neutrality of Bureau of Indian Affairs schools. In 1899 Fort Spokane was refurbished to accept an influx of Indian children and Christine Quintasket was among them. Indian children were now housed in the military barracks of those who had been hired to keep the peace at the confluence of the Columbia and Spokane rivers.

Christine remained at Fort Spokane from 1899 to 1902 when she returned home to a family emergency. That year her mother, Lucy Stuikin, died, as did a four- or five-year-old baby brother, John. Christine's four-year-old baby sister, Marie, died the following year. We can assume that Christine, as the oldest sister in a family of seven, had many responsibilities during those two very rough years. It is notable that she never discussed that family tragedy in the correspondence of later life. While those deaths bound the surviving family members together, theirs was probably too intimate and painful a memory to unfold to others.

In 1904 Joseph Quintasket remarried Cecelia Williams, who was scarcely older than Christine, and Mourning Dove and her younger sisters, Julia and Mary Margaret, traveled to the Flathead Reservation in Montana to live with their mother's mother, Marie. By late 1904 or 1905, Christine had hired herself out as a matron at the Fort Shaw Indian School in exchange for room and board and the privilege of attending classes. She was on her own and had chosen the pursuit of "white" education as the means to make her way in the world.

It was there that she met Hector McLeod, a mixed-blood Flathead Indian, and they married on July 3, 1908, in Kalispell, Montana. Soon they had established a livery business in Ronan. The marriage was an unhappy one. Hector was an alcoholic, and there was psychological, and possibly, physical abuse.[5] In that marriage Christal McLeod, as she called herself then, suffered a miscarriage and was never able to conceive a child again. By 1912 it was clear that she and Hector were either separated, or in and out of separation.

Yet those years on the Flathead were fertile in another way. Christal loved to write, and the crucible of assimilation life, a tough marriage, and the fast-growing white settlement of the Flathead pulled to a focus when she witnessed the last major buffalo roundup (1908) to occur in the United States. She recounts that experience in *Cogewea*:

> But it was pitiful to see the animals fight so desperately for freedom. Although I participated in a way, it brought a dimness to my eyes. They seemed to realize that they were leaving their native haunts for all time. To the Indian, they were the last link connecting him with the past, and when one of the animals burst through the car, falling to the tracks and breaking its neck, I saw some of the older people shedding silent tears. But what else could the owner do than sell them? The reservation had been thrown open to settlement and the range all taken by homesteaders.[6]

Mourning Dove was so moved by the event, so struck by its historical and cultural significance for her people, that she did two things. In 1912 she went to Portland, Oregon, to be alone and to write the first draft of her novel, *Cogewea, the Half-Blood*. Then in 1913 she crisscrossed the Northwest to attend the Calgary Business College in Alberta, Canada. She studied typing, shorthand, and composition. In 1914 she met Lucullus Virgil McWhorter at the Walla Walla Frontier Days celebration. The meeting was propitious, for McWhorter would become her editor, cowriter, and lifelong friend.

The collaboration of Mourning Dove and L. V. McWhorter is a complex relationship that lasted for twenty years. When they met, McWhorter was fifty-four years old, and his work on behalf of native peoples already marked him as one who would be important in Northwest history. His outrage at the treatment of Indians at the turn of the century had just led him to write a very important pamphlet, "The Crime against the Yakimas" (1913), a document crucial in the protection of water rights for the Yakima Tribe. His later work on the Nez Perce single-handedly enabled people to accurately reconstruct Chief Joseph's flight for Canada. *Yellow-Wolf: His Own Story* (1940) and *Hear Me, My Chiefs* (1952) are books that preserve much of the latter research.

Mourning Dove, a member of a group of singers whom McWhorter had hired, was between twenty-six and thirty-two years of age when they met. At that celebration McWhorter discovered that Mourning Dove had begun collecting the legends of her people. Somewhat later he also learned that she already had the rough draft of an Indian Western Romance completed. He offered to help edit her works and to find a publisher. After a year of correspondence, Mourning Dove agreed to stay with McWhorter's family during the winter of 1915–16 to complete the first publishable draft of *Cogewea*. Because of the cost of paper during World War I and changing readership tastes, two publishers who had been interested in the work between 1917 and 1919 decided not to publish it. Years passed and McWhorter worked more and more with the text adding passages and ultimately sections to address the inequity in the treatment of Indians. *Cogewea* became torn by two voices and two purposes. Mourning Dove, the storyteller, wrote of the values, dilemmas, and people she knew. McWhorter, the ethnographer and social critic, inserted both detailed description and diatribes against government corruption and Christian hypocrisy. Their second collaborative effort, *Coyote Stories,* which also drew on the skills of Dean Guie, was a far more successful work. It is a collection of twenty-seven Okanogan traditional tales, which was first published in 1933 and was so well received that it was in its second edition by 1934.[7]

What strikes one in reviewing Mourning Dove and McWhorter's extensive correspondence is that they were self-defining people in chaotic times. They knew that they lived in a period of dynamic change, and they made choices to anchor themselves in values that transcended the self-serving and self-preserving mentalities that surrounded them. In her choice to write and to use her Indian name, Humishuma, as author, Mourning Dove rejected the insistent pressures toward assimilation.[8] She also used the education meant to eradicate her "Indian" identity to preserve what would be denied. An examination of the structure of Mourning Dove's original story for *Cogewea* and the themes she chose to address in that work will illustrate her independence of thought clearly.

Although she wrote imitating the format of the dime-store Westerns available to her, the plot is a radical departure from typical Western Romances. Her story is based on her experiences, Indian family stories, and includes the first transcription of Native American oral narratives as a key element of a novel's overall structure. Moreover, by writing a contemporary novel, she has enabled us to explore the frontier as both psychological and physical space.

A frontier suggests edges, boundaries, transitional possibilities. It is where one must let go, redefine, expand, or contract. Frontiers force one to move forward or to go backward. The static in-between is its own kind of hell. That is where we find Cogewea. She is literally and metaphorically a mixed-blood. Many of the Indians of Mourning Dove's generation were one or both. The choices they faced are highlighted by the structure of the novel, which places Cogewea between two sisters: Julia, who has married a white rancher and who has totally assimilated to western ways, literally marrying into the road to blood purity; and Mary, who lives with her full-blooded grandmother, practicing the daily rituals, wearing the costume, eating the foods of her tribe. In her feistiness, Cogewea wants to claim both heritages, to be accepted by both peoples. She rides her horse in the ladies' race, and she rides her horse in the squaw race. She is capable enough to win both. But the issue is not capability. Blood purity and group allegiance are what enable Indian tribes to survive and non-Indians to thrive. The people in-between, both white and Indian, have no certainty within community.

For Cogewea, and probably Mourning Dove, a certain ambiguous pride comes from walking a middle way—seeing with a broader historical eye than a reservation Indian, voicing defense of her "primitive" people in acceptable logical ways, and perceiving that the Euramerican ideals of equality and Christian charity rarely exist in reality. Certainly they had not manifested themselves in the policies determining the treatment of American Indians. Nonetheless, her political astuteness does not prevent Cogewea from being susceptible to the ongoing corrupt white/Indian dynamic. She is a character who has her eighty-acre allotment, and there is an easterner who wants to "get rich quick" by exploiting her trust and Indian vulnerability.

What saves Cogewea is luck and Stemteema, the grandmother who loves her. It is that grandmother, traditional as she is, who breaks from the past and shares with her mixed-blood granddaughter "The Dead Man's Vision":

> This story I am telling you is true. It was given me by my father who favored me among his many children. I was his youngest child from his youngest wife, who was cherished among his twelve wives. He told me the tales that were sacred to his tribe; honored me with them, trusted me. Treasured by my forefathers, I value them. I know that they would want them kept only to their own people if they were here. But they are gone and for me the sunset of the last evening is approaching and I must not carry with me this history.[9]

Why did Mourning Dove write? Because her people, and their vision of the world, were dying. The buffalo were gone. Cultural and physical genocide were on the horizon for those who had lived but a generation beyond the battle of the Little Big Horn.

In a way, Cogewea is an honor song for the generations of her parents and her grandparents. Mourning Dove was born in the shadow of sexual exploitation. She was one of the children they watched going away to school. Then tragedy struck the family and she became one of the children who seemed to turn away and seek out white knowledge, white language, white modes of being. But in her mid-to-late twenties, she paused and reflected. Then she did a new thing to honor an old way. She wrote a novel, a tribute narrative, a promise not to forget, not to be ashamed, not to dishonor. "I'd rather be Injun."

Notes

1. Lucullus Virgil McWhorter was Mourning Dove's editor, collaborator, cowriter, and friend. Their extensive twenty-year correspondence is housed at the Manuscripts, Archives and Special Collections Division of the Washington State University Libraries, Pullman, Washington 99164. The correspondence is kept in individual folders and each sheet of paper within a folder is numbered. This Feb. 29, 1916, letter comprises sheets 4 and 5 of file 393. All further correspondence from the L. V. McWhorter collection will be indicated as shown in the brackets. The quoted material will maintain Mourning Dove's original spelling and grammar with the exception that a period or comma in brackets is my insertion to help reader clarity. Such additions have been kept to a minimum. The letters are published with the knowledge and permission of the family elders, Mary Lemery and Charles Quintasket.

2. Christine Quintasket's marriage license to her first husband, Hector McLeod, and her allotment record indicate that she was born in 1882. Tribal enrollment records and the listing of children on Joseph and Lucy Quintasket's allotment records indicate 1887. Mourning Dove always states that she was born in 1888.

3. Mourning Dove's novel, *Cogewea, the Half-Blood* (1927), has an excellent account of a powwow celebration at Fourth of July festivities. The powwow is ostensibly the reason the traditional grandmother, Stemteema, has come to visit her nontraditional granddaughters, Cogewea and Julia. Chapters 6–8 focus on the celebratory activities in Polson, Montana, around 1900, and because this section of the novel is edited, but not cowritten, by L. V. McWhorter, it provides a fine example of Mourning Dove's storytelling skill.

4. The Colvile tribe is spelled with one l, while the reservation that includes many tribes is spelled with two l's. Colvile was the name given to those whose traditional territory included Kettle Falls.

5. A reference to Hector McLeod's alcoholism is in the patent-in-fee letter on Christine McLeod's behalf written by the superintendent of the Colville Reservation (May 20, 1910), and in the anecdotes of surviving family members.

6. Mourning Dove, *Cogewea, the Half-Blood* (Boston: Four Seas, 1927; reprint, Lincoln: University of Nebraska Press, 1981), 148.

7. Mourning Dove, *Coyote Stories*, ed. Heister Dean Guie (Caldwell, Idaho: Caxton Printers, 1933; reprint, Lincoln: University of Nebraska Press, 1990). The University of Nebraska Press has also published Mourning Dove's last manuscripts in a work titled *Mourning Dove, A Salishan Autobiography* (1990). This text presents the most complete account of inland Salish life we have on record. Donald Hines edited a more inclusive collection of the legends transcribed by Mourning Dove in *Tales of the Okanogans* (Fairfax, Wash.: Ye Galleon, 1976). Unfortunately, the book is now out of print. For a more in-depth examination of the collaboration of Mourning Dove, L. V. McWhorter, and Dean Guie, see Alanna Brown, "The Evolution of Mourning Dove's *Coyote Stories*," *Studies in American Indian Literatures* 4, nos. 2, 3 (Summer, Fall 1992): 161–80.

8. It should be noted that Mourning Dove used both that name and the Indian name Humishuma on the title pages of *Cogewea, the Half-Blood* and *Coyote Stories*. In the former the Indian name is first, followed by its English translation, Mourning Dove, in quotation marks. In *Coyote Stories* the process is reversed with the Indian name, Humishuma, now in parentheses.

9. Mourning Dove, *Cogewea*, 122.

Bibliography

By the Author

Dove, Mourning. *Cogewea, the Half-Blood: A Depiction of the Great Montana Cattle Range.* Boston: Four Seas, 1927. Reprint. Lincoln: University of Nebraska Press, 1981.

————. *Coyote Stories.* Edited by Heister Dean Guie. Caldwell, Idaho: Caxton Printers, 1933. Reprint. Lincoln: University of Nebraska Press, 1990.

————. *Mourning Dove: A Salishan Autobiography.* Edited by Jay Miller. Lincoln: University of Nebraska Press, 1990.

————. *Tales of the Okanogans.* Edited by Donald Hines. Fairfax, Wash.: Ye Galleon, 1976.

Relevant Literary Texts

Allen, Paula Gunn. *Spider Woman's Granddaughters.* Boston: Beacon Press, 1989.

Deloria, Ella Cara. *Waterlily.* Lincoln: University of Nebraska Press, 1988.

Johnson, Emily Pauline. *The Moccasin Maker.* Toronto: Ryerson Press, 1913. Reprint, edited by A. LaVonne Brown Ruoff. Tucson: University of Arizona Press, 1987.

McWhorter, Lucullus V. *Hear Me, My Chiefs: Nez Perce Legend and History.* Caldwell, Idaho: Caxton Printers, 1952.

————. *Yellow Wolf: His Own Story.* Caldwell, Idaho: Caxton Printers, Ltd., 1940.

Silko, Leslie. *Storyteller.* New York: Arcade Publishing, 1981.

Literary Criticism

Allen, Paula Gunn. *The Sacred Hoop: Recovering the Feminine in American Indian Traditions.* Boston: Beacon Press, 1986.

Bataille, Gretchen M., and Kathleen Mullen Sands. *American Indian Women: Telling Their Lives.* Lincoln: University of Nebraska Press, 1984.

Brown, Alanna K. "The Evolution of Mourning Dove's *Coyote Stories.*" *Studies in American Indian Literatures* 4, nos. 2 & 3 (Summer/Fall 1992): 161–80.

———— ."Looking through the Glass Darkly: The Editorialized Mourning Dove." In *Studies in Native American Literatures,* edited by Arnold Krupat. Washington, D.C.: Smithsonian Institution Press, 1993.

——. "Mourning Dove, an Indian Novelist." *Plainswoman* 11, no. 5 (Jan. 1988):3–4.

——. "Mourning Dove's Canadian Recovery Years, 1917–1919." *Canadian Literature*, nos. 124 and 125 (Spring-Summer 1990): 113–22. Reprinted in *Native Writers and Canadian Writing*, edited by W. H. New, 113–22. Vancouver: University of British Columbia Press, 1990.

——. "Mourning Dove's Voice in Cogewea." *Wicazo Sa Review* 4, no. 2 (Fall 1988): 2–15.

——. "Profile: Mourning Dove (Humishuma) 1888–1936." *Legacy: A Journal of Nineteenth-Century American Women Writers* 6, no. 1 (Spring 1989): 51–58.

——. Review of *Coyote Stories* and *Mourning Dove: A Salishan Autobiography*, edited by Jay Miller. *Studies in American Indian Literatures* 3, no. 2 (Summer 1991):66–70.

——. "A Voice from the Past." Review of *Coyote Stories* and *Mourning Dove: A Salishan Autobiography*, edited by Jay Miller. *Women's Review of Books* 8, no. 2 (Nov. 1990): 19–20.

Brumble, H. David III. *American Indian Autobiography*. Berkeley: University of California Press, 1988.

Clifford, James. "On Ethnographic Authority." *Representations* 1, no. 2 (Spring 1983): 118–46.

Dearborn, Mary. *Pocahontas's Daughters: Gender and Ethnicity in American Culture*. New York: Oxford University Press, 1986.

Fisher, Alice Poindexter. "The Transformation of Tradition: A Study of Zitkala-Sa (Bonnin) and Mourning Dove, Two Transitional Indian Writers." Ph.D. diss., City University of New York, 1979.

——. "The Transformation of Tradition: A Study of Zitkala-Sa and Mourning Dove, Two Transitional American Indian Writers." In *Critical Essays on Native American Literature*, edited by Andrew Wiget, 202–11. Boston: G. K. Hall, 1985.

Green, Rayna. *That's What She Said: Contemporary Poetry and Fiction by Native American Women*. Bloomington: Indiana University Press, 1984.

Krupat, Arnold. *For Those Who Come After: A Study of Native American Autobiography*. Berkeley: University of California Press, 1985.

Larson, Charles R. *American Indian Fiction*. Albuquerque: University of New Mexico Press, 1978.

Lincoln, Kenneth. *Native American Renaissance*. Los Angeles: University of California Press, 1983.

Miller, Jay. "Mourning Dove: The Author as Cultural Mediator." In *On Being and Becoming Indian: Biographical Studies of North American Frontiers*, edited by James A. Clifton, 160–82. Chicago: Dorsey, 1989.

Wiget, Andrew. *Native American Literature*. Twayne's United States Authors Series. Boston: Twayne, 1985.

19. "Myths of the East, Myths of the West": Shattering Racial and Gender Stereotypes in the Plays of David Henry Hwang

Jerry R. Dickey

"I write about Asian-Americans to claim our legitimate, but often neglected, place in the American experience."[1] These are the words of David Henry Hwang, a second-generation Chinese-American born and raised in San Gabriel, California. In the relatively short span of the past decade, Hwang has written a dozen plays and has established himself as one of America's finest and most original playwrights. One of his latest works, *M. Butterfly,* was produced on Broadway in 1988, where it won the Tony and Drama Desk awards for best play. Some of his other major plays include *FOB* (an acronym referring to recent Asian immigrants to the United States meaning "fresh-off-the-boat,") and *The Dance and the Railroad,* set in the Sierra Nevadas during the Chinese-American labor strike of 1867 over working conditions on the transcontinental railroad. In his works, Hwang is concerned primarily with exploring the unique identity of today's Chinese-American, an identity that rejects the westerner's restrictive racial and gender stereotypes toward Asians. In *The Dance and the Railroad* and *M. Butterfly,* Hwang examines these stereotypes in an effort to forge a new, more mutually beneficial relationship between East and West.

The son of a Shanghai-born banker and a Chinese pianist who

272

grew up in the Philippines, Hwang was raised in his California home with strong American middle-class values. During his early years, he was relatively unaware of his ethnic background. "I knew I was Chinese," he has said, "but growing up, it never occurred to me that that had any particular implication or that it should differentiate me in any way. I thought it was a minor detail, like having red hair."[2] By the time he was attending Stanford University in the late 1970s, however, he was well aware of the racial stereotypes that prevailed toward Asian-Americans, and his early plays were often concerned with the denial by Chinese-Americans of their ethnic heritage.

The literary history of Asian-Americans during their 150-plus years in the United States has been slow to achieve national recognition, often obstructed by language barriers, wartime hysteria, reluctant publishers, and the popularization and perpetuation of demeaning Asian stereotypes, such as Charlie Chan and Fu Manchu, stereotypes that were frequently the creations of non-Asian writers. With the advent of the civil rights movement in America in the late 1950s and early 1960s, however, and with the removal in 1966 of the last of legislative restrictions involving racial immigration, Asian-American writing took on a new theme: the urgent need to define a new cultural identity that reconciled the disparate traditions of the Eastern and Western experience. Writers such as John Okada, Richard Kim, Louis Chu, and Maxine Hong Kingston produced novels that sensitively explored their ethnic heritage and cultural environment. In the theater, the dynamic and somewhat angry plays of Frank Chin in the early 1970s heralded the emergence of a vital Chinese-American theater, one that dealt with the daily realities of the Chinese-American experience. This new theater bore no resemblance to the numerous productions of Peking or Cantonese operas so prevalent in any one of America's Chinatowns, works that hitherto served as the most visible form of Chinese-American theater. When the characters in Frank Chin's plays, *The Chickencoop Chinaman* and *The Year of the Dragon*, proclaimed they were not Chinese but rather "ChinaMen," or Chinese-Americans, they spoke for several generations of Asian-American citizens who were frequently torn between an ancient cultural heritage from a land they did not know or had left behind and the lack of total assimilation into the American mainstream.

America, and especially the American West, has always offered the promise of new beginnings, a better life, and the opportunity for quick riches. But the promise of America as a land of perpetual sunshine and endless wealth, a vision the early Chinese immigrants called "Gold Mountain," was often only an enticement by enterprising white businessmen to lure cheap labor to the United States. The reality of Gold Mountain for Chinese-Americans turned out to be backbreaking work on the railroads or in the mines, geographical confinement in work shanties exotically called "Chinatowns," persistent attempts at conversion to Christianity, and the constant tease of buying into the American Dream. All of these realities have become recurring themes in the plays of David Henry Hwang, and it is little wonder that he titled the first anthology of his work *Broken Promises*.

Much of Hwang's writing is concerned with deflating the Western stereotypes of the roles of the Asian male and female. In *The Dance and the Railroad*, Hwang chose a historical incident, the Chinese-American labor strike of 1867, to dispel the notion that the Chinese railroad workers were what Hwang derisively refers to as "little coolies who were always being knocked down by big white men on horses."[3] This belief is symptomatic of one of two long-standing stereotypes of the Asian male: he is either the "good" Asian, a helpless, asexual, broken-English, loyal but docile servant to the white man (such as Charlie Chan or any one of a host of characters from American melodrama and television); or, he is the "bad" Asian, a brilliant but morally bankrupt conniver who threatens to overrun the Western world (such as Fu Manchu or the notion of the "yellow peril"). Frank Chin and the other authors of the preface to the popular and widely influential anthology of Asian-American writing, *Aiiieeeee!*, wrote: "Good or bad, the stereotypical Asian is nothing as a man. At worst, the Asian-American is contemptible because he is womanly, effeminate, devoid of all the traditionally masculine qualities of originality, daring, physical courage and creativity."[4] In *The Dance and the Railroad*, Hwang attempted to show that the early Chinese railroad laborers (perhaps as many as 8,000–10,000 in 1867)[5] were what he termed "strong and hardy and rebellious men who considered themselves warriors, adventurers or soldiers."[6]

In this play Hwang attacks head-on the demeaning stereotypes of Asian males by the West, but does so in a manner that never degenerates into hostile polemics. *The Dance and the Railroad* is set on a mountaintop near the transcontinental railroad camp and depicts only two characters: Lone, a twenty-year-old worker who was forced by his Chinese family to abandon studies at opera school to go to

America to earn money; and Ma, a naive eighteen-year-old worker who arrived in Gold Mountain four weeks previously with dreams of wealth. Lone escapes to the mountaintop each day to practice arduous dance steps he learned in opera school. For Lone, the daily practice is the only remaining proof of his individuality and his distinction from the other workers on the railroad. "They are dead," Lone says. "Their muscles work only because the white man forces them. I live because I can still force my muscles to work for me."[7]

One day, Ma follows Lone to the mountaintop where he pleads to be taught some of the movements associated with the depictions of Gwan Gung, the god of fighters and writers and adopted god of Chinese-America. "I spend a lot of time watching the opera when it comes around," Ma says. "Every time I see Gwan Gung, I say, 'Yeah. That's me. . . . We have the same kind of spirit' " (77). Ma refuses to be discouraged by Lone's pessimistic refusals and, inspired by the striking Chinese workers in the valley camp below, Ma accepts Lone's challenge to adopt and hold a dancer's strenuous physical stance throughout the night.

Lone returns excitedly the next day to the mountaintop with the news that the ChinaMen have won the strike and, further buoyed by Ma's tenacious spirit in holding the dancer's position, agrees to teach him the steps of Gwan Gung. Surprisingly, Ma is no longer interested in the heroic god. He tells Lone: "I don't wanna play Gwan Gung. . . Gwan Gung stayed up all night once to prove his loyalty. Well, now I have too. . . . So let's do an opera about *me* . . . I deserve an opera in my honor" (88–89). Ma recognizes the heroic qualities within himself and within each of the striking workers. Together with Lone, Ma invents and performs his own opera, no longer the glorification of the ancient god Gwan Gung, but the celebration of Ma, the Everyman. The railroad workers in Hwang's play do not submit to the white man like abject coolies but, rather, are depicted as men who "laid tracks like soldiers . . . hung from cliffs in baskets [while] the winds blew [them] like birds," and survived winter snows by living "underground like moles for days at a time" (68). As he did in *FOB*, Hwang suggests that ancient myths alone do not have meaning for the Chinese in America, but rather the spirit of these myths must be embraced and adapted to the spirit of the modern American warriors.

If *The Dance and the Railroad* attempts to correct stereotypical attitudes toward the Asian male, Hwang's finest play, *M. Butterfly*, tackles the stereotype of the Asian female. Typically, the Asian woman is viewed by the Western male as exotically sensual, possessing some inherited or innate knowledge about sexual performance and domestic servitude.[8] If the Asian male is viewed as asexual, the Asian female is seen as *all* sexual, a perfect companion for the Western male who, perhaps subconsciously at least, desires a prefeminist ideal of womanhood, someone less independent and less assertive.

According to Hwang, "Asians have long been aware of 'Yellow Fever'—Caucasian men with a fetish for exotic Oriental women. I have often heard it said that 'Oriental women make the best wives.' (Rarely is this heard from the mouths of Asian men, incidentally.)"[9]

Hwang was immediately intrigued when he first read a brief news article describing the improbable twenty-year romance in China between a French diplomat named Bernard Bouriscot and a male, Chinese spy, whom Bouriscot believed to be a female actress. "What did [the diplomat] think he was getting in this Chinese actress?" Hwang asked himself. "The answer came to me clearly: 'He probably thought he had found Madame Butterfly'... [he] must have fallen in love, not with a person, but with a fantasy stereotype" (93–94). At this time, Hwang was unfamiliar even with the plot of Puccini's opera, *Madame Butterfly*. Hwang wrote:

> ...speaking of an Asian woman, we would sometimes say, "She's pulling a Butterfly," which meant playing the submissive Oriental number. Yet, I felt convinced that [Puccini's] libretto would include yet another lotus blossom pining away for a cruel Caucasian man, and dying for [his] love.... Sure enough, when I purchased the record, I discovered it contained a wealth of sexist and racist clichés, reaffirming my faith in Western culture. (95)

In the hands of another writer, a story with such mistaken sexual identities could easily have become lurid or farcical. Hwang, however, ingenuously used the brief historical event as a springboard to create a highly original commentary on gender relationships and the clash of Eastern and Western cultures.

Early in *M. Butterfly*, the French diplomat (here renamed Gallimard) witnesses a performance of the "Love Duet" from *Madame Butterfly* at a social function at the home of an ambassador. Gallimard is immediately "transfixed" (10) by the story and by the presence of the performer, Song Liling, the undercover male spy. Gallimard reveals his secret attraction in an address to the audience:

But as she glides past him, beautiful, laughing softly behind her fan, don't we who are men sigh with hope? We, who are not handsome, nor brave, nor powerful, yet somehow believe, like [Puccini's] Pinkerton, that we deserve a Butterfly. She arrives with all her possessions in the folds of her sleeves, lays them all out, for her man to do with as he pleases. Even her life itself—she bows her head as she whispers that she's not even worth the hundred yen he paid for her. He's already given too much, when we know he's really had to give nothing at all. (10)

Judging by the persistent appeal of Puccini's work for Western operagoers, there is little doubt that Gallimard's speech would strike a sympathetic chord with audiences in the theatre. Hwang, however, wastes little time undercutting the appeal of the Butterfly myth as he attempts a modern deconstruction of the opera. Gallimard quickly seeks out the singer, Song Liling, and confesses his love for what he calls the "beautiful story" of Butterfly. Song responds:

Well, yes, [it's a beautiful story] to a Westerner.... It's one of your favorite fantasies, isn't it? The submissive Oriental woman and the cruel white man.... Consider it this way: what would you say if a blonde homecoming queen fell in love with a short Japanese businessman? He treats her cruelly, then goes home for three years, during which time she prays to his picture and turns down marriage from a young Kennedy. Then when she learns he has remarried, she kills herself. Now, I believe you would consider this girl to be a deranged idiot, correct? But because it's an Oriental who kills herself for a Westerner—ah!—you find it beautiful! (17)

Despite Song's rebuttal, Gallimard feels he has found and fallen in love with the "Perfect Woman" (77). He quickly adopts the role of Puccini's Pinkerton, alternately loving and abusing his newfound Butterfly. Similarly, Song cleverly plays out the role of the submissive and selflessly obedient lover, all the while gaining secret political information for his rising communist government.

M. Butterfly, however, is much more than an imaginative retelling of a titillating story. It is also a devastating attack on Western attitudes toward the Orient. Late in the play, after the affair has been made public, Song confesses in court how it was so easy for him to manipulate the Western diplomat. He says:

As soon as a Western man comes into contact with the East—he's already confused. The West has sort of an international rape mentality towards the East.... The West thinks of itself as masculine—big guns, big industry, big money—so the East is feminine—weak, delicate, poor...but good at art and full of inscrutable wisdom—the feminine mystique.

...You expect Oriental countries to submit to your guns, and you expect Oriental women to be submissive to your men.

...When [Gallimard] finally met his fantasy woman, he wanted more than anything to believe that she was, in fact, a woman. And...I am an Oriental. And being an Oriental, I could never be completely a man. (82–83)

Hwang implies that personal gender stereotypes by Westerners toward Asians ultimately influence the popular culture and media, which in turn influence the attitudes of political leaders. In *M. Butterfly,* he suggests that the "rape mentality" is one reason the United States had so much difficulty with the Vietnam War. American politicians simply could not comprehend that a small, undeveloped Eastern country could match the "big guns" of the West. As Gallimard states in the play, "Four hundred thousand dollars were being spent for every Viet Cong killed; so General Westmoreland's remark that the Oriental does not value life the way Americans do was oddly accurate" (68).

Hwang's other plays cover a wide range of themes and styles. He has recently completed works with non-Asian subjects, including a domestic play, *Rich Relations,* and an opera about UFOs, *1000 Airplanes on the Roof,* the latter cocreated in 1988 with musician Philip Glass and scenographer Jerome Sirlin. Hwang's work, however, is always concerned with characters outside society's mainstream, torn between embracing and denying their past. His work is an honest and heartfelt plea for all people to recognize the destructive nature of prevalent gender and cultural stereotypes. Hwang's Afterword to *M. Butterfly* states: "For the myths of the East, the myths of the West, the myths of men, and the myths of women—these have so saturated our consciousness that truthful contact between nations and lovers can only be the result of heroic effort" (100). In terms of the continuously changing voice of western American literature, the plays of David Henry Hwang offer a new direction. With Hwang's work, the

Asian-American literary concern has moved beyond a regional experience and now attempts to define a national and international consciousness regarding gender and race relations.

Notes

1. Eric Pace, "I Write Plays to Claim a Place for Asian-Americans," *New York Times,* July 12, 1981, D4.

2. Jeremy Gerard, "David Hwang: Riding on the Hyphen," *New York Times Magazine,* March 13, 1988, 88.

3. Pace, "I Write Plays," D4.

4. Frank Chin et al., eds., *Aiiieeeee!: An Anthology of Asian American Writers* (Washington, D.C.: Howard University Press, 1974), xxx.

5. Ping Chiu, *Chinese Labor in California* (Madison: University of Wisconsin Press, 1963), 45–46.

6. Pace, "I Write Plays," D4.

7. David Henry Hwang, *The Dance and the Railroad,* in *Broken Promises: Four Plays by David Henry Hwang* (New York: Avon, 1983), 73. Subsequent references to this play are cited parenthetically.

8. See Elaine Kim, "Asian Americans and American Popular Culture," in *Dictionary of Asian American History,* ed. Hyung-Chan Kim (Westport, Conn.: Greenwood, 1986), 108.

9. David Henry Hwang, Afterword to *M. Butterfly* (New York: New American Library, 1989), 98. Subsequent references to this essay and play are cited parenthetically.

Bibliography

Chan, Jeffrey Paul, and Marilyn C. Alquiloza. "Asian-American Literary Traditions." In *A Literary History of the American West,* edited by J. Golden Taylor et al., 1119–38. Fort Worth: Texas Christian University Press, 1987.

Chin, Frank. "Back Talk." In *Counterpoint: Perspectives on Asian America,* edited by Emma Gee, 556–57. Los Angeles: Asian American Studies Center, UCLA, 1976.

———. *The Chickencoop Chinaman and the Year of the Dragon.* Seattle: University of Washington Press, 1981.

Chin, Frank et al., eds. *Aiiieeeee!: An Anthology of Asian American Writers.* Washington, D.C.: Howard University Press, 1974.

Chiu, Ping. *Chinese Labor in California*. Madison: University of Wisconsin Press, 1963.

Drake, Sylvie. "Hwang's Metamorphosis." *Los Angeles Times*, Oct. 30, 1988, 5, 55–56.

Gerard, Jeremy. "David Hwang: Riding on the Hyphen." *New York Times Magazine*, Mar. 13, 1988, 44, 88–89.

Hiraoka, Jesse. "Asian American Literature." In *Dictionary of Asian American History*, edited by Hyung-Chan Kim, 93–97. Westport, Conn.: Greenwood, 1986.

Horn, Miriam. "The Mesmerizing Power of Racial Myths." *U.S. News & World Report*, Mar. 28, 1988, 52–53.

Hwang, David Henry. *Broken Promises: Four Plays by David Henry Hwang*. New York: Avon, 1983.

——. *M. Butterfly*. New York: New American Library, 1989.

Kim, Elaine. *Asian American Literature: An Introduction to the Writings and Their Social Context*. Philadelphia: Temple University Press, 1982.

——. "Asian Americans and American Popular Culture." In *Dictionary of Asian American History*, edited by Hyung-Chan Kim, 99–114. Westport, Conn.: Greenwood, 1986.

Meissenburg, Karin. *The Writing on the Wall: Socio-Historical Aspects of Chinese American Literature, 1900–1980*. Frankfurt: Verlag fur Interkulturelle Kommunikation, 1986.

Pace, Eric. "I Write Plays to Claim a Place for Asian-Americans." *New York Times*, July 12, 1981, D4.

Street, Douglas. *David Henry Hwang*. Western Writer's Series, no. 90. Boise, Idaho: Boise State University, 1989.

Wong, Yen Lu. "Chinese-American Theatre. *The Drama Review* 20 (June 1976): 13–18.

Part 5

New Directions for the New West

20. Revaluing Nature: Toward an Ecological Criticism

Glen A. Love

Describing the early rejection of the manuscript for his widely admired book, A River Runs through It, *Norman Maclean recalls in his acknowledgments the cool dismissal from one New York publisher: "These stories have trees in them."*

The renowned English historian Arnold Toynbee, in his narrative history of the world entitled *Mankind and Mother Earth,* published in 1976 at the end of his long career and also at the time of the first worldwide recognition of the possibility of environmental disaster, concluded somberly that our present biosphere is the only habitable space we have, or are ever likely to have, that mankind now has the power to "make the biosphere uninhabitable, and that it will, in fact, produce this suicidal result within a foreseeable period of time if the human population of the globe does not now take prompt and vigorous concerted action to check the pollution and the spoliation that are being inflicted upon the biosphere by short-sighted human greed."[1] In the intervening decade-plus since Toynbee's statement, we have seen little of the prompt and vigorous concerted action that he called for, and we must consider ourselves further along the road to an uninhabitable earth.

The catalog of actual and potential horrors is by now familiar to us all: the threats of nuclear holocaust, or of slower radiation poisoning, of chemical or germ warfare, the alarming growth of the world's population (standing room only in a few centuries at the present rate of growth), mounting evidence of global warming, destruction of the planet's protective ozone layer, the increasingly harmful effects of acid rain, overcutting of the world's last remaining great forests, the critical loss of topsoil and groundwater, overfishing and toxic poisoning of the oceans, inundation in our own garbage, an increasing rate of extinction of plant and animal species. The doomsday potentialities are so real and so profoundly important that a ritual chanting of them ought to replace the various nationalistic and spiritual incantations with which we succor ourselves. But rather than confronting these ecological issues, we prefer to think of other things. The mechanism that David Ehrenfeld calls "the avoidance of unpleasant reality" remains firmly in place.[2] For the most part, our society goes on with its bread and circuses, exemplified by the mindless diversion reflected in mass culture and the dizzying proliferation of activity among practitioners of literary research. In the face of profound threats to our biological survival, we continue, in the proud tradition of humanism, to, as Ehrenfeld says, "love ourselves best of all," to celebrate the self-aggrandizing ego and to place self-interest above public interest, even, irrationally enough, in matters of common survival.[3]

One would hope and expect that our field of English would respond appropriately to the radical displacements accompanying ecological catastrophe. Consider, however, that our society as a whole and our profession in particular have, as Cheryll Burgess points out, been faced with three crises in the past thirty years: civil rights, women's liberation, and environmental degradation.[4] All of these problems have been the subject of widespread social concern. All have become, to a greater or lesser extent, world issues. The discipline of English has addressed the concerns of civil rights, equality for minorities, and women's liberation through widespread attention and no small amount of action in such crucial areas as hiring and promotion practices, literary theory and criticism, and canon formation. Race, class, and gender are the words that we see and hear everywhere at our professional meetings and in our current publications. But curiously enough, as Burgess points out, the English profession has failed to respond in any significant way to the issue of the environment, the acknowledgment of our place within the natural world and our need to live heedfully within it, at peril of our very survival.

Curiosity must give way to incredulity at our unconcern when one reflects that in this area the problem-solving strategies of the past are increasingly ineffectual. We have grown accustomed to living with crises, and to outliving them, or to resolving them in some manner or other with comparatively little harm to business as usual. But as Lord Ashby explains, environmental degradation is more than just another crisis. As he describes it, "a crisis is a situation that will pass; it can be resolved by temporary hardship, temporary adjustment, technological adjustment, technological and political expedients. What we are experiencing is not a crisis, it is a climacteric."[5] For the rest of human history on the earth, says Ashby, we will have to live with problems of population, resources, and pollution.

Given the fact that most of us in the profession of English would be offended at not being considered environmentally conscious and ecologically aware, how are we to account for our general failure to apply any sense of this awareness to our daily work? One explanation might be that we care about these issues, but we don't care enough. It is our second most vital concern, the first position being reserved, as Mark Twain reminds us in "Corn-Pone Opinions," for that which immediately affects our personal economic livelihood.[6] A diminished environment is, for the present, a postponable worry. Without in any way discounting the issues to which we have given first priority, however, there will clearly come a time, and soon, when we will be forced to recognize that human domination—never mind the subdivisions of human—of the biosphere is the overriding problem.

I find myself siding here with the contemporary "deep" ecologists, who argue that we must break through our preoccupation with mediating between only human issues, the belief that, as Warwick Fox puts it, "all will become ecologically well with the world if we just put this or that inter-human concern first."[7] Theodore Roszak, in *Person/Planet*, states that

we have an economic style whose dynamism is too great, too fast, too reckless for the ecological systems that must absorb its impact. It makes no difference to those systems if the oil spills, the pesticides, the radioactive wastes, the industrial toxins they must cleanse are socialist or capitalist in origin; the ecological damage is not mitigated in the least if it is perpetrated by a 'good society' that shares its wealth fairly and provides the finest welfare programs for its citizens. The problem the biosphere confronts is the convergence of all urban-industrial economies as they thicken and coagulate into a single planet-wide system everywhere devoted to maximum productivity and the unbridled assertion of human dominance.[8]

The decision of those of us who profess English has been, by and large, that the relationship between literature and these issues of the degradation of the earth is something we won't talk about. Where the subject unavoidably arises, it is commonly assigned to some category such as "nature writing," or "regionalism," or "interdisciplinary studies," obscure pigeonholes whose very titles have seemed to announce their insignificance. Consider the curious nonreception from our profession of Joseph Meeker's seminal book, published in 1974, *The Comedy of Survival: Studies in Literary Ecology.* Launched by a major publisher at a time of widespread public concern for the environment, with a challenging introduction by the distinguished ethologist Konrad Lorenz, this provocative book offered the first genuinely new reading of literature from an ecological point of view. Meeker wrote:

> Human beings are the earth's only literary creatures.... If the creation of literature is an important characteristic of the human species, it should be examined carefully and honestly to discover its influence upon human behavior and the natural environment —to determine what role, if any, it plays in the welfare and survival of mankind and what insight it offers into human relationships with other species and with the world around us. Is it an activity which adapts us better to the world or one which estranges us from it? From the unforgiving perspective of evolution and natural selection, does literature contribute more to our survival than it does to our extinction?[9]

Meeker's principal contribution in *The Comedy of Survival* is a challenging rereading of tragedy and comedy from an ecological point of view. The book was virtually ignored by reviewers—made uncomfortable, no doubt, by its cross-disciplinary approach. (Nature, unfortunately for the organization of academia, is vexingly interdisciplinary.) But its significance is that it confronts the essential issues that are being forced upon us—and does so even more strongly today, after fifteen years in which the problems it addresses have grown more serious in being deliberately ignored.

Recent historical studies such as Donald Worster's *Nature's Economy* and Roderick Nash's *The Rights of Nature* narrate the history of ecological thinking. Nash's book, in particular, records the powerful influence of environmentalism in several intellectual fields. He describes the greening of liberal thought, the greening of religion and philosophy, even law. (Contemporary events underscore Nash's analysis. Alaska's wildlife, for example, moved to sue the Exxon Corporation for damages as a result of the March 1989 oil spill in Prince William Sound. A San Francisco law firm claimed that bears, otters, birds, salmon, and other animals should have legal standing in court action against Exxon.)[10] The question of rights for nonhuman organisms is one of the most vital areas of concern in several disciplines today. Congressional passage of the Endangered Species Act of 1973 has extended ethical and legal rights to some species of plants and animals, and has thus projected ecological thinking into central public policy. Other fields, such as architecture and urban planning, have been powerfully influenced by such environmental awareness. History, our sister discipline, displays a lively new interest in the origin and progress of conservation movements, in the backgrounds of ecological thought, as the Worster and Nash books indicate. Clearly, a general shift of consciousness is taking place in many fields as past paradigms are found to be irrelevant or even harmful in the face of new circumstances.

In the context of this widespread disciplinary revaluation, why, one wonders, have literary criticism and theory remained so peculiarly unaffected, so curiously unwilling or unable to address questions that are at the forefront of public concern, that occupy the discourse of many of our related contemporary disciplines, and that are—most important of all—engaged implicitly or explicitly in the body of works to which we have given our professional lives? Why are our theory and methodology so oddly untouched by all of this? Why, as Cheryll Burgess asks, are there no professors of literature and the environment?[11] Why no prestigious chairs, or even jobs? There are half a dozen English graduate students at my university—and I hear continually of others elsewhere—who, like Ms. Burgess, wish to work in the field of literature and ecology, and they wonder why none of the fashionable critics and theorists are addressing these vital matters. How can the discipline of English—which purports to deal with the human value systems of the past and the present, which seemingly engages literary representations of our relationship with our surroundings, and which thus both influences, and is influenced by, that relationship—fail to address such issues? Why are the activities aboard the *Titanic* so fascinating to us that we give no heed to the waters through which we pass, or to that iceberg on the horizon?

Besides our tendency to postpone or relegate to lesser priority ecological considerations, we must also recognize, in our failure to consider the iceberg, our discipline's limited humanistic vision, our narrowly anthropocentric view of what is consequential in life. The extension of human morality to the nonhuman world discussed above suggests that the time is past due for a redefinition of what is significant on earth. In our thinking, the challenge that faces us in these terms is to outgrow our notion that human beings are so special that the earth exists for our comfort and disposal alone. Here is the point at which a nature-oriented literature offers a needed corrective, for one very important aspect of this literature is its regard—either implicit or stated—for the nonhuman. While critical interpretation, taken as a whole, tends to regard ego-consciousness as the supreme evidence of literary and critical achievement, it is eco-consciousness that is a particular contribution of most regional literature, of nature writing, and of many other ignored forms and works, passed over because they do not seem to respond to anthropocentric—let alone modernist and postmodernist—assumptions and methodologies. In such a climate of opinion, for example, Hemingway's *The Sun Also Rises,* which is little occupied with ecological considerations, is widely taught in college classes, while his *The Old Man and the Sea,* which engages such issues profoundly, is not.

In what follows, I will be turning increasingly to that nature-oriented literature in which most of us spend much of our professional lives, western American literature (though one could as well focus on other examples, as does John Alcorn on rural England in *The Nature Novel from Hardy to Lawrence,* or on various landscapes, as do Leonard Lutwack in *The Role of Place in Literature* and John Elder in *Imagining the Earth*). Fred Erisman made the point over ten years ago in an essay entitled "Western American Fiction as an Ecological Parable," that much western American literature is an implicit plea for ecological awareness and activism.[12] Even earlier Thomas J. Lyon had posited hopefully that "the West's great contribution to American culture will be in codifying and directing the natural drive toward ecological thought, a flowering of regional literature into literally world-wide attention and relevance."[13] I think that many of us have found ourselves drawn to western literature by such a sense of its significance. Perversely enough, it is just this sort of literature

rooted in a real world that is ignored or devalued by such modish surveys as the *Columbia Literary History of the United States.*[14]

It is one of the great mistaken ideas of anthropocentric thinking,
and thus one of the cosmic ironies, that society is complex while nature is simple. The statement, "These stories have trees in them," conveys the assumption that modern readers have outgrown trees. That
literature in which nature plays a significant role is, by definition, irrelevant and inconsequential. That nature is dull and uninteresting
while society is sophisticated and interesting. Ignoring, for the moment, the fact that there is a good deal of human society in Maclean's
book, we might examine these assumptions that underlie the editor's
put-down. If we are to believe what modern ecology is telling us, the
greatest of all intellectual puzzles is the earth and the myriad systems
of life that it nourishes. Nature reveals adaptive strategies far more
complex than any human mind could devise. Surely one of the great
challenges of literature, as a creation of human society, is to examine
this complexity as it relates to the human lives it encompasses. Indeed, in the pastoral tradition we have a long and familiar heritage in
literature that purports to do just that. But the pastoral mode, in an
important sense, reflects the same sort of anthropocentric assumptions that are in such dire need of reassessment. Literary pastoral traditionally posits a natural world, a green world, to which sophisticated urbanites withdraw in search of the lessons of simplicity that
only nature can teach. There, amid sylvan groves and meadows and
rural characters—idealized images of country existence—the sophisti-
cates attain a critical vision of the good, simple life, a vision that will
presumably sustain them as they return at the end to the great world
on the horizon.

While the impetus, the motivation, for pastoral is perfectly relevant
and understandable, no less today than it was twenty-three hundred
years ago, the terms by which pastoral's contrastive worlds are defined do, from an ecological point of view, distort the true essence of
each. This is as true for ironic versions of pastoral, even antipastorals,
as it is for the conventional pastoral described above. The green
world becomes a highly stylized and simplified creation of the humanistic assumptions of the writer and his or her audience. Arcadia
has no identity of its own. It is but a temporary and ephemeral release
from the urban world that asserts its mastery by its linguistic creation
and manipulation of the generic form itself, and by the imposition of
its self-centered values upon the contrastive worlds. The lasting

appeal of pastoral is, I think, a testament to our instinctive or mythic sense of ourselves as creatures of natural origins, those who must return periodically to the earth for the rootholds of sanity somehow denied us by civilization. But we need to redefine pastoral in terms of the new and more complex understanding of nature.

Western American literature provides us with some appropriate versions of new pastoral. Consider the case of a latter-day western writer, Joseph Wood Krutch. Krutch for many years lived in New York City, where he achieved a major reputation as a literary and dramatic critic and scholar. In his later years, he moved to the New England countryside, and then to Arizona, and became—can it be stated without hearing a snicker from Maclean's dismissing editor?—a nature writer. In this latter role, Krutch authored a book on Thoreau and many other volumes, including *The Twelve Seasons, The Desert Year, The Voice of the Desert, The Great Chain of Life,* and other works on the Grand Canyon, on Baja California, and on other aspects of the natural world. Having argued in his famous early book, *The Modern Temper,* that contemporary science had sucked dry modern life of its moral and spiritual values, Krutch went on to become something of a scientist himself, but a scientist of a natural world in which he found many of the values that he had presumed lost. He became a writer of natural history who, under the influence of Thoreau and Aldo Leopold, came to reassess his dualistic view of man's nature.

Describing how his own version of ego-consciousness had gradually changed to eco-consciousness, Krutch tells of his growing sense that humankind's ingenuity had outpaced its wisdom: "We have engineered ourselves into a position where, for the first time in history, it has become possible for man to destroy his whole species. May we not at the same time have philosophized ourselves into a position where we are no longer able to manage successfully our mental and spiritual lives?"[15] Although Krutch remained in many respects a traditional humanist all his life, he found that his investigation of what he calls "the paradox of Man, who is a part of nature yet can become what he is only by being something also unique," led him to expand his vision of what is significant.[16] The realization took shape for him in the words with which he found himself responding to the announcement of spring by a chorus of frogs: "We are all in this together." This sentence, he recalls in his autobiography, *More Lives Than One,* "was important to me because it stated for the first time a conviction and an attitude which had come to mean more to me than I realized and, indeed, summed up a kind of pantheism which was gradually coming to be an essential part of the faith—if you can call it that—which would form the basis of an escape from the pessimism of *The Modern Temper* upon which I had turned my back without ever conquering it."[17] This growing awareness of interconnectedness between humankind and the nonhuman world led Krutch to risk being labeled with what he calls "the contemptuous epithet 'nature-lover.' "[18] He might have noted that his adoption of the desert Southwest as the subject of his books left him open, also, to the contemptuous epithet "western writer," or, worse yet, "regionalist."

This pattern is not an unfamiliar one. One thinks of Jack Schaefer, who wrote *Shane,* the definitive formula Western, without ever being farther west than Ohio. Yet in later life Schaefer moved west, also to the desert, and gave us a new kind of western, a book about the animals of the desert, *An American Bestiary,* whose introduction tells of his own loss of innocence: "I had become ashamed of my species and myself. I understood at last that...I was part of the deadly conquest called civilization."[19] One may find a similar pattern of awareness in the works of urbanites like Edward Hoagland and Gretel Ehrlich, who seem to slough off their New York or L.A. skins when they confront western landscapes. The tug of eco-consciousness as a corrective to ego-consciousness is a familiar feature of their work, as it is in the great preponderance of those whom we consider western writers by birthright or by long association, writers like Cather and Austin and Silko, Jeffers and Stegner and Snyder. "What disregards people does people good," concludes William Stafford of the wild coastal setting in his 1950 poem, "An Address to the Vacationers at Cape Lookout." Stafford's chastisement, like those in the works of Robinson Jeffers, identifies itself particularly with western settings and the writers of those settings, whose life and work are characterized, to no small degree, by their recognition of a natural otherness, a world of land and sky and organic life that exists outside human life yet seems to command its allegiance. "These stories have trees in them." Much of what it means to be a western writer is to risk the contemptuous epithet, nature lover.

The risk is worth taking, indeed must be taken, if it focuses attention on what appears to be nothing less than an ecologically suicidal path by the rest of the culture. Freud in *Civilization and Its Discontents,* Erich Fromm in *The Sane Society,* and Paul Shepard in *Nature and Madness,* all confront the question of whether a society itself can be sick. All conclude that it indeed can be. The fact that millions of people share the same neurosis does not make them sane, as Fromm and Shepard remind us.[20] And, as Freud says, the means for curing a communal neurosis cannot come from those afflicted by the neurosis. Rather, it must come from elsewhere.[21] John Alcorn finds this "elsewhere" in the English literature of place as revealed in the nature novels of Hardy and Lawrence. For others of us, the literature of the American West constitutes that sort of an alternative, as is demonstrated most recently by Harold P. Simonson in his *Beyond the Frontier.* For still others, it is in the literature of some other piece of earth. One place, properly regarded, serves as well as another. As anthropologist-writer Richard Nelson says, "What makes a place special is the way it buries itself inside the heart, not whether it's flat or rugged, rich or austere, wet or arid, gentle or harsh, warm or cold, wild or tame. Every place, like every person, is elevated by the love and respect shown toward it, and by the way in which its bounty is received."[22] We become increasingly aware, as our technological world begins to crack beneath our feet, that our task is not to remake nature so that it is fit for humankind, but as Thoreau says, to make humankind right for nature.

Recent studies of pastoral ideology reveal the pervasive and tenacious appeal of pastoralism in American literature. Leo Marx, in reconsidering the conclusions he reached in his seminal 1964 study, *The Machine in the Garden,* now allows what western American literature has always suggested, that American pastoral did not retreat into insignificance with the rise of modern industrial urbanism. In a 1986 essay Marx reexamines pastoralism and acknowledges its continuing relevance today. Unfortunately, he continues to underestimate its significance, seeing it only as another in a set of competing political ideologies. Marx does not consider whether the very real loomings of ecological catastrophe preclude pastoral's classification as just another value system.[23] Lawrence Buell, in a significant and wide-ranging survey of pastoralism in American literature and criticism, explores the experience of American pastoral in a variety of frames and contexts—social, political, gender-based, aesthetic, pragmatic, and environmental.[24] Buell gives more attention than Marx to the emergent threat of ecological holocaust, and he sees environmental pressures as tending to increase the importance of pastoralism as a literary and cultural force in the future. Obviously, I agree with him on this last point, although it needs to be said that such an outcome will require a more radical revaluation than any achieved thus far by pastoral's interpreters. Aldo Leopold's "land ethic," proposed in his environmental classic, *A Sand County Almanac,* might well be the litmus test for the new pastoralism: "A thing is right when it tends to preserve the integrity, stability, and beauty of the biotic community. It is wrong when it tends otherwise."[25] An ideology framed in such terms, with the human participants taking their own place in, and recognizing their obligation to, the shared natural world, will be an appropriate pastoral construct for the future. Whether we can accept it or not will say much about our chances for survival.

The redefinition of pastoral, then, requires that contact with the green world be acknowledged as something more than a temporary excursion into simplicity, which exists primarily for the sake of its eventual renunciation and a return to the "real" world at the end. A pastoral for the present and the future calls for a better science of nature, a greater understanding of its complexity, a more radical awareness of its primal energy and stability, and a more acute questioning of the values of the supposedly sophisticated society to which we are bound. These are the qualities that distinguish much of our best western American literature, where writers characteristically push beyond the pastoral conventions to confront the power of a nature that rebuffs society's assumptions of control. Much of the elemental dignity of Willa Cather's fiction, for example, resides in her refusal to limit her conception of the significant in western life to that which can be encompassed in the humanistic preconceptions of the pastoral tradition. She never ignores the primal undercurrent, the wild land that kicks things to pieces, while it may also yield the pastoral farms of Alexandra and Antonia. Nature says, "I am here still, at the bottom of things, warming the roots of life; you cannot starve me nor tame me nor thwart me; I made the world, I rule it, I am its destiny."[26]

Indeed, the western version of pastoral may be said to reverse the characteristic pattern of entry and return so that it is the green world that asserts its greater significance to the main character, despite the intrusion of societal values and obligations. This reversal is implicit in Barry Lopez's claim "that this area of writing [nature writing] will not only one day produce a major and lasting body of American literature, but that it might also provide the foundation for a reorganization of American political thought."[27]

While such predictions may be considered visionary, a reasonable observer must conclude that either through some ecological catastrophe of massive proportions or through a genuinely enlightened new sense of environmental awareness, our profession must soon direct its attention to that literature that recognizes and dramatizes the integration of human with natural cycles of life. The time cannot be far off when an ecological perspective will swim into our ken. Just as we now deal with issues of racism or sexism in our pedagogy and our theory, in the books that we canonize, so must it happen that our critical and aesthetic faculties will come to reassess those texts—literary and critical—that ignore any values save for an earth-denying and ultimately destructive anthropocentrism. And it does not seem unreasonable to suggest that the potential significance of such an awareness for the reinterpretation and reformation of the literary canon could be far greater than any critical movement that we have seen thus far. At a time when the discipline of literary criticism retreats ever further from public life into a professionalism characterized by its obscurity and inaccessibility to all but other English professors, it seems necessary to begin asking elemental questions of ourselves and the literature that we profess.

In anticipation of that inevitable day, I would offer three observations related to the future role of the Western Literature Association:

First, that the discipline of western American literature belongs in the forefront of the predicted critical shift. Its authority to lead such a movement arises not only from the work of its established writers and scholars but also from the contributions of its younger practitioners like Carl Bredahl, Cheryll Burgess, and SueEllen Campbell, who have already begun the thrust into contemporary critical fields.

Second, that the revaluation of nature will be accompanied by a major reordering of the literary genres, with realist and other discourse that values unity rising over poststructuralist nihilism. Certainly we shall see a new attention to nature writing. Although the growing interest in nature writing is by no means confined to the American West, writers and scholars from this region have been at the forefront in the surge of recent publications on nature writing. Important new anthologies, such as Thomas J. Lyon's *This Incomperable Lande*, Robert C. Baron's and Elizabeth Darby Junkins's *Discovery and Destiny*, and Ann Ronald's *Words for the Wild*, have come out of the West recently along with the influential volume, *On Nature*, edited by Daniel Halpern. Two recent books of interviews and exchanges with nature writers, Stephen Trimble's *Words from the Land* and Edward Lueders's *Writing Natural History,* further underscore the growing interest in nature writing in the West, as does the burgeoning number of conferences on the topic throughout the region.

Add these to such evidence of national interest as the new *Norton Book of Nature Writing,* edited by Robert Finch and John Elder, and Alicia Nitecki's recently launched *The American Nature Writing Newsletter,* and one might find the basis for some signs of environmental life in the profession. Recent Modern Language Association meetings have included sessions of interest to ecologically minded critics and teachers, evidence that voices crying in—and for—the wilderness are being heard. These are small steps, but they may mark a beginning.

— Third, that western American literature is not unique in its ecological perspective and that we need to recognize our kinship with nature-oriented writers in New England, in Canada, in Europe, in South and Central America, in Africa, in Australia, everywhere. Ecological issues are both regional and global. They transcend political boundaries. What is required is more interdisciplinary scholarship and more interregional scholarship on common issues. Deb Wylder has suggested the possibility of an international meeting of the Western Literature Association. Such a meeting, with significant participation from scholars in other countries, would be well suited to examining and exploring the literary-ecological connections raised here. Because the American West is a region recognized everywhere through books and film, it now seems appropriate to focus upon the New West and other global regions of threatened landscapes, and upon how current environmental perceptions alter forever our sense of lighting out for the wide open spaces. With the seriousness of these issues, it is perhaps time for Melville's shock of recognition that runs the whole world round.

The distinguished cell biologist Lewis Thomas has cautioned us recently that it is time for human beings "to grow up as a species." Because of our unique gift of consciousness (to which should be added our concomitant gift of language), Thomas observes that "it is up to us, if we are to become an evolutionary success, to fit in, to become the consciousness of the whole earth. We are the planet's awareness of itself, and if we do it right we have a very long way to go."[28] As members of a discipline whose defining characteristics are consciousness and language, we in English are particularly involved here. We have indeed a very long way to go, and we seem remarkably loathe to begin the journey.

The most important function of literature today is to redirect human consciousness to a full consideration of its place in a threatened natural world. Why do nature writing, literature of place, regional writing, poetry of nature, flourish now—even as they are ignored or denigrated by most contemporary criticism? Because of a widely shared sense—outside the literary establishment—that the current ideology separating human beings from their environment is demonstrably and dangerously reductionist. Because the natural world is indubitably real and beautiful and significant.

Paradoxically, recognizing the primacy of nature, and the necessity for a new ethic and aesthetic embracing the human and the natural—these may provide us with our best hope of recovering the lost social role of literary criticism.

Notes

1. Arnold Toynbee, *Mankind and Mother Earth* (New York: Oxford University Press, 1976), 9.

2. David Ehrenfeld, *The Arrogance of Humanism* (New York: Oxford University Press, 1978), 243.

3. Ibid., 238–39.

4. Cheryll Burgess, "Toward an Ecological Literary Criticism" (Paper presented at the annual meeting of the Western Literature Association, Coeur d'Alene, Idaho, October 13, 1989), 2.

5. Quoted in Victor B. Sheffer, "Environmentalism: Its Articles of Faith," *Northwest Environmental Journal* 5, no. 1 (Spring/Summer 1989): 100.

6. Mark Twain, "Corn-Pone Opinions," in *Great Short Works of Mark Twain*, ed. Justin Kaplan (New York: Harper and Row Perennial Classics, 1967), 188–92.

7. Warwick Fox, "The Deep Ecology-Feminism Debate and Its Parallels," *Environmental Ethics* 11, no. 1 (Spring 1989): 18.

8. Theodore Roszak, *Person/Planet: The Creative Disintegration of Industrial Society* (Garden City, N.Y.: Doubleday, 1978), 33.

9. Joseph Meeker, *The Comedy of Survival: Studies in Literary Ecology* (New York: Charles Scribner's Sons, 1974), 3–4.

10. "Unusual claim includes wildlife in oil spill suit," *Register-Guard*, Eugene, Oreg., August 18, 1989: A3.

11. Burgess, "Ecological Literary Criticism," 10.

12. Fred Erisman, "Western Fiction as an Ecological Parable," *Environmental Review* 6 (1978): 15–23.

13. Thomas J. Lyon, "The Ecological Vision of Gary Snyder," *Kansas Quarterly* 2 (Spring 1970): 117–24.

14. See James H. Maguire, "The Canon and the 'Diminished Thing,' " *American Literature* 60, no. 4 (Dec. 1988): 643–52.

15. Joseph Wood Krutch, *The Measure of Man* (New York: Bobbs-Merrill, 1954), 28.

16. Joseph Wood Krutch, *More Lives than One* (New York: William Sloane Associates, 1962), 313.

17. Ibid., 294–95.

18. Ibid., 338.

19. Jack Schaefer, *An American Bestiary* (Boston: Houghton Mifflin, 1975), xi.

20. Paul Shepard, *Nature and Madness* (San Francisco: Sierra Club Books, 1982), xi.

21. See John Alcorn, *The Nature Novel from Hardy to Lawrence* (New York: Columbia University Press, 1977), 108.

22. Richard Nelson, *The Island Within* (San Francisco: North Point Press, 1989), xii.

23. Leo Marx, "Pastoralism in America," in *Ideology and Classic American Literature*, ed. Sacvan Bercovitch and Myra Jehlen (Cambridge: Cambridge University Press, 1986), 36–69.

24. Lawrence Buell, "American Pastoral Ideology Reappraised," *American Literary History* 1, no. 1 (Spring 1989): 1–29. For further contemporary reconsideration of pastoral, see Meeker and Howarth.

25. Aldo Leopold, *A Sand County Almanac* (San Francisco: Sierra Club/Ballantine, 1970), 262.

26. Willa Cather, *The Kingdom of Art: Willa Cather's First Principles and Critical Statements, 1893–1896*, ed. Bernice Slote (Lincoln: University of Nebraska Press, 1966), 95.

27. Barry Lopez, "Barry Lopez," in *On Nature*, ed. Daniel Halpern (San Francisco: North Point Press, 1987), 297.

28. Lewis Thomas, "Are We Fit to Fit In?" *Sierra* 67, no. 2 (Mar./Apr. 1982): 52.

Bibliography

Alcorn, John. *The Nature Novel from Hardy to Lawrence.* New York: Columbia University Press, 1977.

Baron, Robert C., and Elizabeth Darby Junkins, eds. *Discovery and Destiny: An Anthology of American Writers and the American Land.* Golden, Colo.: Fulcrum, 1986.

Bredahl, Carl. *New Ground: Western American Narrative and the Literary Canon.* Chapel Hill: University of North Carolina Press, 1989.

Buell, Lawrence. "American Pastoral Ideology Reappraised." *American Literary History* 1, no.1 (Spring 1989): 1–29.

Burgess, Cheryll. "Toward an Ecological Literary Criticism." Paper presented at the annual meeting of the Western Literature Association, Coeur d'Alene, Idaho, October 13, 1989.

Campbell, SueEllen. "The Land and Language of Desire: Where Deep Ecology and Post-Structuralism Meet." *Western American Literature* 24, no. 3 (November 1989): 199–211.

Cather, Willa. *The Kingdom of Art: Willa Cather's First Principles and Critical Statements, 1893–1896.* Edited by Bernice Slote. Lincoln: University of Nebraska Press, 1966.

Ehrenfeld, David. *The Arrogance of Humanism.* New York: Oxford University Press, 1978.

Elder, John. *Imagining the Earth: Poetry and the Vision of Nature.* Urbana: University of Illinois Press, 1985.

Erisman, Fred. "Western Fiction as an Ecological Parable." *Environmental Review* 6 (1978): 15–23.

Finch, Robert, and John Elder, eds. *The Norton Book of Nature Writing.* New York: W. W. Norton, 1990.

Fox, Warwick. "The Deep Ecology-Feminism Debate and Its Parallels." *Environmental Ethics* 11, no. 1 (Spring 1989): 5–25.

Halpern, Daniel. *On Nature: Nature, Landscape, and Natural History.* San Francisco: North Point Press, 1987.

Howarth, William. "Country Books, City Writers: America's Rural Literature." In *National Rural Studies Committee: A Proceedings,* 11–21. Hood River, Oreg., May 24–25, 1988.

Krutch, Joseph Wood. *The Measure of Man.* New York: Bobbs-Merrill, 1954.

———. *More Lives than One.* New York: William Sloane Associates, 1962.

Leopold, Aldo. *A Sand County Almanac.* San Francisco: Sierra Club/Ballantine, 1970.

Lopez, Barry. "Barry Lopez." In *On Nature,* edited by Daniel Halpern, 295–97. San Francisco: North Point Press, 1987.

Lueders, Edward, ed. *Writing Natural History: Dialogues with Authors.* Salt Lake City: University of Utah Press, 1989.

Lutwack, Leonard. *The Role of Place in Literature.* Syracuse, N.Y.: Syracuse University Press, 1984.

Lyon, Thomas J. "The Ecological Vision of Gary Snyder." *Kansas Quarterly* 2 (Spring 1970): 117–24.

———, ed. *This Incomperable Lande.* Boston: Houghton Mifflin, 1989.

Maclean, Norman. *A River Runs through It and Other Stories.* Chicago: University of Chicago Press, 1976.

Maguire, James H. "The Canon and the 'Diminished Thing.'" *American Literature* 60, no. 4 (Dec. 1988): 643–52.

Marx, Leo. *The Machine in the Garden.* New York: Oxford University Press, 1964.

———. "Pastoralism in America." In *Ideology and Classic American Literature,* edited by Sacvan Bercovitch and Myra Jehlen, 36–69. Cambridge: Cambridge University Press, 1986.

Meeker, Joseph. *The Comedy of Survival: Studies in Literary Ecology.* New York: Charles Scribner's Sons, 1974.

Nash, Roderick Frazier. *The Rights of Nature: A History of Environmental Ethics.* Madison: University of Wisconsin Press, 1989.

Nelson, Richard. *The Island Within.* San Francisco: North Point Press, 1989.

Nitecki, Alicia, ed. *The American Nature Writing Newsletter.* Department of English, Bentley College, Waltham, Mass. 02154–4705.

Ronald, Ann, ed. *Words for the Wild.* San Francisco: Sierra Club Books, 1987.

Roszak, Theodore. *Person/Planet: The Creative Disintegration of Industrial Society.* Garden City, N.Y.: Doubleday, 1978.

Schaefer, Jack. *An American Bestiary.* Boston: Houghton Mifflin, 1975.

Sheffer, Victor B. "Environmentalism: Its Articles of Faith." *Northwest Environmental Journal* 5, no. 1 (Spring/Summer 1989): 99–109.

Shepard, Paul. *Nature and Madness.* San Francisco: Sierra Club Books, 1982.

Simonson, Harold P. *Beyond the Frontier: Writers, Western Regionalism and a Sense of Place.* Fort Worth: Texas Christian University Press, 1989.

Thomas, Lewis. "Are We Fit to Fit In?" *Sierra* 67, no. 2 (Mar./Apr. 1982): 49–52.

Toynbee, Arnold. *Mankind and Mother Earth.* New York: Oxford University Press, 1976.

Trimble, Stephen, ed. *Words from the Land: Encounters with Natural History.* Salt Lake City: Peregrine Smith, 1989.

Twain, Mark. "Corn-Pone Opinions." In *Great Short Works of Mark Twain,* edited by Justin Kaplan, 188–92. New York: Harper and Row Perennial Classics, 1967.

"Unusual claim includes wildlife in oil spill suit." *Register-Guard,* Eugene, Oreg., August 18, 1989: A3.

Worster, Donald. *Nature's Economy: A History of Ecological Ideas.* New York: Cambridge University Press, 1977.

Notes on Contributors

Frank Bergon, a native of Nevada, is Professor of English at Vassar College. He is the author of *Stephen Crane's Artistry* and *Shoshone Mike,* a novel. He is also the editor of *The Western Writings of Stephen Crane, The Wilderness Reader,* and *A Sharp Lookout: Selected Nature Essays of John Burroughs.* He coedited *Looking Far West: The Search for the American West in History, Myth, and Literature* and recently edited the Penguin Nature Library edition of *The Journals of Lewis and Clark.*

Gary Brienzo, having received his doctorate from the University of Nebraska-Lincoln in 1990, teaches at Nebraska Wesleyan University, Lincoln. A Cather scholar, he has focused on the connections between Cather and the American Northeast and Quebec, and the connections between Cather and other writers such as Sarah Orne Jewett, Eudora Welty, and Wright Morris. He is also a student of Irish fiction.

Alanna Kathleen Brown is an associate professor of English at Montana State University. She has focused on research on Mourning Dove since 1986, and has published articles on her in *Plainswoman, The Wicazo Sa Review, Legacy,* and *Canadian Literature,* as well as major reviews in *The Women's Review of Books* and *Studies in American Indian Literatures.* She is currently working on a literary biography for the Western Writers Series and an edition of Mourning Dove's letters.

Nancy S. Cook is assistant professor of English at the University of Montana. She has written about travel writing, American film, and Mark Twain. Currently she is at work on a study of Chief Buffalo

Child Long Lance. Her essay in this volume won the J. Golden Taylor award for best paper by a graduate student at the 1988 Western Literature Association conference, when she was engaged in doctoral studies at SUNY-Buffalo.

Jerry R. Dickey teaches theatre history and criticism in the University of Arizona's Department of Theatre Arts. Previously he served as Acting Director of Theatre at Hobart and William Smith Colleges in Geneva, New York. He is active in the Association for Theater in Higher Education and has presented papers at various conferences.

Betsy Downey, associate professor of history at Gonzaga University in Spokane, Washington, has participated in Lily Foundation and National Endowment for the Humanities seminars at Stanford University, working with Karen Offen of the Institute for Gender Studies at Stanford. She has published and presented papers on various American Studies topics, and teaches courses on women in American history and on the American West as symbol and myth.

Paula Kelly Harline teaches Honors English at Brigham Young University. She is writing *Love Triangles: Nineteenth-Century Mormon Polygamous Wives Write about Marriage,* a work that has evolved from her master's thesis, completed at the University of Idaho. Her research has been funded by the John Calhoun Smith Foundation.

Mary Catherine Harper teaches at Bowling Green State University, Bowling Green, Ohio, where she received her doctoral degree. She is a critic of contemporary American literature, a cultural theorist, and a poet. Her work has appeared in *New England Review* and *Studies in American Indian Literatures.*

Nathaniel Lewis is now completing a doctorate in American literature at Harvard University, after receiving a bachelor's at Yale and a master's at the University of North Carolina-Chapel Hill. He wrote the essay in this volume while studying in Chapel Hill, winning the J. Golden Taylor award for best paper by a graduate student at the 1989 Western Literature Association convention. Lewis has traveled extensively throughout the West, having lived in Colorado, California, and Alaska. His master's thesis was on Montana literature.

Patricia Nelson Limerick is the widely acclaimed author of *The Legacy of Conquest: The Unbroken Past of the American West* (1987). A native of California, she taught at Harvard University after completing her doctorate in American Studies at Yale University. She has been a member of the history faculty at the University of Colorado since 1984.

Helen Lojek teaches American literature and twentieth-century drama at Boise State University, Boise, Idaho. Recent publications focus on contemporary Irish drama, John Steinbeck, and Norman Maclean. She edits *The Rectangle*, the literary journal of Sigma Tau Delta, the national English honor society.

Glen A. Love, professor of English at the University of Oregon and past president of the Western Literature Association, has twice taught on Fulbright grants in Germany. He is the author of *New Americans: The Westerner and the Modern Experience in the American Novel* (1982) and numerous articles and reviews on American literature and western American literature. Co-editor of *Northwest Perspectives* (1979), he is currently developing an anthology of short fiction from Oregon and a study of the relationship between literature and the environment.

Susan Naramore Maher is teaching in the Women's Studies program at the University of Nebraska-Omaha. She has published articles in *Children's Literature Association Quarterly, International Fiction Review,* and *The South Dakota Review.* Currently she is working on a book-length study of adventure fiction written by women.

Barbara Howard Meldrum, as president of the Western Literature Association, was responsible for the development of the 1989 conference program and selection and editing of essays for this collection. She is a member of the editorial board of *Western American Literature* and has published numerous essays on western American writers and a collection of essays, *Under the Sun: Myth and Realism in Western American Literature* (1985). Her monograph on Sophus Winther was published in the Western Writers Series. She has received fellowships from the National Endowment for the Humanities and the American Antiquarian Society, and is currently writing a book on Harriet Beecher Stowe. A Ph.D. from Claremont Graduate School and a native northwesterner, she has taught at the University of Idaho since 1965.

Gerald D. Nash, Distinguished Professor of History at the University of New Mexico, has published extensively on the twentieth-century West. His latest book is a comprehensive analysis of historical and literary writing about the West, entitled *Creating the West: Historical*

Interpretations, 1890–1990 (1991), of which the essay in this volume is a by-product. The book is based on the Calvin Horn Lectures in Western History and Culture at the University of New Mexico in 1990. Nash is a past president of the Western History Association (1990–91) and occupied the George Bancroft chair in American History at the University of Goettingen, 1990–91.

Sheila Ruzycki O'Brien teaches courses in American literature, American Studies, and film at the University of Idaho. Her doctorate is from Indiana University, where she received the William Parker Riley Distinguished Teaching Award. She has worked on a U.S. Forest Service helicopter fire crew and as a motorcycle cop.

Forrest G. Robinson teaches American literature and American Studies at the University of California, Santa Cruz. He has written books on Sir Philip Sidney, Wallace Stegner, Mark Twain, and, most recently, on Henry A. Murray, the eminent American personality theorist and Melville scholar.

Marilynne Robinson is the author of the highly acclaimed novel, *Housekeeping* (1981), which is set in the northern Idaho region of Robinson's birth. She has also published an environmental study, *Mother Country* (1989), which was nominated for the National Book Award. Her reviews have appeared frequently in the *New York Times Book Review*. After living many years in Massachusetts, Robinson is now a faculty member in the writers' program of the University of Iowa.

Elizabeth Simpson is the author of *Earthlight, Wordfire: The Work of Ivan Doig* (1992). She has published essays on folklore and western literature and is currently working on a book on landscape in western writing. With Professor Henning K. Sehmsdorf, she co-edits *Northwest Folklore*. She currently teaches in the Interdisciplinary Writing Program at the University of Washington.

Jane Tompkins, professor of English at Duke University, is a recognized leader in feminist criticism and reader-response theory. She is the author of *Sensational Designs: The Cultural Work of American Fiction, 1790–1860* (1985). Her address at the 1989 Western Literature Association conference has been published as a part of her venture into western American literary studies, *West of Everything: The Inner Life of Westerns* (1992).

Max Westbrook, who has taught American literature at the University of Texas-Austin since 1962, is a past president of the Western Literature Association and a recipient of its award for Distinguished Achievement in Scholarship. Best known for essays on Stephen Crane, Ernest Hemingway, and the literature of the American West, he has turned in recent years to creative writing. Three chapbooks of poetry and three short stories have been published. A book of short stories is currently being circulated.

Index